Subversive Laughter

SUBVERSIVE LAUGHTER

The Liberating Power of Comedy

RON JENKINS

THE FREE PRESS
A Division of Macmillan, Inc.
NEW YORK

Maxwell Macmillan Canada
TORONTO

Maxwell Macmillan International
NEW YORK OXFORD SINGAPORE SYDNEY

The Free Press
A Division of Macmillan, Inc.
866 Third Avenue, New York, N.Y. 10022

Maxwell Macmillan Canada, Inc.
1200 Eglinton Avenue East
Suite 200
Don Mills, Ontario M3C 3N1

Macmillan, Inc. is part of the Maxwell Communication Group of Companies.

Printed in the United States of America

printing number
1 2 3 4 5 6 7 8 9 10

Library of Congress Cataloging-in-Publication Data

Jenkins, Ronald Scott.
    Subversive laughter : the liberating power of comedy / Ron
Jenkins.
        p.   cm.
    Includes bibliographical references and index.
    ISBN 0-02-916405-2
    1. Wit and humor—Philosophy.   2. Laughter—Psychological aspects.
3. Comedy—Political aspects.   I. Title.
PN6149.P5J46   1994
791'.0207—dc20   94-19213
                                                          CIP

to my father,
Manuel Solomon Jenkins
Far got zol men weinen,
far mentshn . . . lakhn.

Next to the universality of medieval laughter we must stress another striking peculiarity: its indissoluble and essential relation to freedom.

—Mikhail Bakhtin, *Rabelais and His World*

Contents

Preface ix
Acknowledgments xiii

1
Urban Slapstick and Survival 1

2
Sacred Laughter in Bali 13

3
Revolutionary Laughter in Lithuania 47

4
Ridiculing Racism in South Africa 79

5
Clowns and Popes in Italy 107

6
Mocking Conformity in Japan 135

7
America's Comedy of Detachment 171

Notes 209
Index 211

Preface

Laughter is a fingerprint of our identity. The things we find funny say a lot about who we are. This is particularly true about authors of books on comedy. My approach to humor owes its strengths and flaws to the comic accidents of my experience, so rather than hide the personal circumstances that shaped this research, I prefer to divulge them from the start.

I could never have understood the full significance of Balinese comedy if I had not spent a year in Bali performing as an apprentice to a troupe of village temple clowns. Hopping through dusty temple courtyards in the costume of a giant green frog was my initiation to the sacred and subversive power of laughter in Bali.

My introduction to the intricacies of Japanese humor came through the generosity of kimono-clad variety performers and their fans who befriended me when I began showing up regularly at sleazy downtown Tokyo theaters. It is unusual for an outsider to be accepted into a Japanese group without formal introductions, but I eventually discovered that an eagerness to break the rules of etiquette was at the heart of the comic impulse in these lowbrow working-class theaters. In South Africa the raw vitality of political satire struck me most forcefully when I was arrested at a demonstration in Johannesburg and put in a cell with eight hundred black protesters who spent hours mocking the police officers who had put them there. Being in jail with the victims of apartheid had a lasting impact on my understanding of the complex relationship between laughter and freedom.

My personal connections to the comic traditions in Italy and Lithuania were enhanced by coincidences of genealogy. The political potency of Lithuanian humor might have escaped my notice if I had not gone to Vilnius to work on a play by Joshua Sobol about Jews who staged satirical allegories in the city's ghetto when it was under Nazi occupation. Born in Lithuania, my

paternal grandparents had fled the pogroms before World War
I, so the jokes of the survivors I met in Vilnius filled in the gaps
of a lost family heritage. When I spent a year in Italy with the
Italian clown Dario Fo, and ended up serving as the onstage
interpreter for his first American tour, I could not help but compare his satirical portraits of the church with the stories my
maternal grandmother had told me about her childhood in
Abruzzi. She spoke of the saints and the Madonna as if they were
members of her family, humanizing them with the same intimate
tones that Fo used to bring biblical figures to life in his comic
renderings of Roman Catholic lore. In Italy, like Lithuania, my
search for the historical roots of popular comedy was guided by
the laughter of my ancestors.

I would never have gone to any of these places looking for
laughter if I hadn't performed in a tent circus after graduating
from the Ringling Brothers, Barnum & Bailey Clown College.
My decision to pursue clowning had come when I was a New
York University pre-med student working in the child psychiatric
ward of Bellevue Hospital. I had planned to become a child psy-
chiatrist, but was disillusioned by the treatment of schizophrenic
children at Bellevue. Their therapy consisted primarily of drug
injections. The psychiatrists would prescribe the medicine and
examine the children without engaging in any real human contact with them. Working in the wards every day, I sensed that the
children needed something more and tried awkwardly to develop
relationships with them. One seven-year-old autistic child named
Eric responded to me when I played silly games that made him
smile. Without knowing what I was doing, I became his personal
clown for the summer. When I first began working at the hospital Eric only repeated the words that were spoken to him and
never looked anyone in the eye, but after a few months of our
improvised goofiness he started to look at me and say my name. I
had won his trust with laughter.

Breaking through to Eric gave me my first real taste of
laughter's power, and I wanted to learn more about it. It occurred
to me that clowns and psychiatrists shared a common goal of freeing the spirit from oppressive tensions, but I knew there wouldn't

be any courses on humor at medical school, so I gave up my schol-
arship to NYU and set out in search of a school for laughter. A
few months later I found myself in a small Mexican village where
a clown named Sigfrido Aguilar taught workshops in the stone
courtyard of an eighteenth-century convent. After several months
of studying with Sigfrido and performing for the children in his
village, I received a hand-painted diploma that certified my expertise in buffoonery. Realizing I still had a lot to learn, I moved to
Los Angeles, where part-time clowning gigs and a winning
appearance on a television quiz show helped me to finance further
studies at the Ringling Brothers Clown College in Florida.

After graduation I got a job touring the country with a
shabby tent circus called Rudy Brothers. My clown character was
a powerless underdog, an innocent dupe who was forever tyran-
nized by the white-faced bullies that surrounded him. I was the
one who got the bucket of water dumped regularly on his head. I
was the one whose baggy pants fell down every day to reveal a
tattered pair of boxer shorts. This comic pathos eventually
became part of my character's strategy for subverting the abusive
behavior of his fellow buffoons. My partner was a far more
aggressive clown than I was and would set up a shouting competition between the children seated on opposite sides of the arena.
The one who screamed the loudest won the privilege of taking
home a dog made out of balloons that he waved teasingly in front
of them. The contest never failed to whip the kids into a frenzy of
greed. They would climb on top of the chairs and step on one
another's heads to get close to the cherished balloon dog.

My clown character could never get the crowd's attention
during these shouting matches, so I just followed my partner
around the ring and applauded feebly in a futile attempt to win
the balloon for myself. He, of course, ignored me completely.
Convinced that the audience was also ignoring me, I was surprised one day during intermission when a little girl came backstage to clown alley and presented me with the balloon dog as a
gift. She said she felt sorry that the other clown was so mean to
me. I was impressed that such a simple gag had undermined the
contagion of avarice that pervaded the arena.

Laughter is a biological imperative, a complex cognitive and physiological response to the human condition that is as necessary for survival as water, air, and freedom. While I have no evidence that comedy is encoded in our chromosomes, it is plausible that a genetic impulse for adaptation and survival might explain the persistence of laughter in life's most urgent moments. Perhaps it is more than coincidence that people who laugh in the face of death are often the ones who live to tell about it. Prisoners who overcame the hardships of Nazi-imposed ghettos and apartheid jail cells often attribute their survival to a sense of humor. Laughter is not our only defense against despair, but it can play a key role in freeing us from the stresses that sap our will to live.

Acknowledgments

During the twenty years of fieldwork, research, and clowning that contributed to the preparation of this book, I have been assisted by a cavalcade of scholars, friends, and comic artists from around the world, and I owe them all more gratitude than can possibly fit into these pages. Nevertheless, like a ringmaster trying to squeeze as many clowns as possible into the confines of a tiny circus car, I will attempt to express my thanks to as many of my collaborators as possible.

First, I want to thank my agent, Kim Witherspoon, for believing in this book long before it was fully conceived. I am also grateful to Joyce Seltzer and her assistant, Cherie Weitzner, for their honest and wise editing of the manuscript. Their insights helped to give this book a focus and economy it would not otherwise have. For permission to use in altered form some of the material that I originally published in the *New York Times*, the *Village Voice*, *The Drama Review*, *Harvard Magazine*, the *Boston Phoenix*, and *Theater Magazine*, I thank the editors of those periodicals, including Andrea Stevens, Ross Wetzsteon, Richard Schechner, and Carolyn Clay. Among those editors Joel Schechter was particularly generous with his support and advice over the years.

For their inspiration as I struggled to master the intricacies of slapstick performance I am indebted to Sigfrido Aguilar, Lou Jacobs, Hovey Burgess, Steve Smith, Janice Gillespie, and my 1973 classmates at the Ringling Brothers Clown College Class. For their dedication to my clown troupe at Haverford College and their support of my postgraduation voyage to Bali, I owe special thanks to Jack Coleman, Joseph Russo, Bob Butman, Paul Desjardins, Sid Perloe, Sue Wohl, Cynthia Grund, and Lydia Stokes.

My first year of research in Bali was financed by a 1976 fellowship from the Thomas Watson Foundation and warmed by the friendship of Ibu Anom and Ibu Arsa of Peliatan, who provided me with food and shelter; Tangguh, Ketut Kodi, Wayan Dhibia, Ni Made Wiratini, I Made Bandem, Ni Suasthi Wijaya Bandem, and Chandri of Singapadu, who provided cultural insights into Bali's traditions; Andy Toth and Elizabeth Young, who helped me keep everything in perspective; and the entire performance troupe of I Made Djimat in Batuan, who adopted me into their family of dancing kings, demons, princesses, clowns, and frogs.

My second trip to Bali was made possible by a faculty research grant and sabbatical leave from Emerson College in 1992. I was aided in Bali by all the people who helped me the first time around with the additional assistance of I Nyoman Catra, Desak Made Suartilaksmi, Gusti Windia, Wayan Wija, Ketut Rupik, Ni Made Rusni, Rucina Balinger, Cristina Formaela, Patti Hartigan, and my translator, I Made Dwi Sutaryantha. I owe a particular debt of gratitude to Dr. I Made Bandem, who in the interim between my two visits had risen from the ranks of the island's great comic performers to the prestigious positions of Director of Bali's Institute of the Arts (S.T.S.I.) and member of the Indonesian President's Advisory Council. He opened both his school and his home to me with a typically Balinese spirit of hospitality.

For my introduction to Lithuania I am deeply grateful to Joshua and Edna Sobol, who invited me to work with them and Jiri Zizka on adapting Joshua's plays about the Vilna ghetto from Hebrew into English. During our residency as master artists at the Atlantic Center for the Arts in Florida we recreated the Vilna ghetto of World War II and formulated plans that later brought me to modern Vilnius as an adviser for one of the plays' Lithuanian premiere. Once I arrived in Vilnius I was touched by the generosity of Dr. Irena Veisaite, who became my adopted Jewish mother and introduced me to an invaluable network of artists, scholars, politicians, and translators. These individuals provided me with boundless personal and professional assistance during my research into the tensions between Lithuanian comedy and politics. They included Joasas Budraitis, Jonas Vaitkus, Ruta Wiman, Eimuntas Nekrosius, Ceslovas Stonys, Khasys Saja, Gintaras Varnas, Albinas Kentras, Jurate Grinceviciute, Larissa Kalpokaite, Pranas Tupikas, Kostas Aleksynas, Lyuba Traup,

Julius Lozoraitis, Lina Ditkovskyte, and Grazina Eimutyte. I am particularly thankful for the help of Daiva Dapsiene, Arvidus Dapsys, Inga Bulotaite, Rimas Tuminas, and all the members of the Little Theater, where I directed two plays by Dario Fo in the spring of 1991. Special thanks as well to my students at the National Theater Academy in Vilnius and to Vytautas Landsbergis, president of the republic, for taking time over breakfast in his office to talk about laughter.

I am indebted to the Whiting Foundation for funding my 1992 sabbatical research in South Africa. Barney Simon, Caroline Creasy, Mark Shute, and the staff of the Market Theater in Johannesburg were helpful in orienting me to apartheid's world of multiracial theater. Further assistance came from informative conversations with Prince Dubu, Manny Manim, Eric Miyene, Patrick Mofokeng, Boy Bangala, Smal Ndaba, Phyllis Klotz, Tale Matepe, Patricia Qhaba, Moses, Mampone Esau, Julian Seleke, Mike Manona, Carol Steinberg, Richard Schechner, Napthali Mlipha, Brenda Glodblatt, Kathy Berman, Charlotte Bauer, Matsemela Manaka, Wally Serote, Mbongeni Ngema, and Percy Mtwa. Peter Dirk Uys and Evita Bezeidenhout were fountains of laughter and insight. Muzi Sithebe at the Film Resource unit in Johannesburg was particularly kind in locating visual documentation of satirical performances and political events. My deepest thanks goes to the men and women of Palm Springs, South Africa, who befriended me after we were arrested together at Johannesburg's Jeppe Street Post Office. From them I learned how laughter can help set a community free. I also appreciated the hard work of Mathole Motshekga, the attorney who fought and won our case in the courts. A special acknowledgment of unrepayable debts goes to Jenefer Shute and her family.

A 1984 Sheldon postdoctoral fellowship from Harvard University supported my research in Italy with Dario Fo and Franca Rame, and a courageous invitation to the couple from the American Repertory Theater led to my serving as onstage interpreter during Fo and Rame's first American tour. Robert Brustein of the American Repertory Theater served as an inspiring role model and mentor as I shaped my graduate studies at

Harvard around the art of the clown, and the opportunity to collaborate with him and his company on bringing Fo and Rame to America was only one of the many cherished gifts he has given me over the years. I am also grateful to Howard Gardner for his key role in guiding my research on comedy at Harvard. His theories of multiple intelligences helped me come to terms with the artistry of clowns wherever I encountered them. In addition to my appreciation of Dario Fo and Franca Rame for their willingness to accept me into their company, I owe much to their friends and colleagues who provided me with ongoing commentary about the couple's place in the world of Italian comedy and politics. Cristina Nutrizio, Piero Scioto, Anna Maria Lisi, Walter Valeri, Franco Ruffini, Fernando Taviani, Eugenio Barba, Cristina Valenti, and Mariella Guidici were all enormously helpful. Francesca Direnzio and her family were especially kind in assisting me in my first awkward encounter with Fo and Rame, but I will always remember most warmly the wise advice and insights of Claudio Meldolesi, his wife, Laura, and their two angelic daughters.

In Japan my thanks begin with Jonah Salz, who secured the 1990 Japan Foundation grant that supported my residency in Kyoto to collaborate with the Shigeyama family of traditional comic Kyogen actors. It was while directing Akira Shigeyama and his son Joji in an adaptation of a satiric novel by Herman Melville that I saw my first *taishu engeki* performance in Osaka. For this first glimpse of lowbrow Japanese comedy I am indebted to Julie Iezzi. In Tokyo my appreciation of *taishu engeki* was enhanced by the scholarly advice and friendship of Masao Yamaguchi. James Brandon also provided me with valuable insights into the form during an early stage of my research. Most welcome was the friendly reception I received from Satomi Yojiro, his mother, Mifuji Kieko, and their troupe of *taishu engeki* actors. In the theater, backstage, and at our frequent postperformance dinners, they always went out of their way to make me feel at home. I also want to thank Midori Kimura, her daughter Yumi, and their friend Miki Mieko for allowing me to see *taishu engeki* through the eyes of its fans.

Above all I want to express my deepest thanks to Sally Schwager, who suffered through all the phases of this book's creation with saintly patience and devilish humor. The chapter on Japan could not have been written without her. She accompanied me regularly to the sleazy *taishu engeki* theaters, translated the slang-filled dialogue of the plays, and established a far more intimate rapport with the actors and fans than I could ever have managed on my own. My understanding of *taishu engeki* was aided enormously by her penetrating insights into Japanese culture and the wit with which she expressed them. Sally's contributions to the book did not begin or end in Japan. Every page I wrote was enhanced by her presence in my heart. While I traveled around the world, and labored diligently in search of laughter's essence, Sally embodied it without effort. The courage, strength, and beauty of the comic spirit reside naturally in her. I could never have wished for a more generous and inspiring muse of laughter.

A metal clown wielding a chain saw in the French circus Archaos. (press photo courtesy of Archaos)

Urban Slapstick and Survival

In a world fraught with danger and despair, comedy is a survival tactic, and laughter is an act of faith. Think of Charlie Chaplin in *The Gold Rush*. He does pratfalls in a cabin teetering precariously on the edge of a frozen precipice, and avoids starvation by eating his shoe. We laugh at his ingenuity in freeing himself from the predicaments that threaten his existence. His sense of humor not only saves his life, it makes him immortal. Chaplin's little tramp will always be remembered as an icon of human resourcefulness in the face of impossible odds.

While comedy takes many forms, Chaplin embodies a global tradition of clowning that offers hope in the direst of circumstances. Clowns of this tradition struggle relentlessly for freedom and survival no matter how bleak their chances for success. Pummeled by cream pies, upended by gravity, and stung by the ringmaster's whip, they somehow manage to persevere. To watch a clown emerge unscathed from impossible dilemmas gives us hope that we too might escape the forces that oppress our daily lives. Everyone can identify with the clown's beleaguered attempts to recover from a stumble, avoid the humiliating impact of a cream pie, or flee a tyrant's whip. His efforts to cope with the mundane constraints of gravity, etiquette, and authority make us acknowledge our own feeble attempts to do the same.

Comic heroes throughout history have tried to break free from the political, social, and economic tyrannies of their times.

Aristophanes mocked the dictators who he believed were corroding the democratic principles of ancient Athens. Harlequin's comic reversals of the master-servant relationship entertained audiences emerging from the rigid hierarchies of feudal Europe. Richard Pryor launched savage comic attacks against racism in contemporary America. When humor undermines the forces that stifle the basic human needs for freedom, justice, and dignity, laughter is experienced as a wave of liberating release.

Some forms of popular comedy still rage against the political, moral, technological, and commercial tyrannies that plague our modern world. In cultures as different as Indonesia, Lithuania, South Africa, Italy, Japan, and the United States laughter is an emblem of resilience. It can help people to escape the oppressive influences of their environment. While colonialism, dictatorship, racism, religious dogmatism, rigid social conformity, and emotional alienation will never be overcome by humor alone, laughter can play a role in subverting their impact.

This defiant tradition of clowning is a measure of its audience's character. Viewed collectively, reports from the front lines of laughter suggest that a nation's sense of humor is inseparable from its sense of values. As individuals and as cultures, our deepest contradictions are embedded in the punch lines of our clowns.

The globally acclaimed films of Chaplin provide a starting point for looking at the deep bonds between comedy, freedom, and survival. Chaplin's tramp is constantly subjected to life-threatening dilemmas that restrict his options. His costume offers the first clues to his central concerns. Chaplin wears the morning suit of a rich man, reduced to the rags of a beggar. Its ill fit confines his upper body with a jacket that's too tight, while leaving his legs free to run and dance in baggy-pants abandon. Tyranny and liberation coexist in the cut of Chaplin's clothes. His physical appearance signals a readiness to challenge barriers of class, wealth, and status. As one of the twentieth century's first great clowns, Chaplin moved beyond the traditional slapstick adversaries of gravity, cream pies, and authority figures to wage comic battles against the oppressive economic and political constraints of contemporary civilization.

Chaplin's most enduring films center on his comic battles with the social forces of industrialization, politics, and greed. In *Modern Times* the tramp fights for his life against the dehumanizing effects of modern technology, a conflict immortalized by the famous still of Chaplin caught in the gearshift of a giant machine. The tramp tackles the political tyranny of racial hatred and genocide when he faces death at the hands of Hitler in *The Great Dictator*. Blinded by poverty and the lust for wealth, Chaplin's antagonists in *The Gold Rush* try to murder the tramp and eat him alive. In each of these classic films the comedy revolves around struggles of life and death.

Chaplin understood that the tramp's escapes became funnier in proportion to the severity of the threats to which he was subjected. To emphasize the brutal underside of his comedies, he often reshot his scenes to make them appear more dangerous. "Tragedy stimulates the spirit of ridicule,"[1] observed Chaplin, who chose to film part of *The Gold Rush* in the same California mountains where the Donner expedition had perished after eating one another's corpses. He hired hobos to play the hordes of prospectors trudging through the snow-covered mountains in hopes of striking it rich. The shadows of genuine poverty, desperation, and cannibalism were essential to Chaplin's comic masterpiece. "Ridicule," he noted, "is an attitude of defiance. We must laugh at our helplessness against the forces of nature or go insane."[2]

Chaplin's "attitude of defiance" was a key component of his character's indomitable resilience. The tramp never gave up. He refused to be straitjacketed by etiquette, logic, or brute force. Whether he was confronting burly policemen, snooty millionaires, or machines that had run amok, Chaplin used his comic ingenuity to free himself from the forces that seemed bent on his destruction. The tramp is always seen subverting the established social order to give power to the powerless, homes to the homeless, and dignity to the poor. The impact of Chaplin's comic defiance can be measured in part by how much it threatened the guardians of the status quo. During the McCarthy era, Chaplin's outspoken criticism of capitalism and social injustice led to his being refused an entry visa to the United States.

At the end of the twentieth century clowns are often fueled by the same spirit of comic defiance that motivated Chaplin's tramp, but their comedy has been remodeled to fit the modern adversaries their laughter is intended to subvert. One of the most popular circuses in Europe now features a troupe of "metal clowns" who wear costumes of corrugated aluminum to battle the cruelty of contemporary society. They have traded in the baggy pants and red noses of traditional clowns for suits of rusted scrap metal that protect them from the onslaught of diesel trucks, motorcycles, and high-tech explosives. Based in France, the circus is called "Archaos," and its darkly violent environment recalls the postapocalyptic setting of films like *Road Warrior* and *Escape from New York*.

Some of the metal clowns cite Chaplin as a direct influence on their work, but their updating of the tramp's dilemmas reveals the unique cruelties of a contemporary urban landscape. The charming vagabond in his frayed morning coat and derby has been replaced by a snarling gang of homeless street people sporting black leather jackets and mohawk haircuts. These punked-out metal clowns are road warriors battling against urban nightmares that Chaplin could never have imagined. They scavenge for scraps of food on junk piles of industrial waste. Where the tramp was forced to eat his shoe, the metal clowns feast on the tubes and wires of discarded television sets. They are assaulted by drug-dealing pimps on steel stilts and sex-starved transvestites who stuff their bras with juggling balls. At moments when the tramp might have twirled his cane and skipped lightly out of danger's way, the metal clowns rev up their chain saws and lunge wildly at the throats of their antagonists. Archaos's director, Pierrot Bidon, himself a former metal clown, says his images are inspired by the violence in the streets of cities like London and New York.

In fact, the habitat of the metal clowns resembles a city street much more than it does a traditional circus ring. Archaos sets up its tent in parking lots, not grassy fields. Instead of a canvas big top supported by wooden poles, the circus takes place in a high-tech plastic structure mounted on steel frames. There is no calliope. The show's musical accompaniment is provided by a heavy metal band that drives in on a diesel truck emblazoned with the motto "Put blood in your tank." The playing area is an asphalt runway, designed to be as suitable for screeching truck tires as the eighteenth-century ring was for the hooves of galloping horses. Archaos's arena is untouched by the droppings of elephants and tigers but filled with oil stains and the stench of gasoline. "The forklift is our elephant and costs less to feed," boasts Bidon. "Instead of roaring wild animals, we have roaring wild motorcycles. Our metal clowns have diesel fuel in their veins."[3]

Archaos is a microcosm of a late-twentieth-century urban jungle, and its set and costumes are created from the trash heaps of Europe's capitals. In the cities that host his show from London to Stockholm, Bidon scours the junkyards for scrap metal and abandoned automobiles to create the bleak landscape that greets the audiences who enter Archaos's tent. The corrugated metal shields of the clowns were devised to protect them from the jagged edges of the rusting steel environment they were expected to negotiate during the circus performance. "To survive the clowns have to mutate and re-use the scraps of society's refuse," observes Bidon, who takes great pride in the amount of physical abuse his mutant metal clowns are able to withstand.

Sometimes a particularly vicious explosion knocks the metal clowns over on their backs, where they writhe gleefully on their aluminum shields and flail their limbs wildly in the air. In this position they resemble a swarm of giggling metal cockroaches, stubbornly refusing to be exterminated. Laughing ferociously in the face of death, the metal clowns take endless delight in their role as human cockroaches, grotesque descendants of evolution's most obstinate survivors.

Chaplin's tramp was belched out of the machine that swallowed him in *Modern Times*, but in the postmodern times of Archaos, the clowns seem to have been fully ingested by and cross-bred with the mechanical devices that threaten to devour them. One clown crawls along the asphalt, his legs enmeshed in the tubing of a giant air-conditioning duct. Another trudges through the harsh landscape with a phone booth lashed onto his back. Resembling genetic accidents induced by toxic doses of urban stress, these dada-esque comic creatures epitomize the difficulty of surviving the modern technological wasteland.

Archaos's clowns are pitted against political tyrannies as well as technological ones. In a scene that echoes Chaplin's bout with Hitler in *The Great Dictator*, the metal clowns confront the fury of a Latin American drug-dealing dictator. Chaplin's strategy was to play the role of the Führer himself. He ridiculed the tyrant as a pompous egomaniac who danced with the globe of the world on his fingertips and displayed his obsession with one-upmanship by pumping up the height of his barber's chair. In a similar but modernized mode of mockery, the Archaos stilt walker plays the modern dictator as an oafish giant who wears a gas mask over his crotch, as if to protect himself from some ghastly sexual disease. He oversees the murder of homeless children by death squads, a detail inserted in the show by Brazilian members of the troupe who witnessed similar atrocities in their home neighborhoods. The stilt-walking dictator is a postnuclear mutation of Chaplin's Hitler, a führer for the age of AIDS.

Having elevated the dictator to the stature of a grotesque colossus, the metal clowns cut him down to size with a subversive act of comic castration. One of them cuts off his stilt with a chain saw, while a mischievous juggler slits open the tyrant's gas mask to uncover crystal balls hidden between his legs. The crippled dictator tries to reclaim his precious possessions but can only drag his broken stilts behind him as the juggler keeps the balls floating teasingly out of his reach. The two of them play out a comic ballet that recalls Chaplin's famous scene as Hitler dancing with the globe of the world. Both gags mock the thirst for power by physicalizing the subconscious urges of a tyrant. For Chaplin's dictator the bouncing ball is the fulfillment of his dreams of conquest. For Archaos's dictator the bouncing balls are the nightmare of his impotence.

The joyous juggling of the dictator's testicles is the first step toward transforming the arena into a carnival of liberation. Freed from fear of the drug-pushing politician, the victims of his tyranny take control of their lives and turn their hyperindustrialized urban ghetto into a mardi gras of wild dancing, throbbing music, and mayhem. This is the legacy of the metal clowns, who invite the audience to dance with them at the end of every Archaos performance. The metal clowns give people at the bottom a place at the top. They overturn the prevailing order to free us to see the world from a fresh perspective, where the truth is not always what we imagined it to be when the world was right side up.

Archaos's vicious urban slapstick is inspired by the street life of cities like London and Paris where the circus performs. Operating in a blighted ghetto landscape, the clowns create black humor that illuminates the dynamics of urban violence and despair. Like inner-city gangs, the metal clowns travel in packs and are frustrated by the things they see but cannot have. In a traditional circus, the clown falls in love with the ballerina on the high wire and pines away with unrequited love. In Archaos, the clowns masturbate while watching a bare-breasted aerialist. The beauty of a trapeze artist on a construction derrick makes one clown so crazy with desire that he climbs up after her, only to be tossed off her perch, his limbs flailing the air as he falls.

Every aerial act in the circus is viewed from the ground by a motley band of marginal characters. They grimace at the images of perfection that loom beyond their reach, like homeless tramps window-shopping in a department store. Their longing for the unattainable echoes Chaplin's dreams of riches in *The Gold Rush*, but their despair is deeper than Chaplin's and their violence more extreme. A metal clown motto expresses the longing to break free of society's restrictions: "Have a laugh, don't take things too seriously, and if anything gets in your way smash it with a hammer."

Frustration is the driving force that animates Archaos's clowns. A typical performance presents the clowns with a series of unsettling annoyances that drive them to fits of frenzied aggression. A tiny remote-controlled jeep winds its way between their feet, but they never succeed in catching it because the remote contol is being operated by someone they can't see. One clown responds by rhythmically smashing himself in the head with his juggling clubs. Others set fire to whatever full-size vehicles come within range of their blowtorches. The old circus gag of trying to see how many clowns could fit into one car is updated by Archaos into trying to see how many cars could be demolished by one clown.

Audiences by the thousands respond enthusiastically to the lunatic antics of the metal clowns, a sign that their violent comedy has tapped an authentic stream of contemporary urban frustration. A performance of Archaos resembles a rock concert, with skinheads, punks, and teenyboppers whipped up into a delirium of wild delight. For many of the young spectators, the hunger for the circus's liberatingly subversive humor cannot be satisfied by simply laughing, screaming, and cheering. They volunteer to join the show. During the 1991–92 tour through England, France, and Scandinavia, hundreds of youths responded to Archaos's attempts to create local squadrons of metal clowns to perform alongside the professionals. The recruiting advertisement read: "Director Pierrot Bidon invites the criminally insane, unbalanced, degenerate, depraved, manic, and masochistic members of the 18 to 25 year old age group to strap on costumes of corrugated iron, crash-helmets and lacerated leathers before running through the burned out scrap heaps and petro-chemical stews of our circus set."

Most of the people who answered the ad were drifters or welfare recipients without many prospects for employment. "You can tell which ones are on the dole by how they run away when the television cameras show up," notes Jackie Toner, a twenty-three-year-old metal clown who dropped out of art school to join the show in Manchester, England. The applicants in London sported shaved heads, nose rings, and tattoos. Like the skid row derelicts hired by Chaplin as extras in *The Gold Rush*, these ragged recruits know what it's like to be left behind in their society's race for prosperity.

Metal clowns learn to survive by overcoming society's efforts to render them helpless. The brutal humor of their urban slapstick is epitomized by the comic adventures of the paraplegic midget who travels Archaos's runway in a motorized wheelchair, an embodiment of bondage and powerlessness. When he matches wits with acrobats and aerialists, his victories make the audience laugh with him instead of pitying him. Comparing their own inadequacies to the superhuman skills of the circus acrobats, the spectators are invited to identify with the entrapped vulnerability of the tiny invalid and take pleasure in his triumphs.

The midget's frailty is emphasized when he is thrown out of his wheelchair and tossed into a garbage can. One of the homeless tramp characters leaps into the midget's motorized chair and rides it away with his broom raised in triumph. In the street life depicted by Archaos, human beings are disposable and it is a step up in the world to achieve the status of a cripple. Meanwhile, the midget keeps comically popping his head out of the trashcan, refusing to be silenced, until he is eventually lifted tenderly into the arms of another clown and restored to his wheelchair. The rapport between the tiny man without legs and his burly rescuer has the intimacy that one usually associates with a mother and her infant, an image reinforced by the midget's earlier surprise entrance from between the buttons of a fat man's coat, like a newborn baby popping his head out of a womb. The scenes of caring in Archaos are inseparable from its scenes of heartlessness. Despite their aggressive fury, the show's metal-clad maniacs are just looking for a family to take them in out of the cold.

The paraplegic midget is the ultimate metal clown, a powerless figure who defies our expectations and survives the perils of an urban nightmare. He has no metal shield, but the electric wheelchair is his source of independence and self-protection, providing him with the mobility to outmanoeuver the forklifts, cranes, and diesel trucks that tower over him. When the performance ends in a carnival of dancing, he joins in the celebration with the rest of the circus troupe. Together they revel in their triumph over the inhumanity of their environment. Their outrageous black comedy has turned their microcosmic society upside down, revealing tenderness beneath the cruelty, generosity beneath the isolation, and freedom beneath the fear. The figures of authority have been humiliated, the fire-belching machines have been tamed, and the paraplegic clown leads a dance of the dispossessed on the grave of a techno-crazed society.

Much of the raw power of an Archaos performance comes from the audience's realization that its fictional universe bleeds into the real landscape of a twentieth-century metropolis. Like Chaplin's *Modern Times*, Archaos's carnival of forgotten souls is a comic slap in the face of the industrialized world, a disturbing reminder of the human cost of technological progress. The wretched comic vagrants of Archaos puncture the myth of their era's prosperity in the same way that Chaplin deflated the economic hypocrisy of his times. In *City Lights*, when the city authorities unveil a monument to Prosperity in an old-fashioned town square, they discover a tramp sleeping on the statue's lap. Creatures of another generation, the homeless clowns in Archaos sleep on a grease-stained tarmac as motorcycles speed obliviously around them. Their black comedy is a challenge to those who would ignore the rising tide of homelessness, unemployment, and urban violence. It shatters the polite silence of social apathy with a chorus of harsh, defiant laughter.

Every generation and culture invents new costumes and settings for its clowns, but the basic confrontation between the powerful and the powerless remains the same. The comic artists described in the following pages are part of the same defiant tradition that includes Chaplin and the metal clowns. Together they form a motley constellation of comic heroes who seem to spring up wherever new forms of oppression threaten a community's physical or spiritual survival.

Whether we are facing annihilation in the physical or spiritual sense, the comic tenacity of these artists suggests that the most deeply liberating function of humor is to free us to hope for the impossible. Our sense of humor is a mirror of our aspirations, reflecting our desires to escape the limitations that circumscribe our lives. This is one of the reasons that comedy is so frequently censored. Authorities that maintain control by relying on the public's diminished expectations are threatened by the power of unbridled laughter. Clowns are emblems of insubordination whose talent for subversion inspires the powerless with a hunger for revolt.

Not all comedy lives up to these lofty definitions of the art. Depending on the context in which it is used, humor can be ugly, cruel, and fascistic as well as liberating, but one way or another, it leaves its mark on our collective psyche. Popular comedy can be a call for perseverance in the face of tyranny, death, and oppression. For an audience with its back against the wall, a clown is a meta-physical escape artist, a Houdini of the soul.

I Nyoman Catra in the mask of a Balinese temple clown. (photo by Rebecca Carman)

Sacred Laughter in Bali

*Laughter is laced into the fabric of Balinese culture in many ways,
but it was the frogs I noticed first. Shortly after I arrived on the
island, my landlady giggled at my startled reaction to a brownish
green amphibian that hopped onto the dirt path in front of me. Her
name was Ibu Anom and the silly incident sparked a long conversation about a troupe of dancing frogs in the village of Batuan. Laughing as she described them, Anom urged me to seek out the dancing
amphibians for myself. I never would have understood the indispens-
ability of the island's clowns if I hadn't taken her advice and ended
up performing in Bali's temple ceremonies as a giant green frog.*

*I Made Djimat was the leader of the troupe in Batuan, and he
adopted me into his extended family of musicians, dancers, and
clowns. I rehearsed with them in Djimat's mud-walled compound
and rode with them in dilapidated pickup trucks to temple festivals
throughout the island. While I never achieved the comic grace displayed so easily by Djimat and his troupe, my apprenticeship gave
me an inside perspective on the Balinese view of laughter as something sacred, a necessity without which no temple festival would be
complete.*

*After I had been training with him for six months, Djimat
asked me to perform with his troupe in the temples. I began with the
mask of the old man, a comic character who is past his prime, infest-
ed with fleas, and barely able to lift himself out of his chair, but
insists on dancing as a tribute to the gods.*

The temple ceremony where I made my debut was a typically chaotic Balinese event. Multiple activities coexisted in eclectic harmony. As families brought ancestral offerings to the shrine, a priest chanted Sanskrit prayers over a loudspeaker. He did not stop when the performance began; his wailing melody simply melted into the texture of the gamelan orchestra of gongs and metal xylophones that accompanied our play. The music attracted an audience to the courtyard where our curtain had been hastily set up. Behind it Djimat sprinkled holy water over me and another dancer who would perform with him that day.

After Djimat finished dancing the warrior mask I shook the curtains from behind to signal the entrance of the old man. The frenetic rhythms of the gamelan lifted my limbs into action. Sweat dripped into my eyes as I looked through the tiny slits cut under the mask's bulging eyes. I saw the spectators: young girls sitting on the ground in their colored sarongs, children in their mothers' laps, and grandparents chewing on beetle nut. They seemed mildly amused by my efforts but equally intrigued by the stray dog barking at me and the women with pyramids of rice cakes balanced on their heads walking through the playing space. I staggered around them and began to improvise with a live duck that one of the women in the procession was carrying to the shrine. The duck quacked indignantly at the old man's halting advances, and the impromptu encounter turned out to be the comic highlight of my performance.

My debut as a clown in the temple marked the beginning of a change in my relationship to the village. Prices I was charged in the market began dropping. Casual acquaintances invited me to their homes. The speed of my acceptance into the community was further accelerated a few weeks later when Djimat tricked me into adding another clown character to my repertoire. In the middle of a particularly rowdy performance, Djimat handed me the mask of a fat-lipped buffoon and told me to follow him out through the curtain. Before I had time to refuse, he had put the mask on my face, and I was improvising an entrance. Being as surprised as the audience at my arrival, and realizing I was wearing a mask that was expected to speak, I just looked around and bellowed, "Kenken niki?" (What's going on here?)

My bad Balinese accent was enough to set the audience roaring. With lack of grace as my specialty, I managed to entertain the crowd simply by chasing Djimat around in circles. The gruff voice I used was frequently imitated throughout the village over the next few days, and before long Djimat invited me to perform other comic characters including the frog.

Dewa Made Gulem, a man in Djimat's troupe who excelled in the frog dance, took me to the rice paddies with a kerosene lantern so that we could get down on our knees in the mud and watch the frogs cavort. Made concentrated on the frogs engaged in rituals of courtship, a key part of the frog story we would perform together. "This is how you should move when the girl arrives," he said, pointing to a frog that had backed away slowly from its mate, jumped forward suddenly, and struck a pose. "When she kisses you, jump in the air, lie on your back, and wiggle your toes with happiness. Then you can sleep on her lap and put your hands wherever you want." When we got home Made Gulem was so inspired by our observations that he tried out some of his new frog steps in a dance with a two-hundred-pound hog that lived in his family's yard.

Once I began performing the frog mask regularly, people in the village started calling me "Kodok" (frog). Djimat's troupe indulged my attachment to the character by inserting a frog segment into plays that had absolutely no connection to frogs. In the middle of the story, someone would stop and say something absurd like, "Look, we must be close to the rice fields because I see a frog coming." That would be my cue to enter in the frog mask and costume that had been patched together for me by my friends with scraps of old army camouflage material and hand-painted cloth. It was as a frog that I felt most at home in Bali.

The significance of clowns to the everyday life of a Balinese village was revealed to me most clearly in a performance I arranged as a gift to Ibu Anom, the woman who had directed me to the troupe on my first days in Bali. She was happy to hear I would be dancing the frog mask in her family temple but disappointed to learn there was no romance planned for the frog. Wanting to please her, I asked Djimat to play the frog's lover in one of his comic female impersonation masks. He agreed, but another dancer surprised us during our duet by coming out in yet another female mask and claiming to be the frog's forgotten first wife from America.

As the performance evolved, more village relationships were integrated into the comedy. Djimat initiated a scene in which I became his dance teacher, reversing our real-life roles. A wood carver came to watch me dance a cross-eyed clown mask he had made for me, and knowing it was his birthday I used the opportunity to congratulate him in the voice of his own creation. I also teased Ibu Arsa, the woman who had cooked for me during most of my stay in Bali, joking about her food as an expression of my appreciation.

The performance was full of personal innuendo and comic references like these. The audience and the performers were part of one another's lives, and their relationships were threaded into the fabric of the comedy. The crowd responded warmly to the croaking frog with the American accent. Formal handshakes and thank-yous would have meant little to them, but the mask of the frog helped me speak to them in a language of laughter that was embedded in their culture and understandable to all.

In one sense the village's laughter was the equivalent of a heartfelt embrace marking my acceptance into the circle of spiritual and mundane connections that link all Balinese clowns to their audiences. But I was not naive enough to believe I had actually become a full-fledged Balinese clown. My performances were tinged with an inescapable irony. As were other foreigners before me, I was an invader whose potential threat to the harmony of village life had been neutralized by laughter. Another awkward, gangling outsider had been tamed by the clowns, stuffed safely into a frog mask and costume blessed by their gods.

Djimat's wily troupe of sacred merrymakers had dealt with me in person the way they are accustomed to dealing symbolically with larger cultural threats. They had incorporated me into the comic dance that the Balinese use to subvert the corrosive forces of Westernization and insure the spiritual continuity of their traditions. The last laugh was on me. There were genuine bonds of

*affection between me and my adopted Balinese family, but I could
not pretend to be anything more than a bit player in the epic
comedy that has been a part of the island's survival strategy for
centuries.*

The clanging gongs of a gamelan orchestra vibrate feverishly in
the Balinese night air. Brightly robed dancers perform a sacred
spectacle in the open-air courtyard of a village temple. Silhouettes of palm trees loom overhead in the moonlight as the audience of rice farmers and their families sit together on the dirt
floor beneath their ancestral altars. Infants wriggle in their parents' laps while old women squat in the dust and listen intently to
the dialogue.

The play is about a sixteenth-century Balinese kingdom
plagued by demons when its citizens forget to pay tribute to their
gods and ancestors. The cautionary tale is meant to remind the
modern audience to follow the teachings of their Hindu-Buddhist
religion, but the plot is interrupted in midstream by an ungainly
figure who bursts through the makeshift curtain shouting shrill
bursts of broken English. He grabs a gong hammer from a musician and the orchestra stops playing. There is a moment of tense
silence as the intruder's eyes dart among the motionless dancers,
musicians, and spectators.

"How much?" he barks, as if the instrument he has snatched
were being offered up for auction. "Five dollar? Ten dollar? I got
many dollar." He turns abruptly and points across the courtyard
to a dancer's gold-leaf headdress adorned with frangipane flowers. "I buy your hat too." The crowd responds to his boorishness
with squeals of laughter.

This seeming act of sacrilege is not intended to defile the
sacred ceremony. On the contrary, its function is to strengthen the
village traditions. The apparent intruder is a temple clown, and
his anachronistic antics are accepted as a natural part of a complex
communal event where laughter helps link the spectators to their
gods, their ancestors, and one another. Balinese religion revolves

around the propitiation of divine and ancestral spirits. One way of pleasing the gods is to present them with prayers and offerings; another is to make them laugh.

Temple festivals, known as *odalan*, are microcosms of Balinese society. They provide a ceremonial affirmation of the complex rituals that give spiritual meaning to everyday village life. The clowning that occurs in the *odalan* plays a key role in the culture's balancing act between the historic forces that sustain the integrity of Bali's heritage and contemporary forces like tourism and commercial development that are poised to destroy it. When the harmony of a temple festival is shattered by a satirical portrait of Western greed, the choice between material and spiritual values is put into sharp focus. The lithe grace of the Balinese dancers is pitted against the neurotic twitches of the tourist, and the audience casts its vote through laughter.

Like the village itself the clown interloper exists at the intersection of Balinese and Western culture. He wears the same hand-embroidered robes that clothe the actors playing gods and kings, but his mask is a garish, wooden caricature of a Westerner's nose. He converses with characters who speak Balinese and Sanskrit, but he himself speaks only fragments of English that might be overheard in a hotel souvenir shop.

A perfect parody of rude and intrusive tourists, the clown grabs a cheap camera swinging from his neck and photographs everything in sight. "Smile, please. Just one more," he shouts, sticking the camera into the faces of every dancer, musician, and child he can get close to. The shiny plastic gadget contrasts sharply with the sacred offerings of palm leaves, rice cakes, and woven cloth that decorate the temple. It is clear that this grotesque embodiment of Western materialism does not fit into the sublime environment of a Balinese ceremony. The audience is directly confronted with the discrepancies between the beauty of their heritage and the hollowness of what the tourist has to offer.

Everyone in the audience understands the performer's intentions. "Our culture needs a filter to modify the influence of Westernization," explains I Nyoman Catra, one of Bali's most sought-after clowns. "When people look at the results of modern development through the eyes of the clowns they see it with a dose of skepticism. The clowns help us filter out the excesses of progress so that we can change and evolve without losing the traditions that make Bali unique."

Catra often shakes up village temple performances by injecting rock and roll into the ancient dramas. His buck-toothed comic character often demonstrates the disco steps that tourists will bring into the temples if the Balinese are not careful to preserve their heritage. The same buffoonish mask plays the part of a Balinese tour guide who sells his rice fields to buy a motorcycle and cater to the whims of foreign vacationers. "Time is money," yells the clown, as he rushes past the landscape in a ridiculously hurried gait that is antithetical to the traditional Balinese sense of time and harmony.

Bali's traditions are rooted in an agrarian village life that revolves around the cycles of rice plantings and harvests. Spiritual values take precedence over material concerns, and offerings to the Hindu-Buddhist gods are made of fresh flowers every day. Enormous amounts of time and resources are devoted to creating beautiful works of art. The Balinese live in a lush, fertile island paradise and feel it is their obligation to thank the gods for their good fortune by making regular offerings of sculpted rice cakes, stone temple carvings, or religious dances. The culture's unique interconnections among nature, religion, art, beauty, and everyday life are now threatened by crasser values imported by tourists and Western entrepreneurs. Souvenir shops are beginning to obscure the view of the rice fields, and devotion to profit is eating away at the villagers' devotion to their gods.

Catra's parodies of progress are so entertaining that the governor of the island regularly invites him to perform his clown routines at state functions. In situations like these, the moral implications of his jokes are pondered by the politicians who will make crucial decisions about the pace of modernization in Bali. Performing at the governor's mansion, Catra implied that the Western sense of progress might not be the best thing for Bali by joking that there are times, as during a game of tug-of-war, when going backward is the only way to win. He went on to compare

tourists to ducks who waddle out to the villages pecking for food
and come back to the hotels to lay their eggs. It was his way of
suggesting that the hotel industry was exploiting village life and
keeping the tourist income for itself. To ensure that his jokes
would be remembered, Catra told some of them dressed in drag
and ended his show by giving the governor a big, wet kiss.

The respect with which temple clowns like Catra are viewed
is reflected in their name. Almost every form of Balinese temple
performance is centered around a pair of comic servants to the
king who are known collectively as *penasar. Penasar* is the Balinese word for foundation, and their title indicates the fundamental
role of the clowns in the temple performances. It is the responsibility of the *penasar* to integrate modern references about
tourism, politics, and religion into the ancient epics with improvisations that make the plays relevant to a contemporary audience.

The *penasar* are two zanies who quarrel, bicker, and tease
each other like tropical reincarnations of Laurel and Hardy, but
the audience pays special attention to the loony dialogue. It provides a living link between history and current events, and a
bridge between the sacred and the mundane. Rangda is a mythi-
cal Balinese figure who serves as a timeless embodiment of evil,
but the clowns who perform with Rangda in the temple spectacles concretize and update the spirit's vague malevolence. In one
play the clowns preface a comic exorcism of Rangda's disciples
with banter about progress, development, and tourism. These
three words (*maju, pembangunan,* and *pariwisata* in Indonesian)
are heard constantly throughout the island, and no village is
immune to the stresses they cause. One clown argues that it is a
sign of progress to see children learning English in schools.
"Yes," his partner answers ironically. "My son learned English.
Now he can say, 'Good morning, Dad. I need some money.'"

This exchange led to an impromptu English lesson for the
children in the audience in which the clowns encouraged their
students to communicate with a tourist who had found his way to
the performance. Unlike the dances staged in Bali's hotels, this
performance was meant for the worshippers of the temple, and
the presence of an outsider was felt to be mildly invasive. The

clowns defused the awkwardness of the situation by making jokes that accorded the tourist the status of a guest while defining the limits of his participation as an outsider. They used humor to exorcise the disruptive influence of the tourist as effectively as the priests use holy water to exorcise the evil spirits of Rangda's mask. Their comedy suggests that tourists might be bizarre earthly manifestations of Rangda, and that running amok for dollars is the modern Balinese equivalent of demonic possession.

To live up to their multiple responsibilities as entertainers, town criers, educators, historians, and priests, the clowns study Sanskrit texts inscribed on manuscripts of dried palm leaves called *lontar*. Their knowledge of the island's heritage is displayed in improvised responses to interruptions of the ceremony. The intrusive tourist is met with historical references and cross-cultural gags that render his boorishness obvious to even a child.

Incorporating the mask of the tourist into the comic dance of the temple ceremony is the clown's solution to the threat of Westernization. The improvisational skills of the performers reflect the adaptive resilience of the culture at large. The Balinese have developed a shrewd system for minimizing the destructive influence of tourism, without sacrificing its economic benefits. Vacationers are housed in luxury hotels and picturesque beach cottages, while the traditional life of the villages continues relatively undisturbed in the fertile highlands of the island's interior. This division is particularly pleasing to the Balinese, who believe that evil spirits live in the ocean, and prefer to be surrounded by fertile terraced rice fields in villages close to the heavenly abodes of their gods. The islanders keep vacationers away from sacred festivals in the center of the island by sending dancers and clowns to perform for them in hotels, restaurants, and roadside arenas. Most tourists are distracted by these secular dances and leave the genuine ceremonies undisturbed.

The clowns' tactics are characteristic of the strategy that Bali has used throughout its history to preserve its cultural continuity in the face of the potentially devastating influence of military and cultural invasions from other parts of the world. Like their clowns, the Balinese owe their success to the fine art of improvisation.

They adapt their traditions to accommodate changing circumstances, preserving their heritage through indirect assimilation
rather than direct defiance of their invaders.

In the fifteenth and sixteenth centuries the island absorbed
the migration of the Hindu Majapahit Dynasty from East Java,
resulting in a hybrid form of animistic Hindu-Buddhism that is
uniquely Balinese. At the turn of the twentieth century the
Balinese were the last major spice island to resist colonization by
Holland, and even after their surrender to the Dutch army in
1908, the Balinese continued their traditional lifestyle with only
slight modifications. The Japanese occupation during World War
II was equally ineffective in penetrating Balinese traditions. And
now, although part of an independent Indonesian state, Balinese
villages continue to govern themselves according to timeless customs that have nothing to do with the practices of the Javanese
Muslim majority that dominates the country's politics.

Across the spectrum of Balinese performing arts from purely sacred ritual to purely secular fun, there is almost always some
element of clowning. The Balinese believe it is much more likely
the gods would grace a performance with their presence if they
could be assured of a good laugh. Laughter, in this context, sanctifies the temples.

As mediators between the world of the audience and the
worlds inhabited by gods and kings, the clowns banter with the
spectators, teasing the royal characters and making ironic comments about the sacred Sanskrit songs that are sung in praise of
the gods. Their words shift easily from ancient Kawi (a Sanskrit
variant used in prayer) to high Balinese (spoken to royalty) to low
Balinese (spoken to commoners) to Indonesian (spoken in reference to official government business) to an occasional phrase of
English (spoken in mockery of tourists). Their polyglot fluency
mirrors the balanced coexistence of a society in transition. The
creative tension between the different dialects and what they represent is expressed in a lively barrage of multilingual puns.

In the Balinese cosmology, good and evil are inextricably
linked to each other. Demons and gods coexist with the same kind
of dynamic tension that characterizes the relationship between

Balinese tradition and Westernization. This concept of interrelated opposites is expressed most directly in the ritual encounters between Rangda and the phantasmagorical lion mask known as Barong. Barong is an archetypal spirit of benevolence, and his clashes with Rangda are charged with extraordinary spiritual potency for the Balinese. Although their battle is enacted regularly in every village, neither Rangda nor Barong is ever allowed to kill the other. They always fight to a draw, achieving the dynamic tension between good and evil that defines the Balinese vision of life.

In the village of Jembaran the yearly struggle between Rangda and Barong takes place in a colorful street pageant. Several clownish characters play subsidiary roles in this important village ceremony, but the most striking comic aspect of the event is Barong himself, a huge masked creature animated by two villagers dancing under a dazzling costume of horsehair, spangles, and gold-leaf brocade. One man is responsible for clicking the big, chattering teeth of the red-and-white wooden mask while the other wiggles Barong's erect golden tail. The coordination of their footwork is reminiscent of a vaudeville duet in a dancing horse costume, and the Barong players heighten the comedy by nuzzling their way into the laps of the spectators who throng to greet their sacred benefactor. Touching Barong brings good luck, and small children try to pull off small clumps of his hair for souvenirs.

Rangda's ghoulish masked servants take even greater liberties with the good-natured Barong, grabbing his testicles in an effort to discourage him from attacking their mistress. The audience enjoys Barong's slapstick response to the assault on his private parts. They are clearly on the creature's side, rooting for him to vanquish Rangda and her malicious servants from their village for another year. Although he is a divine manifestation of goodness, Barong is humanized by his comic antics and takes on the intimate role of an oversized family watchdog. Like the furry, cuddly hero of a Walt Disney fantasy, he plays with the children until it is time to defend the clan from intruders. Then he mounts a display of teeth-snapping ferocity, stymies the advances of Rangda, and ends the ceremony by healing villagers who have been thrown into frenzied trances by the witch's malevolent powers.

A more ethereal form of Balinese clowning occurs in the sacred shadow puppet plays known as *Wayang Kulit*. Here clowns are servants to the heroes and villains of the *Mahabharata*, a classic Hindu epic poem, but they exist only as shadows cast by the flame of a coconut oil lamp. A master puppeteer called the "*dalang*" manipulates animal skin silhouettes of the *Mahabharata* characters between the fire's light and a white cotton screen, creating a universe of pulsating shadows. In a story that uses two warring families as metaphors for good and evil, the *dalang* plays all the parts himself, giving particular emphasis to the clown servants who translate the abstract moral issues of Hindu philosophy into concrete human terms.

As he animates the short, squat clown puppets, the sounds that surge from the mouth of the *dalang* are as warm and richly varied as the flame that is the source of the shadows. The clown voices flicker with laughter, burst into sparks of teasing conflict, fade into smoky wisps of irony, and erupt unexpectedly into fiery tirades of bellowing nonsense. The vibrant musicality of these vocalizations results in the same types of comic banter used by the *penasar* in other forms of drama, and the *dalang* provides percussive slapstick punctuation by hitting his wooden puppet box with a metal clacker lodged between his toes.

Wayang Kulit is usually performed in village temples, and the best *dalang* are highly regarded for their ability to weave religious and philosophical debates into the clown dialogues. Ketut Rupik, a *dalang* from the village of Lukluk, known simply as "*dalang* Lukluk," gives his shows in the back of an old red pickup truck. He drives it from village to village like a mobile movie theater, setting up his shadow screen and gamelan orchestra in the truck bed, while the audience gathers to watch on the ground around his parking spot. While *dalang* Lukluk's stories are still based on the *Mahabharata*, he spices up the ancient epic with shadowy images of motorcycles, jeeps, and airplanes. He jokes about Mike Tyson and borrowing money from local Indonesian banks. In one scene the police arrive to break up an illegal cockfight and a Balinese family escapes by piling onto a motorcycle, only to crash into an oncoming truck. The clash between the forces of change and tradition is jarringly displayed in this wacky junkmobile spectacle. It is a battle in which the Balinese heritage seems to be losing ground to the forces of Westernization. *Dalang* Lukluk's comedy is a warning of what the future might be like in a Bali that surrenders its traditions to progress.

Wayan Wija, a highly respected *dalang* from Sukawati, is just as innovative as *dalang* Lukluk, but he uses his departures from tradition to reinforce the values that have always been central to Balinese culture. Wija's clown puppets go jogging, do push-ups, and make jokes about real estate speculation, but their fascination with the West is tempered by their clearly articulated belief in the preservation of their island's religious values.

"The clowns connect me to the audience," says Wija in the thatch-roofed studio where he carves new puppets from dried animal skins. "Everything that the audience learns about philosophy comes from the clowns." Wija feels that the philosophy of the clowns protects the audience from harm in a way that is analogous to the physiological protection a mother provides for her child. "In Bali we believe that everyone is born with the help of four siblings: the umbilical cord, the amniotic sac, the amniotic fluid, and the mother's blood. These four siblings protect the child until it is born. The four clowns in Wayang Kulit [two pairs of comic servants] are like those four siblings. If you pay attention to those siblings they can help you." In Wija's view of Balinese cosmology, laughter is a biological necessity that nourishes, renews, and invigorates the audience.

This vision of comedy as a form of spiritual sustenance is shared by Balinese artists in all genres of performance. I Gusti Windia, one of the island's most popular clowns, is a specialist in *topeng*, Bali's most sacred form of masked performance. "When I make offerings before a play," says Windia, "I meditate on how to make a performance that connects our religion to our life." Windia has a Falstaffian body that stretches the limits of the bamboo chair he sits in. His wide face broadens into a luminous smile at the end of each phrase, as he thoughtfully articulates the responsibilities of a clown. "There is a lot of philosophy in *topeng*, but I can't be too serious about it, or the audience will get bored, so we use comedy to speak to the audience indirectly, under their skins. Then when people leave the temple they will remember the ideas inside the jokes and think about them at home. It is their homework."

Windia speaks from the porch of his mud-walled family compound in the village of Carang Sari. At the center of the complex of stone altars and thatched huts is an open-air pavilion where Windia rehearses *topeng* with the troupe that has earned a reputation as one of the most entertaining on the island. As the most highly skilled clown in the troupe, Windia is the group leader. He is the one who keeps track of their busy schedule of temple performances and decides which stories will be the best suited to the particular needs of each village they visit. "A good *topeng* play should answer the questions that people need to ask to help them with the problems in their lives."

The masked characters in a *topeng* play recreate the rhythms of life. "Between the morning of youth and the nighttime of old age there are the everyday activities of life. This is shown by the *penasar* clown going through the business of the day. He is the foundation of what people do in their lives."

The second type of Balinese comic characters are called *bondres*, and include the mask of the tourist. They are more eccentric types of buffoons, and Windia animates their description with goofy voices, frustrating stutters, and funny faces. "The *bondres* are the interferences in our lives. Like when you go to the office and are interrupted by something that stops your mind from working. In the plays, the mind is represented by the mask of the king who controls the movements of the kingdom the way our mind controls the movements of our body. The *bondres* clowns are always interrupting the king's plans the way the distractions in our lives interrupt the things we want to do."

When the arc of the *topeng* play has completed its trajectory from morning to night, the last mask to be danced is called Sidhya Karya, which means "The end of the ceremony." This is the most mysterious of all the characters, because it is connected to the end of life as well as the end of the day. "At the end of every activity," Windia notes, "after all the interruptions, there is a finish, and at the end of your life, after all the interruptions, you die. It is hard to know how to die, because people don't know what it means to be dead. It's like being born, or choosing a wife. We never know how it will work out."

The mask of Sidhya Karya is connected to the idea of finishing all activities in the proper way, and for almost any undertaking in Bali, from bargaining at the market to attending a cremation, the element of shared laughter is part of a proper finish. Although Sidhya Karya is not considered literally to be a clown, he wears a mask carved into a perpetual grin. The character is often played by the lead clown in the troupe, and his appearance is greeted by the laughter of children who run away as Sidhya Karya tries to catch them and make the offering that will end the play.

On the holy day of Tumpek Wayang, Windia prepares himself for a performance of *topeng pajegan*, the most sacred form of *topeng*, with an elaborate ceremony at the ancestral temple inside his family compound. A priest has been invited to bless the masks that Windia will use in the show. His children play the gamelan in accompaniment to the priest's chanting, and his wife has prepared offerings of fruit, rice cakes, and a roast suckling pig that are removed from the altar and devoured at the dinner table once it is determined the gods have eaten their fill of the food's essence.

After the meal, Windia and his assistants carry his costume and masks down a dirt road that runs alongside a river. The procession is led by Windia, whose burly body makes huge waddling shadows in the beams of the flashlights they use to find their way in the dark. Chickens and ducks squawk and flutter when the lights pass over their resting places in the foliage that lines the road. Eventually the group arrives at one of Carang Sari's three major temples, where Windia's neighbors are engaged in public ceremonies similar to the ones he has just performed at his home. Their efforts will not be complete until Windia enacts his one-man *topeng pajegan* and finishes the play with an offering from Sidhya Karya.

Sitting on the hard dirt ground of the outdoor temple courtyard, surrounded by hand-carved stone altars and tropical vegetation, the audience could very well be part of the sixteenth-century ceremony being reenacted before them. Windia's *topeng* masks are archetypal embodiments of high- and low-caste characters whose descendants are sitting in the audience. When Windia makes jokes that include his contemporary audience in the action of the historic play, he is fulfilling the purpose of the larger temple ceremony by establishing continuity between the world of the ancestors and present-day reality. The play's characters realize that their lives will be blighted with plague and pestilence if they do not properly complete the ceremony, and the modern audience too must find a way to carry out their ceremonies in the traditional fashion so they can find the same spiritual harmony enjoyed by their ancestors.

By the time that Sidhya Karya comes out to finish the ceremony in the play, the two time frames have become one. The offering that he makes to end the play is the same offering that the villagers need to end their ceremony in the temple, and they are participating in both events at once. The clown in the mask of Sidhya Karya has become their priest. Sidhya Karya, with his grinning face, teases the children, makes everyone laugh, and then sanctifies the ground with rice that has been blessed with holy water. He leaves a tiny palm leaf basket of flowers and incense on the dirt in front of the curtain before making his final exit.

Now that the ceremony is complete, Windia says a prayer of thanks over his masks and places them carefully in the basket, where they rest pressed against one another, the clowns, the kings, the demons, the gods; masks of youth, morning, and life; masks of age, nighttime, and death. One of the temple elders gives him an envelope of cash, from which Windia removes a single bill as token payment and gives the rest back. He slings the mask basket over his shoulder and walks off into the night, his stocky frame shifting rhythmically with each step, like a wind-up toy duck.

Having helped his neighbors complete their temple ceremony, Windia has contributed to the spiritual balance of the village. The Balinese are obsessed with carrying out ceremonies in the proper manner, on the proper day, facing in the proper direction. Every important activity is accompanied by offerings, whose proper presentation insures its propitious completion. The building of a traditional Balinese house involves countless measurements calculated according to where the various pavilions stand in relation to the sacred volcano *gunung agung* (home of the gods) and the sea (abode of the demons). The spaces between the pavilions must be measured according to the foot size of the owner, who speaks the names of demons, gods, and humans as he takes the measured steps that will determine the placement of the different structures. Similarly, the idea of successfully completing a ceremony is implicit in every *topeng* performance, making it an essential part of each village's spiritual life.

In *topeng panca*, a variation of the genre in which five men share the roles of the different masks, the historical stories also revolve around the necessity of completing a ceremony that has been disrupted by some outside force. In the *topeng* play known as *Puputan Badung* (the end of Badung), typical enemies such as a demon, witch, or tyrannical enemy king are replaced by Dutch soldiers who disrupted the spiritual harmony of Balinese life with their 1906 invasion of the island. Although the Dutch were armed with muskets and the Balinese had only swords, the king of Badung refused to surrender. He and his courtiers dressed in ceremonial clothing and marched to the sea in what they knew would be a procession of ritual suicide. The *topeng* play that reenacts this massacre presents it as a spiritual ceremony. The king and his followers are seen completing their lives in a way that brings dignity to their ancestors and descendants. They accept defeat with serenity and are portrayed dancing blissfully to heaven in a choreography that honors the enduring legacy of their sacrifice.

The Dutch, on the other hand, are played as bunglers with big pink noses, bumping into each other and tripping over their own muskets like doltish Keystone cops. The clowns who play these soldiers make it clear that their hollow victory is destined to be short-lived. In reenacting the tragedy, the Balinese use laughter to reclaim their history from the country that colonized them. As the audience laughs at the ineptitude of the Dutch, it is evident that the Balinese turned the loss of the battle into a spiritual victory. The irony is compounded by the spectators' knowledge that the Dutch are gone, while the Balinese traditional culture still remains strong.

Similarly subversive comic portrayals of outside invaders were enacted by *topeng* performers during the World War II occupation of the Dutch East Indies by Hirohito's imperial army, and many clowns were arrested for resistance against the Japanese. Windia's family compound was a center of resistance activities during the war with Japan and again during the war for independence from Holland, which was won in 1949. "It was like a post office," laughs Windia. "People would come here to bring letters, exchange news, and hide weapons." His father, also a *topeng* clown, would pretend to be rehearsing innocent dances when the Dutch searched his home, but he was receiving regular information from the independence movement and passing it on to the public during performances in which the clowns spoke dialects that the colonial censors didn't understand.

Windia's father received a medal of recognition from the Indonesian government for his resistance activities during the war for independence. Windia's acts of comic subversion are less obvious but equally important to the survival of Bali's cultural identity. In addition to performing at temple ceremonies, Windia is often invited to provide entertainment at important civic events like the founding of his village's credit union. Balinese farmers are not in the habit of saving and accumulating wealth, and village credit unions are being established to keep the island's economic development under local control. Healthy savings accounts will enable village farmers to resist outside real estate speculators who threaten to turn Bali's rice fields into tourist shops and hotels. Windia's clown mask translates the complex economics of the situation into a comic allegory about sex. "If you deposit money into the credit union's money box," he explains, "it will grow bigger, just like your wife's belly grows bigger when you deposit something precious inside her." Crude as they were, jokes like these helped the credit union get off to a roaring start.

Windia's most popular clown character is his female impersonation of a mask called *ratu gegek* (beautiful lady). His comic
transvestite has become so famous that people all over the island
refer to his *topeng* troupe as *tugek*, a shortened form of the mask's
name, and farmers have been known to jokingly introduce their
wives as *tugek* when they want their friends to know that their
spouse's beauty is more than skin-deep. "Ratu Gegek is an ugly
woman with a beautiful soul," explains Windia, who sometimes
receives mail in Carang Sari addressed only to "Ratu Gegek."
"The postman knows where to deliver it," he adds proudly. The
homely masked lady has become a cultural phenomenon, spoofing
the disorienting effect of modernization on Balinese village life.

Nothing is stable in Ratu Gegek's universe. Her sentences
begin in Balinese and end in Indonesian. She boasts that her
mother calls her "a gift from the cemetery" (a Balinese malaprop-
ism that comes from her mispronunciation of "a gift from the
gods"). Reversing the usual preparations for an evening on the
town, Ratu Gegek washes her face after she puts on her makeup,
negating the hours of work she has invested in making herself
beautiful. She complains that it is hard to be a woman, because
men always want something from women, but if they damage
what they get they never take responsibility for it. Women in the
audience cheer at her loopy logic. But of course everyone knows
she is only a man pretending to be a woman, so everything she
says is suspect. Ratu Gegek is a Balinese Gracie Allen in drag, a
comic incarnation of the cultural vertigo that plagues her island
home.

Often Ratu Gegek compounds the audience's confusion
without offering any solutions, but her sense of social responsibility compels her to give advice on topical issues like birth control.
In a jungle clearing near the stone demon guardians of Windia's
village temple is a pink-and-blue monument to family planning
whose idealization of a nuclear family with only two children
attests to the government's concern about overpopulation. Ratu
Gegek, like other Balinese clowns, has been asked by the
Ministry of Health to include information about family planning
in her comic routines. Because sex is a favorite topic of Balinese

audiences, jokes about birth control fit naturally into the repertory. Clowns across the island express relief that family planning does not involve chopping off a man's penis. Ratu Gegek and her colleagues cannot take all the credit, but because the public information program began recruiting clowns in the late seventies, Bali's population increase has declined markedly.

Male members of the audience might be content to take advice about birth control from a man in a female mask, but Balinese women are hungry for more authentic role models. *Topeng*, like many other Balinese forms of theater, excludes female performers, but new hybrid genres of temple performance have been developed in which women play increasingly important roles, including some of the most slyly subversive comic characters in the Balinese repertory. In deference to the growing popularity of female dancers and clowns, Windia invites several women to perform regularly with the men in his *topeng* troupe. The men continue to play *topeng* masked characters, while the women create their characterizations with stylized makeup belonging to the performance tradition of *ardja*, an all-female form of operatic temple love stories.

Until the twenties *ardja* was also performed entirely by men, but women began infiltrating the form under Dutch colonial rule, a period that saw the liberalization of many gender-based restrictions, including the custom of suttee, in which the widows of kings were expected to throw themselves into the cremation fires of their husbands. Seen by many young educated Balinese as bellwethers of women's changing status in a male-dominated society, the *ardja* actresses exhibit a fiery independence and sense of humor that has helped them take over the majority of *ardja*'s parts, including the role of the king.[1]

When female *ardja* actors perform together with male *topeng* actors, the resulting mélange is known as *prembon*. One of the funniest and most popular characters in both *ardja* and *prembon* is the *liku*, or crazy queen, and the island's most accomplished master of *liku* acting is Ni Made Rusni, a one-woman theatrical hurricane who shatters the Balinese stereotype of the docile, domesticated female. Even before she comes onto the stage, her voice dominates the male characters as it sings out eccentric rhythms from behind the curtain. The clown menservants who await her arrival complain that she sounds like an old car engine trying to drive up a mountain. When she finally bursts through the curtain, Rusni literally knocks them both off their feet with a wild parody of Balinese classical dance that replaces modestly sinuous curves with aggressive pelvic thrusts.

Rusni uses her body as a comically subversive text, demanding attention in a dance that ends with her hip tilted. As they try to help their queen, the *penasar* clowns embellish their earlier line of automotive jokes with some sexual double entendres:

"Let's get a mechanic. Her shock absorber is broken."

"There's no mechanic here. Use your jack."

"I can't use my jack."

"Why not?"

"It's too small. Why don't you use yours?"

"Mine doesn't work very well either."

In this comic battle of the sexes Rusni always maintains the upper hand, intimidating the two clowns and ultimately refusing to let them treat her body like a machine. Instead she forces them to clean her bottom with their sacred headbands, a humiliating act of comic obeisance. When the king arrives Rusni performs another slapstick reversal of status. She gets down on her knees and folds her hands dutifully before her husband, singing a song that attests to her waiting faithfully for his return, but when she comes to the end of the song Rusni undercuts its passive message by unexpectedly changing the lyrics and tune to an onomatopoetic rendition of an attacking mosquito. Ending the ditty with a ferocious death slap to the annoying insect, her message to the king is that she has no intention of sitting around and becoming food for the bugs. She wants the attention and respect she deserves. "I come in a small package, but I give big results," quips the diminutive queen, in a quote she has stolen verbatim from a radio advertisement for a well-known headache remedy.

Balinese women are usually confined to traditional village roles of mothers and housewives, but Rusni plays the crazy queen as a woman determined to break out of the straitjacket men have fashioned for her sex. To win the king's respect she likens the abused landscape of her body to the sacred landscape of the island. The story is ostensibly unfolding in another century, but the anachronistic jokes about cars and tourists remind the audience that the mountains, rice fields, and temples of contemporary Bali are also in need of special attention to preserve them from harm. By the end of the play she has convinced the king to sing her praises, and he lovingly lists the attributes of her beauty, one body part at a time. Their romantic harmony coincides with the successful completion of an important religious ceremony, so that the well-being of the island is again connected to the respectful treatment of the queen.

At her modest home in the village of Sanur, Rusni seems no different from an ordinary Balinese housewife, serving tea to her husband and helping him prepare food for his pet roosters. She is shy and soft-spoken, a sharp contrast to the extroverted energy of the crazy queen she plays in the temple performances. "On stage I am in control," says Rusni. "I just do the things that women would like to do at home. The crazy queen is just like the women in the audience." Playing the *liku* character, Rusni is free to say the things that Balinese women feel but have no outlet to express. Her comic antics feed their hunger for respect.

In the spring of 1992 Rusni took part in a village *ardja* performance that mixed sexual with government politics. Based on the Greek tragedy of Phaedra, the play epitomized the extraordinary ability of Balinese clowns to entertain audiences while challenging them to think about religious, secular, and moral issues. Initially conceived by Wayan Dhibia as a tribute to his parents and the Balinese gods who blessed him with success during a trip abroad, the play took on deeper dimensions of meaning when the male and female clown characters he had invited to perform began improvising with the basic story. Phaedra's forbidden love for her stepson, Hippolytus, became a catalyst for the queen, her mother, and her servants to discuss a range of contemporary issues in both serious and comic terms. The Greek legend was charged with an immediacy never achieved in Western productions of the play.

Initially the story was grounded in the everyday experiences of the audience. Wearing headdresses of fresh frangipane flowers, the women joked and gossiped about a wife's right to the same sexual adventures men have always taken for granted, particularly in Bali, where it is still acceptable to have more than one wife. While waiting for the arrival of her queen, a maidservant gives marital advice to young girls in the audience. "Don't take a man who likes motorcycles. My friend told me that vespas have big backsides, but their exhaust pipes are too small."

One of the women's raunchiest sexual jokes was based on a campaign slogan for the national elections that were scheduled to take place a few weeks after the performance. A maidservant warns women about men who only want to "stick it in the middle," an obscene pun originated by supporters of the governing Golkar Party. Golkar is listed as the second of three competing parties on the election ballots that require voters to make their choices by punching a hole beneath the name of the party they prefer. The peculiarities of this system lead to endless election joking about the pros and cons of voting for the party that asks you to "stick it in the middle."

Double entendres like these move the dialogue from personal bantering to the realm of politics. They call attention to the fact that the play is actually about the ethical dilemmas faced by leaders who have the responsibility of running a country. Prince Hippolytus, the future king, is faced with the problem of how to deal with his stepmother's advances. As happens in all Balinese drama about royal families, the actions of the monarchs become metaphors for effective government, and the clowns serve as touchstones for discussing the moral implications of leadership in contemporary society.

The Balinese use of theatrical heroes as role models for civic action is rooted in what the anthropologist Clifford Geertz has called "the myth of the exemplary center."[2] Long before modern electoral politics, Balinese kings exerted their authority through a system that used theatrical pageantry to reflect what was thought to be the ideal relationship among humans, gods, and their environment. The cremation rituals, temple festivals, and sacred performances that still proliferate in Bali are remnants of this cultural proclivity toward viewing dramatic spectacles as microcosms of social reality. The jokes of the temple clowns help keep the tradition alive.

Like King Lear's fool, the comic servants in Balinese theater engage in seemingly nonsensical banter with their masters that is resonant with topical and philosophical meaning. Ketut Kodi, an actor known for his mastery of sacred poetry, played the role of clown servant to Hippolytus in the Singapadu staging of *Phaedra*. He gets the audience's attention with some crude jokes about the reason he wears an old smelly costume: "When a woman walks by wearing fragrant perfume, you just watch her go by," he explains, "but if you step in dog shit you don't forget it so easily. People pay more attention to something that stinks."

When Hippolytus (played by a woman) muses on his obliga-tion to act in accordance with the will of the gods, he sings his thoughts in Kawi, a variant of Sanskrit. Kodi's *penasar* clown translates the song into melodic strains of High Balinese that communicate the underlying meaning of the prince's thoughts to the audience. "The sweetness of your voice is like the wind blow-ing through a bamboo reed," warbles the clown. "If you think and live this way, then people will follow you as their model." Suggesting that unseen breath passing through the reed gives voice to the king's sense of sacred duty, the clown has shifted effortlessly from a vulgar joke about animal feces to a lyrical metaphor that links the invisible world of spirits to the responsi-bility of kings. The combination of laughter and poetry trans-forms a Western story into a quintessentially Balinese situation and helps the audience connect the characters' dilemma to their own choices in the upcoming election.

The bond between clowns and politics in Bali goes far beyond the infiltration of election issues into the temple perfor-mances. During election campaigns the same clowns who per-form in the temples can be seen entertaining large crowds at political rallies. It is a measure of the respect accorded to Balinese clowns that politicians want them to appear at their meetings. The clowns are associated with sacred ceremonies and thereby connect the rallies to a sense of historic tradition. Audiences are accustomed to hearing debates and advice on topical issues from these village humorists, and their presence helps turn the rally into a rough facsimile of a temple festival. The rallies are held in open fields, and long banners of bright cloth are mounted on bent bamboo poles to simulate the sacred decorations found at traditional festivals. Gamelan gong orchestras warm up the crowds with the same driving metallic rhythms they hear in the temples. Most important, the clown routines serve as entertaining interludes between the speeches made by candidates and government officials, recreating the same pattern established by the clowns and kings in the temple dramas. In a secular setting, the outrageous excesses of the clowns are interspersed with the endless promises of the candidates.

In the spring of 1992 the issues that dominated the campaign were the same issues the clowns had been joking about regularly in the temples, so there was a natural unity between the political speeches and the clown intervals. The effects of tourism and economic development were raised repeatedly by both the comics and the politicians, particularly in the rallies of the ruling Golkar Party, which was faced with the problem of preserving the island's heritage while continuing the growth of prosperity that resulted primarily from tourism. While bureaucrats spoke prudently about the issues, the clowns' perspectives were more provocative. One clown wore an earring made out of a hotel room key to adorn his traditional hand-embroidered costume.

Touching on the most urgent issue faced by Balinese politicians, the clowns use comic paradox to argue that economic progress and historical preservation can be interdependent. "We have to make progress," insisted a clown who specialized in double-talk. "But we can't make progress if we don't stay the same. If we don't preserve the original Bali, tourists won't want to come here anymore, because Bali will look like everyplace else in the world." The clown's advice was given added impact by the long-nosed tourist mask he wore as he delivered it. In a display of cross-cultural ventriloquism the clown expressed his concern for preservation through the voice of the intruder.

In a Negara campaign rally that often degenerated into numbing shouts of mindless slogans, Kodi used his clown character to inject a little thoughtfulness into the proceedings. Whenever speakers called out the word *"Pembangunan!"* (development), the crowd would yell back, *"Terus!"* (keep it up), as if they were cheering at a football match. Kodi playfully threw off the rhythm of this and other chants by reversing the order of the words and substituting new phrases for the words to which the crowd had become accustomed. Although he was in fundamental agreement with the ideas being expressed in the rally, Kodi's comic disruptions and ironic commentary encouraged people to actually think about what they were saying before they shouted.

Clowns like Kodi give political events an authentic connection to the historic legacy of temple pageants where social issues have been debated for centuries. The Golkar Party uses the symbol of the sprawling banyan tree as its trademark, but only the clowns have the moral authority and poetic gifts to communicate the full implications of that image to the public. They talk about the Hindu ceremonial uses of the tree's leaves for cremation ceremonies and other religious rites. They also alert the audience to the significance of the banyan tree as a metaphor for social change. "If it encounters a rigid obstacle," observes a clown, "the pliant vines of the banyan tree wind around it and adapt to its shape." This is the same flexible survival strategy favored by the clowns when they incorporate tourists, radio commercials, Greek tragedy, and broken English into the ever-shifting world of their sacred temple dramas.

While the pliant vine of the banyan tree is an apt symbol for the adaptability of Balinese culture, it is also an appropriate metaphor for Balinese clowns themselves. Their improvisations and jokes alert their audiences to the positive and negative elements of Westernization. The resilient improvisational spirit of the clowns provides an inspiring model for a population struggling to survive change without losing its traditions.

The political architect of Bali's long-term plan for simultaneously containing and encouraging tourism is himself a former temple clown. I Made Bandem, a leading member of parliament and director of the Balinese National Academy of the Arts, works closely with the island's governor to map out a strategy for economic development in which culture plays a major role. As a child Bandem performed in village temple ceremonies with his father, I Made Kredek, a specialist in comic roles who taught his son that people would remember him if he made them laugh. It is a lesson that Bandem continues to employ on the campaign trail.

Bandem organizes the appearances of temple clowns at election rallies throughout the island, and when he makes his own campaign speeches, they always include comic references to his career as an entertainer, along with eloquent arguments for the reconciliation of tradition and modernization. Using the multiple voices employed by *dalang* in their shadow plays, Bandem makes a playful plea for reelection. He also has a *penasar*'s gift for poetic allegory, summoning up tales from the *Ramayana* to explain how the bridge built across the sea by the monkey king Hanuman is a metaphor for Bali's future bridges to the Western world.

Bandem's father taught him to study the *Ramayana* and other traditional texts from handwritten books engraved on palm leaves. Written in the Sanskrit-based language of Kawi, these books are repositories of Bali's heritage, and their study is mandatory for both clowns and priests. Speaking at a campaign rally in the village of Sukawati, where he gave his first childhood performance, Bandem outlines his plans for balancing Bali's material and spiritual prosperity. He sees the challenge as a battle between ancient books and luxury hotels: "The magic power of our *lontar* is being tested by modern development."

Bandem's political career is a testimony to the respect with which the Balinese regard their artists. More specifically, it is a modern manifestation of the traditional power that has always been wielded quietly by Balinese village clowns. People pay attention to what they say and expect their comic philosophizing to be relevant to issues that are crucial to their survival. Bandem was raised in a household where the power of the Balinese clown tradition was built into the rhythms of everyday life. Neighbors would come to the house to ask his father's advice for all kinds of problems, because in addition to being a clown, Kredek was also a traditional healer (*dukun*). His success in both professions was attributed to the same skill: a talent for reconciling contradictory forces.

"Artists are important in a society because they contribute to the harmony of life," observes Bandem at home as he reminisces over photographs of his dead father, "and clowns do this more than any other artists in Bali."

In his career trajectory from comic performer to political decision maker, Bandem has preserved the traditional Balinese link between clowns and kings. He most vivid memory of his father performing was a scene in which the comic servant transformed himself momentarily into a monarch. It was part of a *topeng* story about a prince who is about to inherit the kingdom of his aging father. Kredek, playing the clown servant to the prince, gives him a lesson in kingly comportment, mimicking the gestures of the monarch in a dance that alternated between devilish mockery and transcendent grace. "That was a wonderful moment," recalls Bandem, imitating his father's gestures as he describes them. "He transformed himself into the most elegant king imaginable. Then a moment later he lapsed back into the movement of the clown and everyone laughed, but they never forgot how beautifully he danced as the king."

Bandem proudly displays a photograph of his father wearing the mask of a king that was given to him by a real monarch. The king of Bangli had carved the mask as a self-portrait and gave it to Kredek in appreciation of a performance the clown gave in his palace. The wooden mask is white with a black moustache and a third eye made of a sapphire set in real gold. The third eye is a traditional Hindu symbol of wisdom, but what makes the mask truly unusual is the mark of dignity carved into the space above the mother-of-pearl teeth. "This dark space heightens the king's dignity," explains Bandem. "It is there so that only four of the king's teeth will be exposed. Monarchs should never show more than four teeth when they smile. It ruins their dignity. It's true," he insists. "Queen Elizabeth always smiles like this." Bandem makes his point with an imitation of the queen's constipated grimace that would have made his father proud.

The peculiar Balinese talent for intermingling the worlds of clowns and kings, past and present, public and private, can be seen clearly in the family history of Kredek and Bandem, but their story is representative of a phenomenon that permeates all aspects of Balinese life. The intermingling of social, spiritual, political, and symbolic realms is essential to the dynamic vitality of Balinese society, and clowns are simply the most visible stage managers of that ongoing cultural spectacle.

As a university administrator, nationally known politician, and distinguished performing artist, Bandem redefines the relationship between Bali's past and future with the wily charm of a master clown. At his family's ancestral home in Karangasem there is a photograph that distills Bandem's varied accomplishments into a single image. Wrapped in the traditional gold-leaf costume of a *kebyar* dancer, his body is tilted at eccentric angles that complement the odd curves of his impish smile. "Visit Indonesia," reads the lettering beneath the photo, which is in fact a travel poster commissioned by IBM, executed by a Dutch photographer, and distributed around the world. In a photo of himself as a dancer, taken by a descendant of the island's Dutch colonizers and sponsored by a multinational corporation, Bandem stands at the intersection of Bali's history and its promise. Like his father and all the clowns that grace the island's temples, Bandem is an enigmatic figure of continuity and change.

Bandem's dream of adapting to change without disrupting tradition is central to the genius of Balinese clowning and to the remarkable resilience of the culture at large. Bali is an incongruous mix of terraced rice fields, tourist hotels, sacred rituals, modern politics, and clowns who facilitate the interpenetration of these disparate realms as models of improvisation with shrewdly adaptive responses to the unexpected. At a temple festival in June 1992, a few days before the national elections, I Made Djimat was in the middle of performing a solo *topeng pajegan* in his home village of Batuan when the governor of the island arrived ahead of schedule to make a speech. Djimat was performing for a crowd gathered outside the sculpted stone temple gates when the governor's blue Volvo limousine drove up the dirt road and stopped behind the crowd. As he happened to be wearing the mask of the priest, Djimat opened the car door for the governor and welcomed him to the ceremony.

"Do you speak English?" he asked the governor in English, as if he were a visiting tourist. To the crowd's delight the governor played along and replied that he did indeed speak a little English. Without missing a beat Djimat had incorporated the governor into the performance, turning a possible disruption into an entertaining sideshow in which the politician followed the cues of the clown like a seasoned second banana. Djimat's improvisatory skill enabled the audience to accept the secular invasion of their sacred play as a minor interruption that could be easily assimilated into the overall stream of the ceremony.

As soon as the governor was out of his car, an elaborate procession of village children in traditional costumes danced out to greet him, and the gamelan gong orchestra struck up a medley of welcoming songs. Knowing that his *pajegan* performance was essential to the ritual fulfillment of the temple's obligation to the gods, Djimat simply switched masks and joined in the performance of the children, dancing alongside them and mimicking their steps as if they too had been sent to perform as extras in his ever-expanding one-man show. When the governor had been safely led away to an interior enclave of the temple, Djimat changed into the mask of a constipated bureaucrat who grumpily began directing traffic. The car and jeep drivers he rerouted also became part of the performance.

Moments later, the temple priests conformed to the governor's schedule by beginning their group prayers earlier than expected. Adapting quickly to the new situation, Djimat put on the mask of Sidhya Karya and joined the worshippers outside the temple gates. Circulating through the worshipers, Djimat was both clown and priest, playfully assisting the temple elders in dousing the crowd with holy water. As had been the case all day, people laughed for a while and then ignored him, accepting his masked presence as an ordinary part of the ceremony in which they were all participating. The boundary between spectacle and everyday life had disappeared completely.

One high-spirited elderly woman teased the priests as they walked by. "More holy water," she pleaded. "It's hot out here. I need a little shower to cool off." Everyone chuckled, including the priests. Not only had Djimat lived up to his responsibility to render the temple sacred with laughter; he had also inspired his audience to respond to the difficulties of the situation with some spirited clowning of their own.

The massive assembly of men, women, and children praying together in a dirt road, overseen by a masked clown and a few bearded priests, was a tribute to the faith of the Balinese people and the power of their laughter. With all the interruptions of limousines, politicians, and motorcycles, there was every reason to assume that the sanctity of the ceremony would be diminished. But the prayers were conducted as they had been for centuries with frangipani petals dipped in holy water used to bless devout villagers dressed in sacred sashes and handmade sarongs. The continued existence of this ancient ritual in 1992 defies one's expectations for an island deluged with a tidal wave of tourism and Westernization.

Clowns like Djimat, Kredek, Windia, Wija, Rusni, and Bandem have skillfully injected bits of modernity into Bali's central nervous system of temples, shrines, and ceremonies. Tourist masks, English phrases, motorcycles, and other foreign incongruities are ridiculed in a way that helps the Balinese live through a wave of economic development with their traditional beliefs unscathed. Living up to their heritage as village healers, Bali's clowns play a subtle but necessary role in the survival of their culture.

The power of Balinese temple clowns is rooted in the social complexity of the laughter they evoke. Their comedy is both subversive and cohesive. They mockingly subvert the destructive potential of Western development at the same time that they reinforce the spiritual and cultural bonds that make their audiences a community. Modernity and tradition are reconciled in a web of sacred slapstick that touches all aspects of Balinese life. The temple clowns perform in luxury hotels, campaign rallies, and civic anniversaries as well as in sacred ceremonies, ritual exorcisms, and wedding celebrations. In the midst of disorienting change, they offer reassurance by connecting their audience to an extended family of ancestors, kings, tourists, gods, demons, heroes, servants, and frogs in stories that speak to the problems of the times.

The Balinese public acknowledges the necessity of all this laughter by continuing to include clowns in the most meaningful rituals of their lives, both sacred and secular, even as those rituals are under tremendous pressure to change. To celebrate the anniversary of Bali's independence from the Dutch, the governor of the island, Ida Bagus Anom, organized a monkey dance called *kecak* with a liberal dose of clowning. The bare-chested chorus of monkeys was played by the Balinese parliament, and the king of the demons was played by the governor himself. He took lessons in clowning from Bandem, Catra, and Kodi to prove to the Balinese that their officials are artists as well as statesmen. "We would like to show the people that we know how to laugh," said the governor, explaining that comedy is as important as bureaucracy. He proved his point when the vice-governor, playing the part of the monkey king, stuck his head between the governor's legs and bit his crotch during the battle scene. It won a big laugh from the crowd.

In spite of competition from television, movies, and the lure of tourist dollars, villagers still stay up all night to watch the antics of the *penasar* clowns. These laugh makers provide the foundation for sacred plays that are crucial to the success of temple festivals, which in turn are essential to the preservation of the island's religious heritage. And because the religious faith of the Balinese people has been a major factor in protecting the island's traditions against the onslaught of Westernization, the clowns' role in the constant renewal of that faith makes them a cornerstone of Bali's cultural identity.

None of the other seven thousand islands in the Indonesian archipelago have preserved their culture as successfully as the Balinese, and at least part of the island's good fortune can be attributed to the irrepressible resourcefulness of its clowns. Strategically positioned at the heart of the island's most sacred ceremonies, the clowns are always improvising, adapting, and laughing their way out of the dilemmas that fate throws in their paths. Their ingenuity inspires the Balinese to be equally inventive in freeing themselves from the lures of the West. Balinese popular comedy is forged out of the island's ongoing conflict between tradition and modernity. Evil spirits are dressed in imported galoshes. Legendary heroes are introduced to government family planning. Fifteenth-century battles are interrupted by tourists looking for souvenirs. Deftly outwitting the demons, bureaucrats, and sightseers that threaten the integrity of their heritage, Balinese clowns personify the resilience of their culture's instincts to survive.

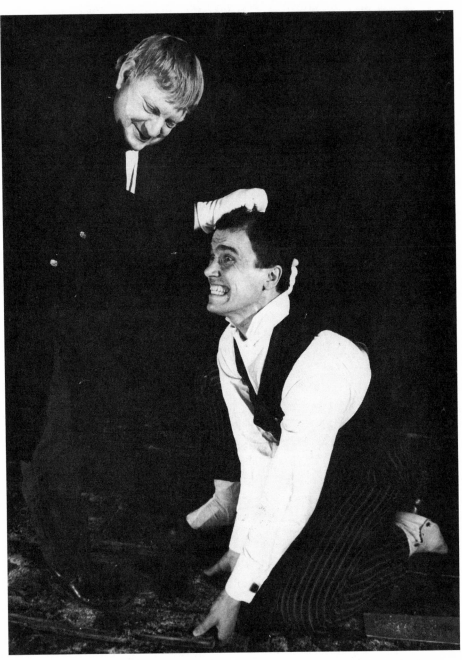

A Lithuanian adaptation of Chekhov's Cherry Orchard *as performed by the* Little Theater of Vilnius. (photo courtesy Little Theater of Vilnius)

Revolutionary Laughter
in Lithuania

*Lyuba Traup arrived at the offices of the Vilnius State Theater
wearing a drab green overcoat, a kerchief, and short, plaid socks.
Wisps of white hair fell across her wrinkled forehead, and her clear
eyes seemed on the verge of tears. With no word of introduction she
sat down on the sofa and sang to me in a frail voice, as if her song
were a greeting. She had learned the comic Yiddish lyrics fifty years
ago as a child in the Lithuanian ghetto where she lived under the
Nazis. As she sang about smuggling food behind the backs of stupid
ghetto guards, she laughed.*

*Mrs. Traup had been invited to speak about her memories of the
war to a Lithuanian theater company staging a play about a Jewish
theater troupe that performed comedy and satire in the Vilna ghetto
before it was liquidated by the Nazis. The company found it hard to
see how people could laugh under those conditions, but Mrs. Traup
made it clear that a sense of humor was necessary for surviving in the
ghetto. She showed us that for prisoners of the Nazi occupation,
laughter was an act of resistance. Fifty years later the comic song she
had used to defy the ghetto guards continued to give her strength.*

The play being rehearsed was called Ghetto. *Written by the
Israeli playwright Joshua Sobol, the script was recommended to the
Vilnius State Theater by Irena Veisaite, another ghetto survivor. She
sat with Lyuba Traup while the actors read the script. The two
women nodded and smiled at jokes like the ones they remembered as
girls in the ghetto. A Nazi asks a Jew the difference between total*

*and partial liquidation. "Kill 50,000 Jews and not me, that's par-
tial liquidation," answers the Jew. "Kill me. That's total."*

*The two women had sung in a Communist propaganda opera
after the war. They remembered the words and began singing. It was
something about marching toward the sun of the Soviet Union,
where there would be no more injustice. They laughed at the stupid-
ity of the lyrics, especially ironic in the winter of 1990, when
Lithuanians were still suffering under the injustices of a totalitarian Soviet regime.*

*In the course of a few minutes the two survivors had moved
from laughing at the Nazis to laughing at the Soviets. The parallel
between the two tyrannies was also being emphasized by the director, Jonas Vaitkus, in his Vilnius production of Ghetto. One of
Vaitkus's boldest directorial choices was to portray a Nazi officer as
a hysterical hermaphrodite who could easily be interpreted as a
send-up of a KGB agent. For Vaitkus Ghetto offered an opportunity
to mount a subversive challenge to Communist authority.*

*Watching rehearsals and performances of the play in Vilnius
gave me a taste of the comic spirit that had been a part of Lithuania's
resistance to Communist domination for years. A few days after the
first Ghetto rehearsal, Mrs. Veisaite told a joke that typified the prevailing cynicism toward the Soviet state. It was about a Jewish musician famous for singing through his anus. He could play anything
from folk songs to Beethoven with the musical notes he made by passing wind. Stalin summoned the artist to the Kremlin and ordered him
to learn the Communist Party anthem, "L'Internationle." When he
came back the next week and confessed that he could not play the song,
Stalin threatened to have him shot. "I've been trying all week," said
the Jew. "It goes along fine until I get to the lyrics about building a
new world, but then only shit comes out."*

*The story of the man who defecates on the false promises of the
state combined anti-Soviet cynicism with the chutzpah that had
characterized laughter in the ghettos. It reminded me of how my
father had laughed in the face of fear. His parents were born near
Vilna and would probably have been incarcerated in its ghetto if
they hadn't left Lithuania before World War I to escape the pogroms.
Instead they fled to America, where my father later enlisted to fight*

the Nazis in the allied invasions of Africa and Europe. He remembers running and laughing on the rooftops of Casablanca as German bombs exploded around him. "We knew we might get killed any second," he told me once during a night of war stories, "but we didn't want to let that scare us, so we just laughed."

I went to Vilnius looking for traces of the laughter that was part of my family's heritage. Sobol had been denied an entry visa to Lithuania and asked me to represent him at the rehearsals of Ghetto. *Having immersed myself for months in writing English adaptations of his trilogy of plays about the Vilna ghetto, I looked forward to seeing the old buildings depicted so meticulously in the scripts. When I actually located the former Yiddish gymnasium that had housed Vilna's ghetto theater, I was taken aback by the sound of laughter coming from behind its closed doors. The square, drab auditorium was now a children's theater, and I had arrived in the middle of a puppet show about a big bad wolf that devoured everything in sight. "Watch out for the wolf," screamed the giggling children to a chicken that was about to be eaten alive.*

I smiled at the ironic historical resonance of the child's warning. The puppet fable was the same kind of comic allegory the Jews had staged in that same room fifty years ago when they mocked the Nazis who threatened to devour them. The puppet show in the ghetto theater was only one of many links between the comic survival strategies of my Jewish forebears and those of modern Lithuanians fighting for freedom from Soviet rule. My most intimate encounter with Lithuania's comic spirit of resistance came while having breakfast with the president of the republic.

To get to his office in the parliament building, I walked past the concrete barricades and barbed wire that had been set up to protect the building against Soviet army attacks, which had already killed over a dozen civilians in attempts to crush Lithuania's drive for independence. There were bullet holes in the glass walls of the parliament foyer and burlap sandbags were stacked behind all the doorways. But even in this state of siege President Vytautas Landsbergis retained his low-keyed sense of humor.

When I walked into his office Landsbergis was seated alone at a large table calmly eating a bowl of puffed rice cereal without milk.

A former music professor, the president looked more like a pudgy, balding, bespectacled scholar than a political leader steering his nation through a crisis. He paused thoughtfully before speaking, taking time to lift a spoonful of cereal to his mouth between each of my questions. The clinking of his spoon against the plate became a metronome that slowed the pace of our conversation to a fascinating crawl.

Landsbergis explained that nonviolent resistance to military power requires the use of symbolic weapons like art, music, and theatrical representations. The president paused, clinked his spoon, and slowly chewed his puffed rice before continuing. "Even if the flames of freedom were extinguished by Soviet forces," he observed, "the fire's sparks would remain alive in the music, the songs, and the art of Lithuania."

In Landsbergis's vision of art and politics, one of the most effective means for making these artistic symbols of freedom accessible to the public at large is to express them in comic terms. "Laughter is a contact," he reasoned. "It is an understanding between people that is immediate and of the moment. It's clear to all." Pause. Clink. Chew. "Wisdom from our history has deep roots," continued the president, "and some of this wisdom is passed on through common laughter."

Landsbergis often used jokes to emphasize the illegitimacy of the Soviet occupation. When asked how it would be possible to get Soviet troops out of Lithuania, the president quoted a Lithuanian peasant's one-liner to a Russian soldier. "You knew how to come, so you must know how to go." In a period of violence and uncertainty there was something reassuring about the slow, methodical rhythms of Landsbergis's voice. No sharp edges. No crescendos. The stylistic opposite of a Soviet dictator, Landsbergis disappeared into his sentences the way one imagines the leader of an ideal democracy disappearing into the will of the people. His humor had the same comforting effect. Nothing shocking. No belly laughs. Just a gentle stream of irony based on a bedrock of common sense. The besieged population of Lithuania responded instinctively to their leader's laughter. Ridiculing the enemy became a collective ritual that helped give them the courage to fight for their freedom against all odds.

On November 7, 1990, a troop of Soviet soldiers parading down the main street of Vilnius was stopped by the sound of laughter. An actor on a balcony above them was entertaining a crowd of onlookers with a comic impersonation of Leonid Breznev. Wearing a masked likeness of the former Soviet president, the actor staggered in a drunken attempt to hold himself up on the railing and read a speech. He mocked the catchphrases of Soviet propaganda by burying them in an unintelligible sequence of inebriated mumbles.

While Lithuanians on the street below laughed at the impromptu performance, the Soviet soldiers were outraged that such a mockery was being staged on a holiday set aside to commemorate the glory of the revolution. The troop's captain pointed aggressively toward the balcony, and one of his men leaped onto a first-floor window ledge and began climbing up the wall in pursuit of the clown. The Breznev impersonator disappeared inside the building. He had attacked the occupying army with a well-aimed comic barb. Physical violence was unnecessary.

This public display of comic insubordination is emblematic of the way Lithuanians used laughter to subvert Soviet authority during their struggle for independence from 1940 to 1991. Although direct clashes between clowns and soldiers were rare, the dynamics underlying this encounter were played out repeatedly through the years of the Soviet occupation. Landsbergis's official strategy of nonviolent resistance that eventually led to independence was complemented by an unofficial strategy of comic resistance. The relentless assault of laughter in theaters, parks, and meeting halls helped to undermine the credibility of the Soviet system at the same time that it enabled Lithuanians to express common values essential to the survival of their cultural identity.

Lithuania has a rich history as a crossroads of pagan, Christian, and Jewish cultures. The clashes between the country's past and present are embedded in its architecture. Once glorious medieval churches are only now being renovated after years of Soviet neglect. From Pilius Street in Vilnius you can look up and see the Lithuanian flag flying over the fifteenth-century castle built by the pagan king Gediminas. It stands in the spot once occupied by the hammer and sickle of the USSR. Three holy crosses on a hill near the castle have been restored to the spot where they had once been forbidden by the Communists. Many of the town houses on the cobblestone streets of Vilnius's historic district were built under the rule of the Russian tsar, and one of them is famous as the spot where Lithuanian patriots declared the country's independence in 1918.

Twenty-two years later Moscow annexed the country as part of a secret treaty between Stalin and Hitler, but it wasn't long before Hitler went back on his word and occupied Lithuania in the name of the Third Reich. After the war the battle for control between Vilnius and Moscow was reflected in the slapstick conflicts of Lithuanian comedy. The nation's history was reclaimed by its clowns. Their double takes unraveled the lies that had been perpetrated by the Communist Party and revealed the injustices committed in its name. For half a century the Soviets had promised a utopian Communist society, while delivering nothing but a corrupt government that robbed Lithuanians of their freedom and their lives. Stalin had sent tens of thousands of Lithuanians to die in labor camps, but atrocities like these were omitted from Soviet schoolbooks, which claimed Lithuanians had freely chosen to become part of the USSR. Often the only alternative to this propaganda was underground satire.

There is a long history of political satire in Lithuania. The archives of the folklore institute at Vilnius University are crammed with shelves of satiric songs, stories, and anecdotes that date back to the nineteenth century, when the tsar and his entourage were the targets of anti-totalitarian humor. In 1991 Professor Kostas Aleksynas conducted research into these files near a window that looked out onto a Soviet army outpost. "When the soldiers stand on the roof with their rifles," he laughed, "they have an unobstructed aim at my desk."

The short, gray-haired scholar is only half-kidding. The Soviets had in fact persecuted and imprisoned many of the people responsible for circulating the jokes that had been reprinted in his latest book. (An example: "Breznev's eyebrows are nothing more

than Stalin's moustache raised to a higher political level.")
Aleksynas believes that humor like this was censored for so long
because it undermined the carefully orchestrated version of history the Soviets presented to the public. "These jokes reflect the
attitude of Lithuanians to the so-called Soviet reality," he writes
in the introduction to the collection. "They mock the creators of
that reality as well as the words and deeds of its ideologists." The
reforms of *glasnost* had made possible the publication of Aleksynas's work, but they had not yet removed the machine guns from
outside his window.

The ingenuity with which Lithuania's comic artists were
able to subvert Soviet authority helped resurrect their public's
faith in the feasibility of resistance. This was particularly important during the period of uncertainty between March 1990, when
Lithuania declared its independence from Moscow, and August
1991, when its statehood was formally recognized by Russia and
the rest of the world. The country's comic heroes personified the
power of the powerless to defy the seemingly invulnerable Soviet
forces that had been arrayed against them. Humor had always
been an antidote to terror, but *glasnost* helped bring the laughter
out in the open. Audiences that laughed at the absurdities of
Breznev and the KGB were exorcising the fear that had prevented them from resisting Soviet pressure in the past.

There were many strands to the complex web of Lithuanian
laughter that preceded the winning of independence. Slapstick puppet shows mocked the myths of Soviet history with satirical jabs at
Stalin, Marx, and Gorbachev. Prominent Lithuanian stage directors reinterpreted the comedies of Chekhov through the lens of the
Soviet occupation. New works lampooned the hypocrisy and sense-
lessness of the Communist bureaucracy. These were not lighthear-
ed farces intended to help people laugh their troubles away.
Lithuanian comedies of this period were as brutal as the occupation
they depicted. Their comic situations were sculpted from the hardships that their audiences had endured for fifty years, and their
laughing heroes were never far from the threat of death.

Theaters playing these politically charged comedies were
always packed with appreciative audiences, but the spirit of comic

defiance was not confined to legitimate theaters. It spilled over into public meetings, demonstrations, and political rallies. A candidate for parliament toured the schools, lecture halls, and prisons with a show that presented historic documents from the reign of Stalin as absurdist comedy. Another politician wrote allegorical comic dialogues that he performed in venues ranging from collective farms to the living rooms of his supporters. The barbed wire barricades around the parliament building in Vilnius were festooned with anti-Soviet cartoons, some of them painted by children. And when the building was threatened by Soviet tanks, pro-independence demonstrators camped out in front of these barricades and sang satirical folk songs.

The debates inside the parliament were charged with the same subversive irony that animated the children's drawings and graffiti outside on the barricades. Khasys Saja, a newly elected parliamentary deputy and a well-known playwright who entered the political arena after a career as a dissident artist, shapes many of his arguments in parliament around comic anecdotes and parables. Once, while accusing Lithuania's ex-Communists of stealing the country's resources for Moscow's benefit, he told the story of a man who found a thief in a crowded room by shouting, "Thief, your cap is burning!" When the Communists objected, he asked them why, if they were not guilty, did they think the story was about them.

"The Parliament is now a theater," observed Saja in his Vilnius apartment, sitting beneath a painting of a jester on the throne of a king. His sense of theatrics and satire is part of a political process that took place on the stage and in the streets, as well as in the halls of parliament. For Lithuanians there is a remarkable sense of continuity between the events that occurred in all these arenas. During Saja's election campaign, he also traveled to town halls, collective farms, and private homes, performing satiric dialogues that expressed his opposition to the Communist regime. Voters came to understand Saja's positions by paying attention to the targets he chose to ridicule.

One of Saja's dialogues is called "The Flea Killers." Its title refers to the curious fact that Lithuania has no fleas. The protagonist is a KGB informant who claims that a colleague has been spreading the theory that human beings under the stress of fear emit an odor lethal to fleas, and that the absence of fleas in Lithuania is due to the overpowering stench of fear that was unleashed during the years of Stalin's terror. The informant is a history teacher who, in spite of his desire to please the KGB, is possessed by involuntary fits of obscenity whenever the Soviet government is mentioned. "The teacher has a psychological disorder called coprolalia," explains Saja, smiling mischievously over a cup of tea. "It is a condition which makes it impossible for him to restrain himself from uttering obscenities. The disorder is particularly troubling when he gives lectures on Soviet history."

Ceslovas Stonys, one of the actors who performed with Saja in dialogues like "The Flea Killers," tapped into the repressed rage of his audiences with a satiric cabaret based entirely on historic documents from the years of Stalin. The entire text of his show was taken verbatim from transcripts, letters, newspaper stories, and propaganda songs that were circulated in the 1950s. At a performance in a museum that the Soviets had built to glorify the Communist revolution, Stonys and a trio of musicians sang a toast to Stalin that was popular in the early years of the dictator's regime. To the jaunty accompaniment of a red accordion, they lavished syncopated praise on the man who had sentenced thousands of their countrymen to death in Siberian labor camps:

> *The Party is leading us to happiness.*
> *And we thank dear Comrade Stalin*
> *From the bottom of our hearts.*

The Bolshevik fervor of their-four part harmony had a powerful effect on the audience. Hundreds of Lithuanians responded to the absurdity of the Stalinist propaganda song with a mixture of astonishment and horror that eventually erupted into a chorus of deep, sustained laughter. One woman in the third row, old enough to have lived through Stalin's regime, shook with laughter until tears rolled down her face.

"Our performances are like group psychotherapeutic seances," says Stonys, who believes his satirical revue helps to exorcise the demons of Lithuania's history. The title of the piece, "Who's in Favor? Who Objects? Who Abstains?," invites the audience to ponder the nation's receptiveness to these fragments of propaganda when they were originally disseminated in Lithuania. He and his colleagues perform the documentary texts exactly as they were written. There is no need to exaggerate for comic effect. In the context of the political changes sweeping through the Baltic states, history becomes its own parody.

"Audiences are shocked when they hear these texts," says Stonys. "They are shocked that people actually wrote and read such idiotic words and sang these stupid songs to the health of Stalin. Before the performances I always warn the audience that even though they lived through these times, they will be persecuted by one thought as they listen: `It cannot be.' But it happened, and we became anesthetized to it, because fifty years of Soviet rule in Lithuania drove us out of our minds. Our socialist society was a huge loony bin that turned us into psychic invalids. And that's why I created this revue. Now that the gates of the loony bin are open, the theater can give us a form of group psychotherapy."

Stonys was not the only artist who used humor to help release Lithuanians from the madness of their political history. The same psychocultural dynamics that fueled his documentary satire were apparent in dozens of other performances that referred to dying icons of the Soviet regime. A grotesque mask of Stalin's face was a central prop in a play called *The Awakening*, by Antonas Skema. Staged in Vilnius's Academy Theater by the director Jonas Vaitkus, the story is set in a prison where Stalin's caricatured features are carved into the desk lamp of a KGB interrogator. The mask's oversized mustache and bulging eyes intimidate the Lithuanian political prisoners who pass through the office, but when one of them shoots his interrogator, the wounded KGB agent grabs the lamp and staggers through a dance of death with his inanimate patron hero. Each slapstick stumble confirms Stalin's impotence and elicits howls of delight from the audience. When the mask crashed to the floor, the crowd's triumphant applause stopped the show.

The emotion that flooded the auditorium made it clear that the laughter had unleashed more than a mood of simple pleasure. The comic demise of Stalin's image had triggered the celebration of an imagined victory over the totalitarian forces that had oppressed Lithuania for half a century. The impact of the slapstick victory lingered on during intermission. A memorial display was set up in the lobby so that members of the audience could light candles in memory of prisoners killed in Siberia by the KGB. The performance brought together the imagined world of the stage and the real world of the audience by blurring the boundaries among laughter, memory, suffering, and insurrection.

To a population living under the repressive Soviet occupation, the power of laughter offered welcome relief from the anxiety of waiting for political change. Lithuanians channeled their hope for freedom into ridicule aimed at the hypocrisy of the Communist regime. Denied free speech, they resorted to coded forms of comic speech, waging an underground war of laughter in which parodies, jokes, and satire undermined the credibility of Soviet propaganda.

The official Soviet version of history taught in schools censored all references to Lithuania as an independent nation and never mentioned the illegal nature of its annexation to the USSR. Stalin's secret deal with Hitler and other stolen fragments of Lithuania's history were made public for the first time in a satirical puppet show by Sepos Theater. Performed in a tiny wardrobe-shaped stage with puppet caricatures of famous figures from Karl Marx to Boris Yeltsin, Sepos's carnivalesque inversions of official history drew large audiences while inciting significant scandal and debate.

"Our puppets are braver than our politicians," claims Gintaras Varnas, the director of Sepos Theater, who proudly points out that his animated characters demanded freedom for Lithuania months before the republic's parliament announced its official declaration of independence. One skit, broadcast on Lithuanian television on the last night of 1989, was a parody of the three kings visiting the newborn baby Jesus. It featured a puppet figure of Gorbachev traveling to Vilnius to give gifts of graft and plunder to the head of Lithuania's Communist Party, Algirdas Brazauskas, whose refusal to support the independence movement branded him as a Soviet patsy. Brazauskas, who had been scheduled to appear on the same New Year's Eve telecast, refused to go on, and the director of Lithuanian television was forced to step before the cameras and apologize for any offense the puppets might have caused.

Varnas's troupe was banned from further television appearances but continued performing their puppet satires in theaters across the country. They refused to cut out the controversial segments of their show, so their diminutive Gorbachev look-alike kept audiences laughing with bouncy propaganda jingles like, "Perestroika, holy shit! glasnost I will never quit." Sepos Theater also demystified the political manoeuvering that led to Gorbachev's selection as the head of the Soviet Communist Party. According to the puppets, Lenin leaned out a window in heaven and spit down onto a meeting in Moscow. When his spittle landed on Gorby's head, he was anointed as the new Party leader. This political baptism also explains the famous birthmark on Gorbachev's bald spot.

In the spring of 1990, shortly after the Lithuanian parliament had formally announced its intention to sever ties with Moscow, Sepos Theater premiered a new show called "Communist Nostalgia," expressing the rage that was only recently being acknowledged as a legitimate response to the legacy of Communism. The play began with Friedrich Engels chasing God out of heaven to make room for Karl Marx, whose puppet body consisted of a large red book with arms and a bushy gray beard. "I'm the boss now," shouts Marx to the angels, just before giving birth to baby Lenin, who runs around the atheist garden of Eden clothed in only a fig leaf. President Landsbergis, who was one of the puppet characters in the show, was also in the audience for the opening. He watched the puppets perform a farcical reenactment of the Soviet annexation of Lithuania that included all the facts left out of the official history books. Hitler and Stalin were presented as a violently goofy Punch and Judy team, conspiring to rob Lithuania of its freedom.

At the heart of the puppet show's comedy was the contradiction between Moscow's myth of a Communist utopia and the brutal reality of the Soviet occupation of Lithuania. This dichotomy was established by the double frame of the puppet stage, which was modeled after the traveling fairground shows of the Middle Ages. The upper stage represented actions taking place in Moscow and the lower stage was Vilnius. While the Kremlin in Moscow was filled with puppet tyrants whose bodies moved with the flailing rhythms of fevered propaganda, Cathedral Square in Vilnius was peopled by singing demonstrators. The moral consequences of the events taking place in these two frames were emphasized by the presence of an angel in heaven above them and a figure of death in a hell below.

The most startling scene in the Sepos Theater repertoire is a fantasy sequence that reverses the historical balance of power between Lithuania and its Soviet occupiers. Landsbergis's puppet persona has a dream that the Russian people ask him to liberate their country, and he rides triumphantly into Moscow on top of a tank. The Russians thank him and ask to be annexed by Lithuania, as Gorbachev and his wife, Raisa, bow down at his feet. Landsbergis teaches them a new song to replace Gorby's worn-out *perestroika* jingle, and everyone sings together:

> *We were freed by Lithuania.*
> *Now we're civilized at last.*
> *The Lithuanian flag is flying*
> *Over Moscow's gloomy past.*

This kind of political comedy appealed overtly to the Lithuanian spirit of defiance. Other comic artists expressed a yearning for freedom without tying it to specific current events. The Little Theater of Vilnius was particularly skilled in translating their public's impulse to be free into emotional terms. In their production of *There Shall Be No Death*, the company used the same historical source material of Soviet documents, songs, and newspaper clippings that inspired the satire of Ceslovas Stonys and the puppets of Gintaras Varnas, but these political elements are submerged into the background of the play. The freedom

fought for by the characters in *There Shall Be No Death* is the
freedom to love, and the play's laughter erupts from their painful
struggles for emotional release.

Conceived and directed by Rimas Tuminas, the Little
Theater's play examines the Soviet persecution of the postwar
Lithuanian poet Paulius Sirvius. The forces of terror that silence
Sirvius's poetry are presented with dramatic poignancy. The
same terror becomes fuel for poetic farce when it juxtaposes the
crudeness of Soviet dogma against the delicacy of human feelings.
Delicate love songs are drowned out by harsh patriotic anthems.
Light-stepping village polkas are absurdly interrupted by the
violent stomping of Bolshevik dances. The cast took painstaking
care to insure that the staged fragments of Lithuania's past would
be authentic. "Our parents cried when they saw the play," says
actress Larissa Kalpokaite. "All the details of the clothing, the
songs, the hairstyles, and atmosphere were so real that they felt
like they were watching their lives as they had lived them in
Lithuania after the war." Another performer said that the white
shoes worn by the women on stage reminded her aunt of times
she dressed up for parties by whitening her shoes with tooth
powder.[1]

The play's tragicomic tone is established when two young
lovers at the cultural center encounter a lieutenant in the Red
Army. Before his arrival they are holding hands and blowing a
feather into the air. The tenderness of their relationship is seen in
the gentle ways they move together to keep the feather floating
above them on the streams of their breath. Their reverie ends
when the lieutenant crassly grabs the feather with his grimy fist
and snorts on it with puffs of air. He sets the feather on fire and
watches it burn while munching on a fistful of pig fat and smack-
ing his lips. The gluttonous buffoonery of the soldier shows the
comic side of the collision between love and the Soviet system,
but the charred feather provides a threatening omen that darkens
the laughter.

The young couple's relationship is attacked more directly by
a Communist Party functionary who makes a pass at the girl
while denouncing the boy for misappropriating the village radio.

As his punishment the young man is buried under a pile of radios blaring speeches by a Communist minister of education, while the party official takes his girlfriend outside for a lesson in "revolutionary culture." The ridiculous image of a man besieged by radios is emblematic of the villagers' helplessness against the barrage of propaganda that flooded their lives under Stalin's regime. The boy is literally imprisoned by the relentless stream of words until the girl returns and lovingly frees him from the radios, one by one.

The debilitating effect of fear on the lives of the villagers is demonstrated in a comic scene where the children stage a concert for a group of Soviet representatives from Moscow. The performers try to please their audience by reciting revolutionary poetry, singing Soviet songs, and acting out political parables, but their efforts are thwarted by ludicrous attacks of stage fright, memory loss, and uncontrollable bouts of hysteria. Terrified of embarrassing themselves in front of the party officials, the young actors close the curtain prematurely each time a song or sketch begins going wrong. Onstage their mishaps are laughable, but behind the curtains the characters reveal a compassion for one another that is free to emerge only once they are safely hidden from the glowering eyes of the party dignitaries.

Funny as it is, this scene of rampant paranoia touches serious chords of recognition for the Lithuanian spectators, whether or not they are old enough to remember the postwar era depicted in the play. Shifting from the children's onstage public personae to their backstage moments of intimacy, the comedy is based on the incongruity between official proclamations and unofficial feelings that was a fact of life for everyone who had received a Soviet education. Thirty-year-old Daiva Dapsiene says the play brings back anguished memories of growing up with lies. "I lived a double life," says Dapsiene. "I knew the truth about Lithuanian history from my mother and father, but I had to go to school, pretend I didn't know anything, and recite Lenin."

The Little Theater's audiences walked through streets patrolled by hostile Soviet troops. They remembered the night in January 1991 when those soldiers killed unarmed civilians.

Spectators in Vilnius viewed the frightened characters in *There Shall Be No Death* through their own remembered dread. When they laughed at the fear-ridden charade performed for Stalin's henchmen, they were laughing at the double life from which they were in the process of wrenching themselves free.

The same sense of urgency that animated *There Shall Be No Death* could be found in the Little Theater's slyly comic production of Anton Chekhov's *Cherry Orchard*. Here the signs of political turmoil are buried even further beneath the surface of the action. There are no overt references to the Soviet occupation of Lithuania, but the characters are portrayed in a state of anxiety that mirrored the mood of a country under siege. In Chekhov's play the inhabitants of an old family estate are forced to move out. At a crucial turning point of their lives, the characters are struggling to adapt to a change they don't completely understand. Writing at the turn of the century when his country was at the threshold of the Russian Revolution, the playwright labeled his work a comedy and was disappointed that the famous first production by Konstantin Stanislavsky's Moscow Art Theater was staged with such solemnity. Chekhov envisioned a family that would not surrender to the gloominess of their predicament. In the Little Theater's Lithuanian translation of the play, Chekhov's vision of laughter through tears was brought to life with authentic passion and vital humor.

At the heart of the comedy in this Lithuanian *Cherry Orchard* is the indomitability of the characters. Despite their oppressive circumstances, the characters regularly break into song, laughter, and fits of frenzy. The oddness of these outbursts is touchingly funny, particularly in occupied Lithuania, where so many simple emotions are stifled by the threatening presence of soldiers and an uncertain future. Early in the first act a bookcase falls halfway through the ceiling and hangs over the rest of the action like a slapstick sword of Damocles. Its presence is both dangerous and ridiculous, like the presence of a foreign army in a country that imagines itself to be free. Occasionally the characters engage in some comic confrontation with the bookcase and the crumbling plaster that drops down from it onto their heads.

Their estate is in ruins. The ceiling is rotting. The floorboards are collapsed. In a less resilient household these signs of decay might be tragic, but here they are treated as comic obstacles to be overcome with patience. While their house falls down around them, the characters' humanity remains unextinguished.

When two of the protagonists return home to announce that the estate has been sold at auction, they do not fall into despair but instead sing of their wish to be loved by a woman who waits for them by the sea. Their eccentric behavior becomes even more ridiculous when a family friend joins in with off-key harmonies in the voice of a drunken horse. The audience laughs as the bumbling quartet sings, but as they laugh, they are moved by the tenacity of their dreams in the face of catastrophe.

The song is a Lithuanian addition to Chekhov's text. The Little Theater has taken a Russian classic and appropriated its themes so completely that the few remaining fragments of its original language seem paradoxically intrusive. The lyrical cadences of the Lithuanian translation are interrupted by the harsh Slavic accent of the boorish postmaster who recites from Tolstoy at the ball. Where Chekhov interrupted the musings of his characters with the recurring sound of a distant breaking string, the Lithuanian director, Tuminas, has inserted a sound that could be interpreted as the rumbling of tanks.

This sobering sound effect is followed by the arrival of a menacing vagrant with a Russian icon that he asks the family to kiss as he begs them for money. He is a comic lout who shouts about the glories of the Volga River and pulls out a knife as he absconds with their gold. Clearly identified with the Soviets, this barbaric intruder is another distinctively Lithuanian variation of the original play. The irony of using a Russian play to mock the Soviets is not lost on anyone. When Tuminas was asked how Russians might respond to his making fun of them in his version of *The Cherry Orchard*, he answered wryly, "We always take the Russians very seriously. When the soldiers come we say, `Look. It's Chekhov. Don't shoot.'"

The play's final dark moments are relieved by the flickering of comic hope. Firs, a dying old man locked up in the condemned house, walks across rotting floorboards, under a collapsing ceiling, past a ladder to nowhere, up a staircase that leads to an empty room, muttering about futility. In one sense it is tragic, but the fact that he doesn't stop walking makes us smile at his cantankerous resilience. The gentle comedy of this closing scene brings the production to a point where the quaint vanishing world of Chekhov intersects with the bleak modern universe of Samuel Beckett, who wrote that "nothing is funnier than unhappiness."

Beckett's observation could also be aptly applied to another Lithuanian adaptation of Chekhov that was enormously popular during the Soviet occupation. Like the Little Theater's *Cherry Orchard*, the National Youth Theater's production of *Uncle Vanya* cut to the core of Chekhov's text in a way that revealed the intersection of laughter and pain. Directed by Eimuntas Nekrosius, the Lithuanian *Uncle Vanya* lurches back and forth between moods of inconsolable despair and playful absurdity. The director defies conventional Russian interpretations of Chekhov by letting the quiet desperation of his characters erupt into spasms of raw emotion.

The atmosphere is permeated with an oppressiveness that gives Vanya's household the feeling of an occupied territory. When the extended family gathers together for a group portrait, they unexpectedly break out into an ominous rendition of the prisoner's chorus from Verdi's *Nabucco*, an operatic plea for freedom that was not in Chekhov's original text.

The stifling atmosphere of this iconoclastic *Vanya* is fertile ground for comic intrusions. Characters are constantly bursting through the oppressive story frame in silly ways that give them a sense of release. Even the scene breaks and set changes provide excuses for liberating bursts of irrationality as silent servants ignore their masters and launch into clownish vaudeville dances while dusting off the antique furnishings on the stage. Their carefree play is interrupted by the scowling presence of Professor Serebrakov, who patrols the household in an effort to extinguish all human joy in his path, but the zany servants are only temporarily subdued. They get their revenge in act two when, in a madcap orgy of comic insubordination, they leap onto the love seat and indulge in lewd and boisterous parodies of their masters' mannerisms. The subversive pantomime is accompanied by loud bursts of loony circus music that heighten the impression of a clown show run amok.

The comic rebellion of the servants refers implicitly to Lithuania's legacy of political oppression, but Nekrosius never allows politics to overshadow the specific human dimensions of Chekhov's characters. His directorial choices allow actors to condense a multiplicity of personal and historical associations into the simplest of stage actions. When Vanya is asked to return a vial of stolen morphine, he is thrown to the ground and pinned under the legs of a chair. Traditionally the scene is played with Vanya politely turning over the drug to his accusers, but Nekrosius raises the stakes of the action through the ferocity with which Vanya holds on to the morphine and the brutality with which it is wrested away. There is no heavy-handed allusion to the tyranny of the tsar, the atrocities of Stalin, or the Soviet tanks that killed civilians in Vilnius, but the chair that crushes Vanya to the floor carries the weight of all these events, at the same time that the cruel encounter conjures up contemporary associations of drug addiction, false hopes, and violent desperation.

Although it was performed regularly during the final months of the Soviet occupation and has become part of the permanent state repertory, Nekrosius's *Uncle Vanya* premiered in 1986 and seems to have foreseen the Lithuanian independence movement in the same way that Chekhov intuited the revolution that was brewing when he wrote the play in 1897. "Every great writer has premonitions," says Anatoly Smelyansky, the literary manager of the Moscow Art Theater, where Chekhov's plays were directed by Stanislavsky at the turn of the century. "Nekrosius understands the premonitions of Chekhov and merges them with his own premonitions based on life a hundred years later. This 'Vanya' shows us the meeting of two cultures a century apart."

An astonishingly comic example of Nekrosius's ability to fold modernity into Chekhov's world occurs when Astrov tells Sonya about his ideas to save the forests from the ravages of civilization. Astrov's vast plans are drawn on postage stamps that he presents to Sonya with a ridiculously tiny pair of tweezers. The scene offers a ludicrous portrait of a man whose horizons are shrinking. Sonya needs a giant magnifying glass to see the trees that her friend describes so lovingly, and when she lifts the glass to look at his drawings her face is reflected to the audience as if it were being blown up in a fun house mirror. Nekrosius's bizarre sight gag reduces freedom's terrain to the size of a postage stamp and magnifies human incomprehension to laughably unforgettable proportions.

"I know there is a parallel in our work to the present day situation," muses the actor Kostas Smoriginas, who has worked with Nekrosius since 1979 and plays the role of Astrov with tragicomic eloquence. But he insists that the political references are not explicit. "With Astrov I thought only about his love for the forest and the freedom of the animals that lived there. I imagined him seeing a beautiful gazelle in the woods and wanting to save it, though he knows it was impossible."

"Chaplin is my teacher," he explains. "Not just for eccentricity and buffoonery, but how he thinks about the world and the place of little people. Like Chekhov, he always moves back and forth from tears to laughter." Smoriginas's Astrov drinks a lot and dresses up in funny costumes to shake up the complacency of the household. At the end of the play he enigmatically crawls across the floor with an animal skin on his back. At first his charade is seen as the cavorting of an incorrigible drunkard, but the tone changes when he pathetically tries to walk into the painting of a forest.

Clothed in the hide of a slaughtered animal, Astrov tries to find freedom in an imitation of a landscape that does not exist. The desperate futility of his action is accompanied by the hollow comfort of Sonya's closing monologue about hope and the agonizing screams of Vanya that drown out the optimism of her words. The curtain closes on this tortured tableau of frustrated aspirations, but Smoriginas imagines the play continuing in the minds of the audience. "When I act," he says, "I want to say to the audience, `Maybe this is your feeling. Maybe this is your house.

Maybe this is your story too.'" Rooted in tragedy, this production's irrepressible comic yearnings for freedom made Lithuanian audiences feel that it was their story.

Uncle Vanya and Nekrosius's other major productions have appealed to Lithuanian audiences with the kind of intimate immediacy that Smoriginas hopes for. Like all great comedy, they are rooted in tragic circumstances, but their expression of the irrepressible yearning to be free spoke to the most urgent concerns of their public. The company played to sold-out audiences throughout the period leading to Lithuania's independence, and Nekrosius is acknowledged as one of the country's most visionary directors, an artist who captures the soul of his nation in the pictures he sculpts on the stage. In the years before *glasnost* his bold expressions of rebellion were subject to the scrutiny of Soviet censors, but he circumvented them by staging mediocre Russian scripts, throwing away the texts, and creating his own work under the title of the officially sanctioned playwright.

This subversive tactic was particularly successful in his 1979 production of a play called *The Square*. When Smoriginas saw the script, he thought it was awful, but after months of improvisation, the cast created a masterpiece that played successfully for over twelve years. It is a story of a man in a tiny square jail cell who conducts a romance by mail. Smoriginas played the prisoner with a Chaplinesque mixture of slapstick and heartbreak. "Nekrosius gave me the structural limits of a square cell, but within the confines of that square I was free to make all the circles and curves that were necessary to establish the world of the prisoner's imagination. I have lived in this country for 38 years, and I never knew the meaning of the word freedom until I lived in that cell."

The ironies in Nekrosius's stage productions are shaped by the absurdities that shape the lives of his audience. Under Soviet rule Lithuanians spent an inordinate amount of time waiting in lines. For shoes, for bread, for ice cream, for underwear. Nekrosius tapped into this collective cultural frustration in the sly stage adaptation of Gogol's *Nose* that he premiered in the spring of 1991. Gogol's hero has lost his nose (in Nekrosius's version the man's sexual organ has disappeared) and tries to place an advertisement in a newspaper asking for its return. There are a lot of angry people ahead of him in line, and he has to pretend to have a baby to work his way to the front, where he discovers that the man responsible for typing people's advertising orders is Lenin.

The first clue that this is no ordinary newspaper clerk comes from the fanaticism of his typing, but it is not until he begins responding to the noseless man in Lenin's familiar style of melodramatic gesticulation that the audience begins to howl with laughter. Nekrosius's conceit has confirmed their suspicion that the ideologically crazed spirit of Lenin is in fact at the front of every line in which they have ever stood, impeding their progress with ridiculously irrelevant demands that have no relation to their real needs. Lenin responds to the man's simple request for assistance with a raving monologue about political dialectics and refuses to print the ad until it has been given to a writer who "can describe this extraordinary phenomenon of nature in a way that will serve as a useful lesson to society."

The hero is so infuriated that he sets fire to Lenin's office. As his newspaper goes up in flames, Lenin shouts hysterically, "It's burning! *Respublica* is burning. *Tiesa* is burning. . . ." He continues listing the names of the Communist propaganda newspapers as he is wheeled away in a haze of smoke. Nekrosius's scene is a farcical fulfillment of his audience's wish to rid themselves of Lenin's legacy. They had already erased his name from Vilnius's main boulevard (Lenin Prospect became Gediminas Prospect in 1988), and all were looking forward to the day when they could cart Lenin's statue out of the park that faces the headquarters of the KGB. The audience greets the hero's satiric act of arson with howling cheers of approval.

Nekrosius's protagonist is venting a frustration that parallels the way Lithuanians feel about surrendering their independence to the Soviets. Losing his "nose" is a kind of castration that is the equivalent of losing his freedom, his history, and his soul. His comic determination to regain what he has lost helps resurrect the audience's faith in the feasibility of resisting Soviet tyranny.

Watching over the scene is the figure of Gogol, who adds yet another dimension to the comedy. Nekrosius parallels the hero's loss to the writer's loss of artistic freedom, a misfortune represented by the painful scraping away of the feathers on Gogol's plumed pen. In the play Gogol's feathered pen is both the instrument he uses for writing satirical stories (including the one enacted before him on the stage) and the wing with which he tries vainly to fly to freedom. The antagonist who clips Gogol's wings and obstructs his escape to the sky is a demonic doctor who forces the writer to drop his trousers and submit to a series of clownishly grotesque medical examinations.

The only free spirit in this story of oppression is the delightful character of the castrated sexual organ, who romps through the production like an animated libido. "At first I thought it would be a problem to make my character believable," says Smoriginas, who was assigned the unusual role. "Then I understood that it is not so unrealistic. Our world is ruled by penises. People always believe what these penises say and even build monuments to them. You can find them in every city in the world."

Smoriginas not only makes the character believable, he turns him into a lovable, Chaplinesque everyman (or every-organ) who follows his impulses without shame. At the opera he runs onstage to dance a comic can-can with the ballerinas. At the theater he leaps out of his box seat and volunteers to marry Cordelia when King Lear disowns her. His desires are boundless, and his encounters with the man from whose body he was severed are hilarious variations on the old formula of comic buddy teams. The hero and his penis become great friends. They eat together. They sing duets in two-part harmony. They get into fights. They even fall in love with the same woman (Cordelia). There is nothing vulgar in their escapades, but the situations are full of suggestive innuendo that mocks the idea of male sexuality at its most basic foundation.

When he first began work on *The Nose* in 1990, Nekrosius wondered what the public's reaction would be. "He asked me if people would think he was crazy," said Ruta Vanagaite Wiman, the artistic director of Nekrosius's company. "Everyone was talking about politics and independence, and here he was doing a play about phalluses."

During rehearsals it became clear that the play was about politics and independence as well as phalluses. The subsidiary characters lived in trash receptacles on wheels, squeezed into unlivable units that mirrored the squalor of Soviet standardized housing. Even the smallest bits of comic business had their origins in social observation. Smoriginas gets big laughs in a cafe scene in which he twirls his wet socks on a fork as if they were strands of spaghetti. His hunger leads to acts of comic desperation that recall the famous scene of Chaplin eating his boots, but his more immediate inspiration was the shortages that plagued Vilnius's grocery stores. The goofiest gag in the cafe involved Smoriginas pretending to be a bon vivant and washing his toes with vodka. This too was born from experience. "A Soviet war hero came to Vilnius," recounts Nekrosius. "He went out drinking, but his feet were cold, so he took off his shoes and socks and poured vodka on his toes! I was there. I saw it." The director speaks with the same tone of laughing disbelief used regularly by Lithuanians when describing the outrageous behavior of the Soviet authorities.

Nekrosius's overlapping themes of personal, artistic, and political repression merge together in the play's ironic climax. The severed phallus is forced to endure its own castration. In a gory symbolic ritual of cracked eggs and chopped candles, the character who epitomized liberation is robbed of his freedom and ends up as an agent of tyranny himself. Hearing songs of lamentation from the inhabitants of the trash receptacles, the castrated phallus jumps on top of their tiny tin dwellings and forces them to sing the revolutionary anthem, "L'Internationale." "Enough of democracy," shouts Smoriginas, imposing a state of absurd musical dictatorship that strips the singers of their dignity, their poetry, and their freedom all at once.

The rehearsal process through which this scene was developed provides insight into the relationship between comedy and freedom in Lithuania. The actors improvised a chaotic scene of musical jack-in-the-boxes where the characters would jump out of their trash receptacles with a song, only to be beaten back inside by the tyrannical phallus, who silenced them with a smack on the head with his mallet. Each time he hit one of them, two more popped up singing in another receptacle. Nekrosius rarely speaks during rehearsals, preferring to let his actors discover the line of their action by trial and error. For this scene, however, he jumped onstage with the singing actors and urged them to defy their persecutor with more vehemence. Then he directed Smoriginas to meet their increased defiance with increased fury of his own. "Spit at them," he barked. "Hit them harder."

Nekrosius was sculpting comedy out of the raw confrontation between brutal oppression and fierce resistance. The scene that resulted was frighteningly violent and funny. His adjustments had made it more authentically comic by raising the stakes of the action, so that it was closer to a life-and-death battle for survival than a lighthearted sing-along. The level of laughter evoked by the musical savagery was directly proportional to the level of danger it evoked. No one could watch the beatings without thinking of the recent clashes between soldiers and civilians on the streets outside the theater. This scene, as was the entire farce, was orchestrated by Nekrosius as a slapstick symphony in which each note is fashioned out of a genuine cry of pain.

As a tribute to the indomitability of Lithuania's subversive comic spirit, Nekrosius concludes his play with a funeral of laughter that refuses to expire. When Gogol dies at the end of *The Nose*, he dies laughing. The demonic doctor sits ghoulishly on the writer's coffin, but he cannot silence the sound of Gogol's laughter. The giggling noises from his tomb seem to rise skyward with a freedom that not even the devil can crush.

The grotesque surrealism of *The Nose* might seem on the surface to be far removed from the urgency of everyday life in occupied Lithuania, but Nekrosius was attracted to Gogol's story by the gritty details on which the comedy was based, and the director uses his comic stage pictures to bring his audience into heightened contact with the harsh reality that surrounds them. "Gogol begins with certain facts of life," says Nekrosius, "and transforms them into facts of art. Then the documentary details become fantastical and the facts start to fly."

Flying facts. A runaway phallus. A laughing corpse. Like Gogol, Nekrosius begins with mundane details of suffering and absurdity, then transforms them into comic art. The flying facts in *The Nose* and other plays staged by Nekrosius are grounded in Lithuania's history of oppression. The laughter they elicit is a potent expression of Lithuania's determination to be free.

One leaves Nekrosius's theater in the old quarter of Vilnius with a renewed awareness of the essential bond between the facts of art and the facts of life in Lithuania. A few blocks away is an extraordinary living sculpture that confirms that sense of continuity between the country's symbols and its reality. The sculpture is a huge barricade initially constructed around the parliament building to defend it from Soviet tanks and troops. In January 1991 the Soviet army had tried to remove Lithuania's independence-minded government by force, and citizens of Vilnius responded by setting up an impromptu barricade of concrete slabs and barbed wire. More important, they reinforced this barricade with hundreds of protesters, forming a human wall to block the advance of the armed soldiers and rolling artillery. These freedom fighters sang songs, built fires, camped out all night, and managed to prevent the attempted coup. To commemorate that collective act of resistance the Lithuanians left the barricade standing and embellished it every day with symbolic objects, drawings, and graffiti that expressed their determination to be free.

Although the barbed wire and concrete provide a grim foundation for the populist monument, its adornments were marked by a vital sense of humor that reflected the ability of Lithuanians to combat oppression with laughter. Every day people would make personal contributions to the communal sculpture, painting satirical likenesses of Stalin and Lenin on the concrete barriers, or nailing their Communist identification papers to a plank in an ironic announcement of their resignation from the Party. All available flat surfaces were transformed into cartoon documentaries of current events. One drawing of Gorbachev pictured him dripping blood into three bowis labeled Lithuania, Estonia, and Latvia. He wore tanks instead of shoes, and between his legs was a cynical note to the free world, "Thanks for the Nobel Peace Prize."

The barricades were dotted with ironically arranged scrap heaps of discarded Sovietica. People would gather around stacks of obsolete propaganda buttons, mutilated books on Marx, and torn Soviet passports to discuss politics and ridicule the Communist leaders who had lied to them for so long. An old woman laughed at a defaced portrait of former Soviet President Leonid Breznev that was taped to a junk pile of party propaganda. "That's where he belongs," she muttered. "He was a stupid old drunkard." A passerby agrees and imitates Breznev's drunken syntax to the amusement of everyone around.

There was a carnival atmosphere to the parliament barricades that captured the essential characteristics of Lithuanian laughter: it was shaped by the memory of tragic circumstances; it inspired a subversive attitude toward Soviet authority; and it fostered a sense of solidarity among people working toward independence. As did the complex humor it evoked, the remarkable public sculpture gave a voice to the hopes and frustrations of ordinary people.

The eccentric monument was a tangible embodiment of the country's complex comic spirit and its relationship to political events. It was constructed around the home of the country's president and lawmakers as if its visual paradoxes and tragicomic contradictions were protecting the fragile new democracy from foreign threats to its survival. The makeshift satire was literally attached to the concrete and barbed wire blockades erected to keep the Soviet troops at bay. The central joke of the edifice is found in the ironic placement of a stolen traffic sign over the main doorway to the parliament building. It is the international symbol for "Do Not Enter!"

This comic monument is a concrete manifestation of the defiant humor expressed by Lithuanians in more ephemeral forms

of performance. In each case they are declaring their independence through laughter and assaulting the hypocrisies of the
Soviet system with satirical gestures that expose its weaknesses
and encourage bolder steps of political confrontation.

This courageous spirit of comic resistance was displayed by
Lithuanians who gathered regularly at the fence around Vilnius's
occupied television broadcasting facilities, where Soviet troops
killed thirteen unarmed Lithuanians in 1990. The site of the massacre became a place of pilgrimage where people expressed both
their grief and their satiric anger. People made a point of showing
their children the Soviet troops who were holding their country
captive. Families stared at the soldiers through a chain link fence.
They turned the visit into an educational experience, like a family
trip to the zoo to look at monkeys in a cage.

"Let's go see the fascists," laughs an old woman as she takes
her grandchild's hand and leads her up a muddy slope to get a
better view of the soldiers in green battle fatigues and bulletproof
vests leaning against their tanks. Arvidas Dapsys, an actor who
lives nearby, points up at the red Communist flag flying from the
top of the tower and jokes that the emblem of the Soviet empire
"looks a little dirty. Like a rag for shining your shoes."

Dapsys is a comic performer who was also part of the
human shield that prevented Soviet soldiers from entering the
parliament building. "The night the people went to defend the
Parliament," he remembers, "I felt there was hope they would win
because some of them were laughing." For Dapsys their laughter
was a sign that they weren't afraid. The memory continues to
encourage him as he watches the soldiers parade through Vilnius
every day. Dapsys has a recurring daydream about a laughing
man standing alone as a tank rolls toward him and the steel is
dissolved by the sound of his laughter. It is an impossible fantasy
but only slightly less probable than tanks being repelled by
unarmed demonstrators who laughed and sang in their path.

The memory of that improbable victory was kept alive by
the ornamented barricades that surrounded the parliament
building. For a time it served as a primitive collage of the nation-

al psyche, expressing the brutal ironies that animated all political discourse in the period between the March 1990 declaration of independence and the August 1991 achievement of statehood. It was a time when the country was simultaneously free and occupied, functioning under the rule of two irreconcilable sets of laws, one originating in Moscow, the other established by the Lithuanians themselves.

The existential limbo of the nation's political status created the kind of irrational landscape that is a fertile realm for comedy. Life in Lithuania could be seen as the social equivalent of the classic cartoon where the clown steps off a cliff and casually keeps walking on air as if his body obeyed a system of rules that was independent of the laws of gravity. Sooner or later there is either a fall or the miracle of flight. Lithuanians were unsure which of these fates awaited them, but they were conscious of the absurdity of their condition. Moscow viewed them as a Soviet state, while they saw themselves living under foreign occupation. The incompatibility of these two visions had provided a source for humor throughout fifty years of Communist domination, but now the clash was reaching epic proportions of absurdity, both on the stage and in the streets.

"Much tension is created by the absurdity of our relationship with the USSR," said President Landsbergis. This tension and absurdity were evident in all forms of humor found in Lithuania during the last years of struggling for independence. The incongruity at the core of the country's political reality inspired an outpouring of ridicule that in turn inspired an outpouring of personal and political resistance to Soviet domination.

Long before the collapse of the USSR, Lithuanian artists had begun a satiric assault on the hypocrisies of the Soviet system, and their public's cheers affirmed the country's determination to break away from Moscow's influence. Humor provided Lithuanians with a psychological weapon for reversing the terror tactics employed for decades by the KGB. People who had been paralyzed by the fear of unspecified reprisals were liberated by the exhilarating force of their own laughter. The tyranny of the totalitarian state was subverted by the teasing suggestion of its comical vulnerability. If Stalin could be reduced to a buffoonish target of ridicule, then there was hope that the stranglehold of his legacy might be broken. The public's belief in the fallibility of the once invincible Communist monolith was nurtured by years of laughing at its flaws.

Pieter Dirk Uys in drag as Evita Bezuidenhout joined Nobel Peace Prize winner Desmond Tutu in the struggle against apartheid. (photo courtesy Pieter Dirk Uys)

4

Ridiculing Racism in South Africa

*Two years before South Africa's first democratic election, I drove
past Johannesburg's infamous John Vorster Prison with a young
black activist named Prince Dubu who had been incarcerated there
for his involvement with the African National Congress. Dubu
pointed up to the window where the police had held him over the
ledge and threatened to drop him if he didn't give them the information they wanted. He was a writer and we were on our way to the
black township of Soweto to see his latest play, in which the interrogation had been transformed into a terrifying comedy.*

*"I'll strangle you until you die," Dubu whispered to me dur-
ing the rehearsal. "That's what the policeman said when he ques-
tioned me." Dubu turned the grim dialogue into slapstick when he
showed his actors how to imitate the way the white cop said it to
him. His body tensed and quivered with mock spasms of rage. His
arms thrashed absurdly in the air, and his high-pitched bark
sounded as if every syllable were being beaten by a club: "I'll
strangle you until you die." Dubu's parody transformed his tortur-
er into a buffoon.*

*My personal encounter with the targets of Dubu's satire came
a few days later. Out of curiosity I stopped to watch a demonstration
at the Jeppe Street Post Office in Johannesburg. Before I knew what
was happening, police with machine guns appeared at the door and
barred the entrance. When the officers stormed the building for a
mass arrest, they escorted me into the bright yellow paddy wagons*

*with everyone else. Their guns and dogs provided an effective
deterrent to reasonable argument.*

*In defiance of their captors, the protesters began joking and
singing protest songs as soon as the caged door of the prison van
slammed shut. When we arrived at the jail, the music and laughter
flowed out of the vans into the cells. It brought a feeling of familiarity to the bleak gray jailhouse. Everyone knew the words to the
protest songs from having sung them for years. The more people the
police stuffed in, the more festive the mood became. Before long there
were over six hundred men in the cell and spirits were skyrocketing.
When an exhausted prisoner suggested we take a break from singing
and dancing, one of the revelers laughed, "Why should we be quiet?
We can do anything we want. We're in jail!"*

*The man had shouted "We're in jail" as if it were a cry of
emancipation. Here in the cell these blacks were determined to
escape the invisible prison of apartheid and act as free men. Having
been arrested at gunpoint and caged in a cell so cramped it was
almost impossible to sit down, the men laughed at the injustice of
their situation until it couldn't hurt them anymore. Surrounded by
hostile police, they formed a collective organism that responded to
threats with protective roars of laughter.*

*The men in the cell had all come to Johannesburg that morn-
ing from a government-sponsored housing development called Palm
Springs. The crime that got them arrested was asking for the basic
services of plumbing, mail delivery, electricity, and sewage removal
the government had promised them when it lured them into buying
houses there. Their demonstration at the post office was part of an
ongoing effort to improve their living conditions.*

*South African President F. W. de Klerk was one of the targets
of their protest. My cell mates took turns waving a red poster with
his photograph that read "wanted for crimes of apartheid." In the
carnival realm of our jail cell, the politicians were the criminals
and the prisoners became their judges. It was a world of comic
reversals, but the comedy was rooted in a history of pain.*

*Eleven other men and I eventually left the cell to meet the
lawyer sent to defend us by the African National Congress. We had
been selected by our cell mates to go to night court to try to secure*

everyone's release without bail. Our first stop was the fingerprinting department, where the laughably incompetent guards got the forms all mixed up and couldn't determine which prints belonged to which prisoner. After the fingerprinting no one knew where to send us, so we picked out a room for ourselves and began moving furniture through the halls to have a place to sit while waiting for the lawyer. The men joked that they were now working for the South African police force as volunteer furniture movers. It tickled them to be taking charge of the hallways in a building where they were imprisoned. One of them found a kitchen employee on his way to serving the guards and convinced him to part with a stack of buttered bread. Soon we were having a picnic in John Vorster Prison, passing around the rations meant for our captors while making ourselves comfortable on the hijacked benches.

Although the men's mood was cheerful enough on the surface, there was a grim undertone to their banter. The subtext of violence remained constant. One man denounced boxing as nothing more than glorified barbarism. Another defended it as part of South African culture. "That's not our culture," quipped a third. "You've been brainwashed spending too much time in the John Vorster jail."

"How can you justify beating somebody on the head and calling it civilized?" asked the biggest man in the room.

"If he comes over and shakes your hand afterwards, then it's justified violence," answered the boxing enthusiast.

"Well, how about if we ask the guard to come in here and knock you down?" continued the skeptic. "If he picks you up and shakes your hand afterwards, we'll call it justified violence."

Whites had been trying to justify the use of violence against blacks since the beginning of South African history, and the hypocrisy behind their arguments was transparent to everyone in the room. Their jokes about boxing were animated by memories of the people they all knew who were beaten, shot, burned, hacked, and stabbed to death every day in what white politicians called "the New South Africa."

Two weeks after we got out of jail, I visited my former cell mates at their homes in Palm Springs and found their defiant humor undiminished. A town meeting had been called in a dusty

field to discuss strategies for dealing with grievances against the
government. The proceedings opened with a comic yell.

"Down with de Klerk! He's bald!" shouted Mlungisi
Hlongwane, the head of the Palm Springs Civic Association. "Viva,
the spirit of no surrender! Viva!" His neighbors laughed at the
barbed reference to the cranial deficiencies of President de Klerk and
endorsed the spirit of no surrender with a rousing chant of their
own. "Viva!" they answered, "Viva!"

When the meeting adjourned we drove by a tacky wall mural
that marked the entrance to Palm Springs. The town's name was
spelled out next to a painting of a palm tree, as if it were a luxury
resort. The illusion was shattered a few meters away by ditches
filled with trash. There are no palm trees in Palm Springs. There
aren't any schools, hospitals, or telephones either. The phony mural
is an apt emblem of the "New South Africa" promised by de Klerk
before the transition to majority rule. Its fraudulent advertisement
of a nonexistent paradise echoed a quip I'd heard in John Vorster
Prison: "If everything was fine, like the government keeps saying, we
wouldn't be locked up here in this cell."

When Nelson Mandela, then President of the ANC, called for a
mass action march against the white government in Pretoria on
August 5, 1992, nearly a hundred thousand black demonstrators
showed up to stage the largest protest in the history of the South
African capital. Thousands of people lined the city's main street
to cheer the protestors as they swarmed toward the union buildings that housed the offices of President F. W. de Klerk. At the
head of this historic parade, leading the masses to the spot where
Mandela would make a speech demanding majority rule, was a
clown.

The clown that led the marchers was not a simple figure of
fun. Wearing the khaki uniform of the ANC's military branch,
he carried a painted toy machine gun made of wood and entertained onlookers with wild acrobatic stunts. The comic commando performed dazzling flips, rolls, and somersaults but

always managed to land in a combat-ready position with his machine gun poised to fire. His feistiness tickled the audience into laughter and applause. They knew he wasn't aiming his weapon at them but at the policemen lined up behind them, waiting to intervene with rifles, riot helmets, and tear gas canisters if the demonstration got out of hand. With their bright yellow gas masks dangling around their necks and stiff hulking movements, the real police stood in ridiculous contrast to the swift, lithe antics of the clown.

South African officers had fired on unarmed demonstrators a few months earlier in the aftermath of the Boipatong massacre, and there was no assurance that this march would not end in a bloodbath. The risk of actual violence made the clown's performance all the more extraordinary. His militant pantomime was poised precariously on the border between slapstick and political confrontation.

There was an edge of tension to the crowd's laughter. No one was pretending that violence was an insignificant issue. On the contrary, killing and torture had marred the struggle over South Africa's future with increasing frequency ever since February 1990, when the ANC had been legally permitted to pursue its goal of majority rule. By playing with the theme of violence, the clown soldier was cutting to the heart of the nation's fears.

The link between the comic warrior and real political violence became more apparent as the parade continued. Occasionally the clown would stop to pull a walkie-talkie from the inside pocket of his uniform. He looked down the street at the territory the parade was about to enter and spoke into the handset to report the conditions to his colleagues in the rear of the procession.

The acrobatic commando was in fact a security guard helping to clear the path for the ANC dignitaries marching behind him. His charade of imaginary gunfire was intended to ensure that no real bullets would be fired that day. The strategy worked. There were no injuries during the demonstration, a remarkable achievement given the volatile climate of the country at the time.

Of course, the success of the demonstration cannot be attributed entirely to the performance of the clown. He was only a

figurehead, but his comic defiance was a lightning rod for the
crowd's upbeat determination. The protesters expressed their
exuberance in raucous songs, dances, and laughter. A man strut-
ted down the street in a four-foot-high party hat bedecked with
slogans of liberation. Nestled between his "Mandela for President" buttons and bumper stickers calling for "democracy now"
was a red horn that he tooted vigorously through a rubber tube
in his mouth. Jumping up and down to the rhythms of a revolutionary dance called the *toyi-toyi*, the demonstrators literally
bounced their way to the capitol steps.

Mandela greeted them on the capitol lawn wearing a blue
track suit, brown moccasins, and a jaunty cap that matched the
festive atmosphere of the event. His speech was peppered with
ironic jabs at President de Klerk, who had accused him of intimidating blacks into staying away from work during the recent ANC
boycotts. Wryly claiming to be flattered that de Klerk considered
the ANC powerful enough to intimidate millions of people,
Mandela urged de Klerk to give blacks the vote. "I can't see him
here," said the ANC leader with a smile as he turned to the windows of the president's office behind him, "but I hope he's
listening."

The audience hooted their approval. They had come to take
back their home and were convinced that the next time they gathered on this lawn they would be celebrating Mandela's installation
in the president's office now occupied by de Klerk. For them the
march was a carnival of inversion. The derisive chanting had
reduced de Klerk to a laughingstock, and for a day at least, the
capitol belonged to the powerless who had planted green, yellow,
and black ANC flags all over the government lawns.

Even the somber giant statue of the white pioneer Louis
Botha that dominates the presidential gardens was transformed
into a comical parade float for the revolution. Black children
scampered up the statue and draped Botha's horse in red banners
that called for majority rule. One little boy sat on the brim of the
statue's hat and pounded on Botha's head as he waved the ANC
flag for Mandela. Another stuffed ANC flyers into the bronze
horse's mouth.

When Mandela looked at the crowd spread out in front of him by the tens of thousands, singing, dancing, and shouting for their rights, he called them part of a "tidal wave" for democracy. It did not diminish the seriousness of the march to acknowledge that a motley clown soldier was riding the crest of its tidal wave toward freedom. His presence was simply a visible manifestation of the comic subtext that has always infused the nation's ongoing dialogue on democracy. Battered by the long-term effects of racial injustice and political violence, South Africans displayed a sense of humor that signaled their refusal to surrender their lives, their identities, or their dignity to the dehumanizing tyranny of apartheid.

The same satiric songs that were sung in Pretoria were sung in demonstrations throughout the country. Mock trials in which de Klerk and his followers were subjected to scathing ridicule were common forms of political protest. Laughter in South Africa is part of the process through which blacks and whites continue to come to terms with the brutal facts of their political landscape.

During a march in Soweto strikers engaged the police in a sarcastic duel of words. "Do you know who you look like?," shouted a protester into a police van.

"Who?" shot back the cop.

"You look like me!" taunted the marcher.

"I'm no kaffir," barked the policeman, using the highly insulting Afrikaans word for "black."

"Yes you are," taunted the marcher. "Haven't you ever seen a black asshole. It's pink like yours. That makes you nothing but a white kaffir."

The policeman was infuriated by the marcher's reversal of the racial slur, but his fellow officers laughed at the absurdity of anyone being called a "white kaffir." The nearby marchers laughed too, and the fury of the moment subsided.

The incident is emblematic of South African humor. It was fraught with the same riskiness that marked the comic relationship between the clown soldier in Pretoria and the policemen who warily watched him shoot his wooden rifle. Racial tensions were defused by laughter, but more significantly, the joking signaled a demand for mutual respect and equality. The volatile relationship between rage and humor in South Africa was acknowledged by Mandela when he urged the protesters in Pretoria not to taunt the police as they left the demonstration. His parting advice to the crowd was an indication that he understood how potent a weapon laughter can be.

Much of the growing black rage is aimed at the hypocrisy of a white government that freed Mandela from prison and unilaterally declared the existence of a "New South Africa" without making any fundamental changes in the economic and political systems. Whites created the illusion of reform without giving blacks any real freedom. Their state of limbo in the frustrating period of transition paralleled the condition of Lithuanians who had declared independence but were still living under the rule of the Soviet Union and its soldiers. As in Lithuania, the absurdity of the situation made audiences particularly receptive to comedy that lampooned the hypocrisy of double standards.

When South African President P. W. Botha first introduced the idea of a "New South Africa" in 1981, a series of cosmetic changes were introduced. "Colored" citizens were given the right to elect representatives, but their delegates had no power. "Independent" black homelands were established under the leadership of repressive puppet dictators totally dependent on subsidies from Pretoria. Gradually apartheid laws were taken off the books, but economic discrimination left blacks as impoverished as ever. The "New South Africa" was a hoax invented by an illegitimate white government to convince the world to lift trade sanctions against it.

The clash between the illusion of a "New South Africa" and the racist reality experienced by its citizens gave birth to a powerfully subversive style of comedy that expressed the nation's outrage. The two most influential satires in the country's history premiered in the year that President Botha publicly unveiled the idea of a "New South Africa." Fulfilling an essential public need to come to terms with contradictions that the government was content to ignore, both comedies were received with enthusiasm by black and white audiences.

One of these two satires took its title from a pun on an ultimatum made by Botha in a 1981 speech. The leader shocked his white constituents by declaring that the apartheid system would have to change and challenged them to "Adapt or die." It did not take long for the white satirist Peter Dirk Uys to incorporate the phrase into the title of his newest monologue: *Adapt or Dye*. The other play, entitled *Woza Albert*, ridiculed the supposedly Christian principles, on which Botha's party had governed the nation for decades, by speculating on what would happen if Jesus Christ chose the land of apartheid as the site of his Second Coming.

Reverberations from both these plays continue to have an impact on the interracial dialogue in South Africa more than a decade after their premieres. *Woza Albert* went on a successful world tour that launched the international careers of its creators, Percy Mtwa, Mbongeni Ngema, and Barney Simon. The original version of the play ran until 1985 and was revived in 1990 by Peter Brooks's Paris-based company, which performed it around the world yet again. Mtwa and Ngema both brought subsequent plays to Broadway and Lincoln Center in New York City, where they played a role in fueling the international public outrage against apartheid that helped force the white South African government to repeal many of the country's most unjust laws. Mbongeni Ngema used the fame of *Woza Albert* to win backing for his worldwide hit, *Sarafina*. Barney Simon followed his work on *Woza Albert* with other interracial collaborations that challenged the country's censorship laws. As artistic director of Johannesburg's Market Theater he defied the apartheid system by creating the only theater in the country where black and white artists and audiences could mix freely.

Woza Albert is the quintessential South African comedy, a play that laughingly dissects the hypocrisies of racism as it calls for social change. Created by the two black actors in collaboration with the white director Barney Simon, *Woza Albert* captures the complexity of South African culture in a multifaceted collage of oral history, physical comedy, muckraking, and political protest.

The first scene set a tone of comic defiance that enabled the audience to identify immediately with the actors' dilemma. Mtwa and Ngema are two black performers being arrested by a white policeman for playing their music in the streets. The actors convey the spirit of the outdoor concert without real instruments, using an array of melodic and percussive sounds to give the impression of an orchestra in full swing. Mtwa and Ngema are humming, scatting, and whistling a slapdash version of Hugh Masekela's "Stimela." The song is doubly evocative, reminding people of the apartheid laws that forced Masekela to go into exile to find the freedom to play his music without harassment, and telling the story of black workers taken from their homes to work for slave wages in the gold mines of Johannesburg.

The scene is structured so that the outrage evoked by the song is channeled into derisive laughter directed at the buffoonish white policeman who takes the musicians to prison. Mtwa transforms himself into the policeman by putting on one of the pink round noses that both actors wear around their necks throughout the show. These clown masks are ever-present icons of the white race, emblems of apartheid that encircle the throats of the black actors like a ball and chain. Whenever a scene calls for a white character, one of the pair slips on the clown nose and assumes the awkward gait and hypocritical grin of a racist. In the opening scene the pink-nosed policeman tells the black musicians that they should go "back to the bush with the baboons. That's where you belong."

By ridiculing whites as cartoon caricatures *Woza Albert* exposes the ludicrous foundations of apartheid. The white soldiers, guards, politicians, and TV announcers who appear throughout the play speak in hollow, comic voices expressing idiotic sentiments. The duplicity inherent in their devotion to apartheid is gradually revealed as the play's premise unfolds. Because white South Africans claim that apartheid is based on Christian values, the play explodes the myth of divinely sanctioned apartheid by envisioning what would happen if Christ himself arrived in South Africa and saw how his teachings were being applied.

Woza Albert's fantastical treatment of the Second Coming is a comic jam session based roughly on the New Testament. The imprisoned and exploited blacks await a savior, but when Christ arrives by jumbo jet in Johannesburg and denounces the injustices of apartheid, he is betrayed, persecuted, and martyred by the white government that had initially used his appearance to justify their policies to the world. Wearing a pink clown nose and a sly smile, the prime minister tells an international barrage of television cameras that Christ "is back and South Africa has got him." He cannot hide his contempt for the world leaders who had imposed sanctions on his country and will now be jealous of the public relations benefits bestowed by Jesus' visit. "Tough luck, friends," gloats the politician. "He chose us."

Having welcomed Christ with the key to Sun City and a hospitality tour of its sex shows and gambling casinos, the government is surprised when he denounces the disparities between the excesses of rich whites and the deprivations of poor blacks. Christ is denounced as a terrorist rabble rouser and imprisoned on infamous Robben Island, where Mandela and other ANC leaders were still being held at the time of the play's creation. When Christ makes his escape from the prison island by walking on the water, he is spotted by two doltish air force pilots who lament that they have forgotten to bring their cameras and missed a chance to get a souvenir photo of the miracle. Following a nonsensical dialogue worthy of their pink clown noses, the pilots drop an atom bomb that destroys Christ along with half of South Africa.

Christ's betrayal had been predicted by an old black vagabond who had appeared earlier in the play. In a comic monologue spoken while trying to sew a button on his coat, the hobo recounts the famous story of Piet Retief. Retief was a revered leader of the nineteenth-century Afrikaans settlers, and his fate at the hands of the Zulu King Dingane has assumed mythic proportions for blacks and whites in South Africa. Dingane invited Retief and his soldiers to put down their weapons and join him in a feast that ended in their massacre by the Zulus. The tramp laughingly predicts that the same thing will happen to Christ when the prime minister invites him inside to "enjoy the fruits of apartheid."

The vagabond's rendition of the encounter between Dingane and Retief is full of comic details that play off the audience's knowledge of African history. Embellishing his tale with snatches of a Zulu liberation song warning that whites cannot be trusted, he contradicts the standard history book version of the event used by whites to justify their mistrust of blacks. The national Voortrekker Monument in Pretoria celebrates Retief's martyrdom in a stone frieze while vilifying Dingane's warriors with a sculpted black wildebeest that symbolizes "the barbarism that yielded to civilization."

Civilization for the whites meant the destruction of black culture, but the tramp's revisionist retelling of the tale suggests that Dingane was protecting his people from Retief's intention to steal their land. We know whose side the hobo is on when he imitates the gleeful smile on Dingane's face as he invites Retief inside for dinner. The expression of mock beatitude parallels the look on the face of ex-Prime Minister Hendrik Voerwoerd in a famous newsreel clip from the fifties in which he defends apartheid as nothing more than a harmless "policy of good neighborliness."

Woza Albert's wry use of Dingane's legend calls attention to how the story is used frequently by both blacks and whites to appropriate history to their own ends. Mtwa, Ngema, and Simon offer it as yet another comic salvo in a satirical battle that can be traced back to the nineteenth century when black Africans were caricatured on the English-speaking stage as ooga-booga Zulus in grass skirts.

A large part of the black struggle for political power in South Africa is waged in the arena of international public opinion, and popular comedies like *Woza Albert* have played a role in exposing the injustices of the apartheid system to the outside world. In 1982 *Woza Albert* was presented in London to a storm of critical acclaim. The play overturned the tradition of racial caricature that had become an institutionalized part of European culture. Now it was the whites who were depicted as comic savages, brutalizing blacks and nuking Jesus with their silly pink clown noses. *Woza Albert*'s fierce comic indictment of white savagery can be imagined as the Zulus' revenge for having been caricatured as barbaric cannibals in the past. Somber tragedies, like those of the white South African playwright Athol Fugard, have also been influential, but the resilience of the black liberation movement is most eloquently expressed in the cathartic release of laughter.

Comedies have happy endings, and the political comedies of South Africa end on a note of hope for the future rather than despair over the past. Because *Woza Albert* is a comedy that combines religion with politics, its happy ending takes the form of a resurrection. Christ is killed by the white government's atomic bomb, but he comes back after three days and brings back to life the ghosts of South African freedom fighters who were also victims of the government's repressive policies. The finale is an exhilarating musical duet sung by Christ and the grave digger as they call out the names of Steve Biko, Ruth First, and other political martyrs they will bring back to life. Each of the names is proceeded by a shout of *"Woza,"* which is Zulu for "rise up." Their resurrection of the Nobel Peace Prize–winning black activist Albert Luthuli gives the play its title, *Woza Albert*.

Woza Albert expresses the frustrations and longings of black South Africans with pithy comic grace. Its protagonists are put in jail, but they find freedom. Its heroes are killed, but they come back to life. There is a lot of suffering at the hands of the whites, but there is also a lot of laughter at their expense. The play is imbued with the same irrepressible spirit displayed by the clown commando at the head of the march on Pretoria when he challenged the government's soldiers with a mock machine gun. Displaying the power of the powerless, the characters created by Mtwa and Ngema use laughter as a weapon to ensure their survival.

Mtwa, Ngema, and Simon shaped their satire from personal experience with the raw suffering of South African blacks. Mtwa received a lesson in the caprice of the legal system when he spent weeks in jail for going to a restaurant without his identity papers. When he and Ngema first began working on the script, they didn't have enough money for food or bus fare and depended on the largesse of a Soweto gangster who bankrolled their project with a stipend that amounted to little more than pennies a day. Simon, a director with a passionate commitment to socially relevant theater, encouraged Mtwa and Ngema to gather material for the play by interviewing street vendors, bricklayers, and children of Soweto. This authenticity resulted in rapt audience attention whenever the play was presented in black townships.

Woza Albert was created during a time when censorship laws in South Africa were tightly enforced. Black people had no opportunity to see their suffering portrayed realistically in films, television, or newspapers. The play's gritty comic realism fulfilled their hunger to see the hypocrisy of white authorities publicly unmasked. Nothing like this had ever appeared before on the South African stage. Audiences in black townships like Soweto thronged to performances and responded to its bleak humor with wild enthusiasm. From the opening sequence they were totally engaged in the play's mockery of the white regime that had restricted their movement, limited their economic opportunities, and imprisoned their heroes. In the repressive conditions of 1981 all this injustice had to be endured without question. Laughing at *Woza Albert* was the only permissible form of public insubordination.

Many young black South African theater artists were influenced by *Woza Albert*'s bold style of epic comedy. Prince Dubu, a political activist who spent five years incarcerated on Robben Island, joined forces with a group of actors from his neighborhood in Soweto to create a play about their township's violent past. Entitled *Which Way, Ma-Afrika?*, the play depicts police brutality, political rioting, and children's funerals with a combination of grim humor and stark realism. The performers have lived through these hardships and make no attempt to soften the facts. *Which Way, Ma-Afrika?* is a heartfelt cry from a community trying to come to terms with its past. "God gave us bread," jokes one of the actors trying to make sense of life under apartheid. "But he forgot the butter."

Dubu's play begins with an unjust arrest, an experience so common among black South Africans that it enables the township audiences to identify immediately with the characters onstage. As was the case in *Woza Albert* and many other plays influenced by that classic work, the white police are played by blacks in a demeaning slapstick style. There are no clown noses, but the police are portrayed as neurotic buffoons. They sputter when they speak, and their bodies convulse in ridiculous spasms. Dubu models these caricatures of police officers after the absurd portrayals of power-crazed Nazis in American movies from the forties. They are insecure bumblers who are tripped up, taunted, and teased by the far more dignified victims of their brutality. Black spectators join in the satiric fun by heckling and hooting at these comic emblems of injustice whenever they enter the stage.

Like much of South African humor, *Which Way, Ma-Afrika?* celebrates the courage that enables the black community to transform its losses into victories of the spirit. In a scene eulogizing the Soweto children killed by police in 1976, a character whose daughter has died notes ironically that it takes a mother nine months to bear a child, while the police can destroy it in only a few seconds. A woman in the audience laughed at his graveyard humor and sighed, "It's so true."

The show played just a few blocks away from the Soweto monument to thirteen-year-old Hector Petersen, the first child to die in the 1976 massacre. Sowetans still cover it with fresh flowers every day. Dubu recalled hiding in a church during the shooting while the woman next to him bled to death from a gunshot wound. The public's response to his play is intensified by this kind of living memory.

Which Way, Ma-Afrika? depicts the bravery of black activists in the face of repression, while making it clear that a sense of humor is an essential element in their resistance. The play's funniest moments are in its most violent scenes. A prisoner being brutally interrogated by the police insults his questioners with sarcastic remarks that leave them quivering ridiculously with rage. He laughs at their weakness and sings freedom songs in their faces. His voice is echoed by an offstage chorus that swells in power. By the end of the scene the audience has joined in the song with cheers and applause of their own.

The music and slapstick of the interrogation are followed by scenes of domestic comedy in which a Soweto family struggles

with the hardships of poverty and discrimination. The beleaguered father tries to keep his family together, but his ability to
provide them with food and education is hampered by the injustices of the South African system. Even the battle between the
sexes is colored by the shadow of apartheid, as can be seen in
jokes he makes about injustice after death. "Why do funerals have
apartheid?" he complains to his wife. "When women die, they
sing nice songs like, 'What Have We Done,' and the cemetery
buses have ads for 'Chicken Lick'n.' But when men die, they sing,
'Get out of here, pack your bags and go home,' and the bus ads
say, 'Keep Soweto Clean!'"

In spite of the nominal ending of apartheid, funerals, violence, and injustice are still everyday facts of life for blacks in
South Africa. *Which Way, Ma-Afrika?* is only one of many new
plays that transform these elements into cathartic comedy.
Following in the pioneering footsteps of *Woza Albert*, these popular entertainments are rooted in the suffering of black communi-
ties but transcend that suffering with laughter that fuels their
audience's determination to do whatever it takes to build a home
where their children can grow up to be free.

White South Africans are also deeply concerned about their
homes, and as do their black neighbors realize that the resolution
of their country's racial conflicts is a matter of life and death.
When President Botha urged his constituents in 1981 to "adapt
or die," he was speaking to the white population, and they
responded to his unsettling ultimatum with conflicting emotions
of fear, greed, anger, and guilt. The process of adaptation since
then has been slow and laborious, but it has also been laced with
laughter. Sometimes the humor is dark and bitter, like the racist
jibes of the neo-Nazi leader Eugene Terre-Blanche, who sarcasti-
cally offers to dress up President de Klerk in the wig of Nelson
Mandela's wife so that the whole country can see the confusion
that will be wrought by the dismantling of apartheid. The anxieties of white South Africans give birth to bizarre forms of laughter that reflect the ambivalence of their attempts to "adapt or die."

One of the most fascinating manifestations of this white survival humor is the popularity of Evita Bezuidenhout, the fictional

diplomat in drag who made her stage debut in Pieter Dirk Uys's 1981 farce, *Adapt or Dye*. (More than ten million South Africans have seen the video version of this play.) Evita is not simply a comic character; she is a cultural phenomenon, embodying the ambiguities and hypocrisies of the "New South Africa" as the ambassador to the fictional black homeland of Bapetikosweti. One of the most instantly recognizable stage personalities in the country, Evita is a blatantly racist member of the "South African diplomatic corpse" who unwittingly demonstrates the absurdity of apartheid through the wacky logic with which she defends it.

Famous for her comic stubbornness in refusing to "adapt" or "dye," Evita enjoys a popularity as a cultural icon that has led to her receiving fan mail from actual political celebrities of all persuasions. In July 1992, the Sunday magazine of the *Johannesburg Times* ran an article featuring Evita as one of the decade's ten most influential South Africans, a list that included former President P. W. Botha and Nelson Mandela. An aristocratic matron with shapely legs and a crafty smile, Evita epitomizes the "New South Africa" by being firmly rooted in the old South Africa. She is a politician who owes her career to apartheid and is clearly unwilling to adapt to anything new. As does the government itself, she pays patronizing lip service to change, while clinging tenaciously to the perks of power, which include a mansion called "Blanche-Noir" in Bapetikosweti, where she serves as South Africa's ambassador.

The genius of Uys's characterization and the source of Evita's enormous popularity is the astonishing degree to which this fictional transvestite comes across as a plausible representative of the South African state. Everyone knows that Evita is really a man in woman's clothing, but Uys plays her with such understated dignity that she becomes a completely believable and sympathetic character. She is so charming that you want to believe in her sincerity, but when you look closely at the substance of what she says, it is founded on the same deceptions and lies that have led to decades of injustice. "There are two things I can't stand about South Africa," she confesses in an attempt to demonstrate her dedication to reform, "apartheid and the blacks."

Evita's sugar-coated manner was a perfect symbol for the white government's illusory commitment to change. Since 1981, when the National Party began talking about a "new South Africa," there had been cosmetic alterations of apartheid, but the economic disenfranchisement of blacks remained unchanged. Even winning the right to vote will not bring true equality to the black and colored populations. In a country where democracy had been reduced to a political charade, Evita's status as an illusion made her uniquely qualified to speak for her government. The imaginary black homeland where she worked was no less absurd than the real black homelands created by the Nationalist government to create a false impression of black independence. Before majority rule these homelands were run by puppet governments loyal to the white South African politicians who financed their treasuries. They were not recognized as independent nations by any government in the world but Pretoria's.

In Bapetikosweti Evita enjoyed an excellent relationship with the nominal black president because he used to be her garden boy. Like the white politicians in South Africa, she seemed blissfully ignorant of the contradictions in her actions and advised her audiences to adapt to the coming political changes by saying one thing and doing another. This practice, she reassured the public, has guided government policy for years. Like a kindly aunt encouraging a child to take its medicine, Evita reminds us that "hypocrisy is the vaseline of political intercourse."

In 1986 Uys closed his Evita shows by having her parade down the aisles and leave the theater in a pink Cadillac convertible. Fans would crowd around the car and ask for her autograph. When the convertible was stopped for speeding, a policeman recognized Evita and let her go without a ticket, essentially according her the same diplomatic immunity that would be granted a real ambassador. Years later an elderly housewife attending one of Evita's 1992 Johannesburg performances remembered wistfully seeing the diplomat in her pink Cadillac. She whispered to me that some of her friends believe Evita is a real person, and though she herself knows it's only an act insisted that "Evita would make a wonderful South African representative to the United Nations."

Evita could be accepted as an honest political fiction, because South Africa's real politicians perpetrated fictions all the time without ever admitting it. Uys makes this point explicitly when he impersonates Foreign Minister Pik Botha. Clothed only in Evita's fur coat, Uys as Botha denies he has ever had an affair with the woman for the simple reason that "Evita doesn't exist. Like apartheid doesn't exist. Like there are not political prisoners in South Africa."

There are many stories about people who laugh whenever the real Botha begins a speech, because he looks so much like Uys's accurate comic impression of him. Uys's sketch ends with Botha muttering a line that follows logically from the rest of his implausible denials. "I'm not here," he growls threateningly. "I don't exist. Like political prisoners don't exist." Like Evita, Botha's semifictional stage persona is a challenge to the public's faith in what the government presents as truth.

This ironic manipulation of fact and fiction is perfectly pitched to the anxieties of a period in South African history when everyone knew the political situation would change, but no one believed anyone else's version of what the country would become. These anxieties of life in the "New South Africa" were manifested in the questions asked by the public when they had a chance to speak directly to Evita. In August 1992 Uys staged a performance in Johannesburg called *An Audience with Evita.* Every evening for three weeks the ambassador to Bapetikosweti fielded questions on apartheid, sex, and democracy. She became the South African Ann Landers in drag, a sounding board for the doubts and fears of the nation. People asked how Evita would cope with a transition to real democracy in which the black majority actually controlled the government. Would she join the African National Congress? Would she learn to dance the *toyi-toyi?* Would she move in with the newly divorced Nelson Mandela?

The questions were asked in a spirit of fun, but most of them dealt directly with the uncertainties of political change. Even the silly questions about Evita's rumored sexual encounters with the nation's leaders reflected the need for escapist gossip

that possesses a nation gripped by fear. When answering inquir-
ies about South Africa's future, Evita shakes up her audience by
forcing them to look at their national symbols from a fresh perspective. When a man asks if the flag of the new South Africa will
be a black background with a white dot (representing the insig-
nificance of a white minority population in a government dominated by blacks), Evita turns the tables and says it would be better than a white background with a black dot, because that might
look too much like a bullet hole. With her quick wit, Evita shifts
the focus from worry over the loss of white power to a stark
acknowledgment of the violence that results from the disenfranchisement of blacks. Sometimes Evita stops joking to confront
more directly the nation's symbolic acts. Referring to a national
holiday commemorating the victory of white settlers over Dingane's Zulus at the massacre of Blood River, she wonders aloud,
"How long can you keep celebrating the death of black people and
calling it a gift from God?"

Evita's dialogue with the audience is an extension of South
Africa's ongoing dialogue with its own conscience. Powerful emotions are exposed in a comic context, and because Evita is not
real, the public airing of fear, anger, and guilt is not as threatening as it would be in a political gathering. People feel free to
reveal themselves more openly in their questions and their laughter than they might in other circumstances.

Uys keeps the conversation centered on the nation's most
explosive issues, so that the stakes are high. The subject being
examined and debated in the playful exchange between Evita and
her public is nothing less than the survival of the nation. White
South Africans are terrified of what the future will be like when
the black majority is given the vote. Their encounter with Evita's
comedy is a tentative exploration of the consequences of real
democracy.

Evita is a creation of apartheid, and it is both funny and
reassuring to watch her cope with its demise. Before her entrance
in *An Audience with Evita*, another character says that Evita is
backstage swinging from a chandelier, clothed in the traditional
dress of a white Afrikaans settler and singing the revolutionary

anthem of the black liberation movement. In its garish splendor Evita's response to changing times offers a vision of racial harmony that combines ridiculous charades with an eccentric dash of hope.

Evita's satiric persona and *Woza Albert*'s aggressive comic style both emerged at the beginning of a tortured period of transition ushered in by Botha's 1981 command to "adapt or die." The "New South Africa" that was promised has yet to come into being, and these two distinctively South African comic forms reflect the absurdities of life in a country that pretends to be something it is not. The continuing success enjoyed by the creators of both these comic masterpieces has a lot to do with the ways in which their respective audiences have tried to come to terms with Botha's ultimatum. Blacks and whites are all coping with political changes of enormous importance, and the invigorating, comforting release of laughter is one of the forces that helps them endure the difficulties of those changes.

Although Evita speaks most directly to white experience and *Woza Albert* speaks most directly to blacks, attempts to segregate the laughter evoked by both these forms of comedy are as artificial as apartheid itself. In fact, the audiences for these comedies are often mixed, and the core concern for both the performers and their public is how to turn the racially divided country into a place where blacks and whites can make their homes in peace. *Woza Albert* was created by two black actors in collaboration with a white director. All three shared the writing credits. Their first commercial success was in South Africa's first integrated arts complex, The Market Theater. Pieter Dirk Uys frequently collaborates with a black actress who plays Evita's militant maid in a style that shatters the stereotypes of master-servant relationships in South Africa. Uys also performs frequently at the Market Theater, and one night in 1990 held successive performances of Evita for the Johannesburg Police Union and the African National Congress Youth League.

The racial turmoil in South Africa does not provide much opportunity for blacks and whites to laugh together, but when they do, it is a sign of their mutual desire for reconciliation. In a

1992 comedy about racial reconciliation called *Born Again*, which owes much to the spirit of *Woza Albert*, the Sakhile players joke that the nation's predicament likens it to a zebra: "It doesn't matter if you shoot it on a white spot or a black spot. The zebra will still die."

The slow and painful transition from institutionalized racism to a black majority government has been lubricated by a remarkable outpouring of mockery and mirth. This ironic discourse pervades the country's newspaper headlines, political speeches, theater performances, protest demonstrations, and the graffiti scrawled on walls everywhere. The ongoing comic dialogue demonstrates that people of all persuasions are at least listening to one another. In the absence of mutually agreeable solutions to their problems, they answer each other's challenges with taunting one-liners.

When it became clear that white South Africans were terrified by the idea of giving equal rights to the black majority, the Pan African Congress developed a ghoulish slogan that parodied the unfulfilled promise of "one man, one vote." The radically militant black organization asked the white colonialists to consider instead the possibility of "one settler, one bullet."

The phrase caught on and became an endless source of defiant humor for blacks and whites alike. It was carved into the back of a wooden bench in the Johannesburg Magistrate's Courtroom, where blacks are regularly arraigned for trespassing. White extremists retaliated with their own variation of the slogan, painted on a wall near a highway in Johannesburg: "One bomb, many kaffirs." A colored (mixed-race) humorist performing in a Grahamstown cultural hall called the "1820 Settlers' Monument" expressed his opposition to the white colonists memorialized in the building's name by suggesting it be changed to "1820 Settlers, 1820 Bullets." In the *Johannesburg Times* even a seemingly innocent photograph of a woman feeding crumbs to the birds was accompanied by a caption that kept the dialogue going: "One pigeon, one mealy pip."

At the heart of this continuing debate is the fundamental human need for a home. The violence and political hypocrisy that dominate the South African landscape make it impossible for blacks or whites to build a family life with any sense of security. Jokes cannot change the circumstances, but shared laughter can minimize the paralyzing impact of fear and fuel hope for change. It provides a tentative foundation on which South Africans can begin to imagine a future where having a safe home is a possibility for everyone. Even the combative irony of a slogan like "one settler, one bullet" reaches back in history to the time when blacks were defending their land against white colonists. The dark humor of the phrase was born of desperation, but its subtext is simple: "Give us back our homes."

Ekhaya is Zulu for "home." It is also the title of a comic play by Matsemela Manaka that links the longing for home with the longing of black Africans for political and economic equality. The play's drunken narrator stumbles onto the stage in a comic stupor that mirrors the confused state of the nation and reminds the audience that *ekhaya* is "not just the home where you were born, but home where you can make life worth living."

The protagonist is a black exile who returns to South Africa to fulfill his father's dreams by building a museum in Soweto. In his absence the black township has become so full of contradictions that he ends up needing a map to find his way around. The hero's comic sense of disorientation establishes the need for a home, for some new kind of *ekhaya*.

Manaka invites his audiences to experience the metaphor of *ekhaya* in surprising ways that go beyond the mechanics of his plot. He has actually built a museum in his home in Soweto and invites black and white visitors to watch him make paintings with collaborators from different nations. Sometimes exhibitions of these artworks are combined with performances of the play *Ekhaya*, where members of the multiracial audiences are invited to dance and drink home-brewed beer with the actors.

Maintaining a skeptical attitude toward the white philanthropic organizations that fund his museum home and performances, Manaka does not intend his celebratory comedy to be a sugarcoated reconciliation of the races. It is full of ironies and warns blacks to "beware of progressive slavery in the name of development aid," but the beer, dancing, and laughter of the finale offer both the characters in the play and the spectators in the audience a note of hope in their collective search for *ekhaya*.

The same longing for a home where life is worth living can be found in many South African political farces that followed the trailblazing success of Evita and *Woza Albert*. Homelessness is the central metaphor of a tragicomic play called *The Cause* that follows the hardships of three hoboes living in Johannesburg's Joubert Park. Using interview techniques developed by Barney Simon during the development of *Woza Albert*, the actors spent weeks living with homeless blacks in the park while writing the script. Their research adds an unsettling realism to the slapstick gags that include eating flies out of the garbage. Predicting that if the political system in South Africa does not change, whites and blacks will soon be starving together, the hoboes invite the audience to join them in squalor and sing ironically, "Long live the homeless. We are free."

Another satire called *Artimo* features a slapstick eviction scene in which a black man is driven from his home by clown police officers wearing gas masks fashioned out of aluminum foil and fruit juice cans. They spray his house with an insecticide labeled "DOOM." The play was created by actors in the black township of Sebokeng, an area so completely ravaged by the violent aftermath of the nearby Boipatong massacre in March 1992 that six months later the streets were still impassable, cratered with holes dug by residents to keep out police vehicles. Living in homes without regular food deliveries or sanitation service, the creators of *Artimo* express their rage in slapstick imagery that cuts straight to the painful truth. "We are like flies to the police," says actor Sipho Buthelezi. "They shoot doom at us."

Political meetings in South Africa often express the struggle for home more potently than plays. In Capetown on August 17, 1992, to commemorate the tenth anniversary of the death of the political activist Ruth First, the African National Congress sponsored a memorial gathering that paid tribute to the white woman with honors equal to those accorded to black freedom fighters. First was one of the heroes whose name was invoked in

Woza Albert's climactic scene of resurrection, and her memorial gathering was animated by the same spirit of defiant humor found in the play. Nelson Mandela was one of many speakers of both races who came to pay their respects in a ceremony enriched with a generous measure of music, dancing, and jokes.

Ever since Mandela's release from prison two years earlier, he had become a symbol of impending freedom for everyone. His twenty-seven years as a political prisoner had established him as a symbol of resistance, but his release had catapulted him into a role that crystallized the hopes of his fellow citizens that they too would soon be released from their bondage to apartheid.

The laughter that greeted Mandela's opening remarks was a sign of his followers' confidence that freedom was just around the corner. He joked about the incompetence of the police who claimed that the tape-recorded evidence needed to investigate the Boipatong massacre of thirty-two innocent blacks had been accidentally erased.

Like the humor of Evita, *Woza Albert,* and the clown commando leading the march on Pretoria, Mandela's irony tapped into serious concerns about the devastating effects of political violence. No one lost sight of the grim problems that still remained before political justice could be achieved, but Mandela's resilient joking helped generate belief that the violence could be overcome. Before leaving he reaffirmed that faith by joining the crowd as they sang "Nkosi Sikeleli Afrika" ("God Bless Africa"), a salute to a free nation that did not yet exist.

As Mandela and his followers raised their fists proudly in the air, their song promised the creation of a home where freedom could be enjoyed by blacks and whites alike. This is the kind of *ekhaya* imagined in the subtexts of comedies like *An Audience with Evita Bezuidenhout, Woza Albert,* and the newer plays for which they cleared the way, as well as in political rallies and demonstrations against apartheid.

Giving blacks a genuine feeling of home in South Africa will require more than just giving them the right to vote. When the black writer Can Themba was informed by his friends that the idea of political equality for blacks in South Africa was threatening to

whites, he quipped, "They can keep the vote. We want the country. Then we'll give them the vote."[1]

Themba's joke captures the spirit of South African humor at
its indomitable best. The popular comedy that has emerged in the
country's theaters, streets, and meetinghouses is intended to subvert the tyranny of a system that leaves its people spiritually
homeless. In the tumultuous political landscape of South Africa,
defiant laughter is the birth cry of democracy.

Dario Fo mocks the perpetrators of political and religious corruption in Italy.
(photo by Eugenio Bersani)

5

Clowns and Popes in Italy

Every June in the mountain village of Venafro, Italian peasants and priests gather to honor the three saints martyred there by the Romans in the fourth century A.D. A candlelight procession winds through the cobblestone streets from the Church of the Annunciation to the bleached stone ruins of a medieval castle, and the townspeople stage a pageant that reenacts the lives of the saints. The sacred play is enlivened by a clown servant who brings food to the imprisoned saints but can't resist eating a little bit of their spaghetti himself.

I first heard about the comedy of the saints' spaghetti from my distant cousins who live on a farm on the outskirts of Venafro. Our family has cultivated olives and grapes there for generations. Sitting by the fire in her ramshackle farmhouse, my gray-haired cousin Celeste Cambio recalled taking her daughter Carmelina to the pageant: "When the saints ate the spaghetti, Carmelina cried out, `I want to eat some too,' and everybody in the village laughed." Celeste's stony features beam with pride when she remembers her daughter's impulse to join the saints for dinner.

Steeped in the traditions of folk religion, my relatives live in a peasant culture much like the one imagined by Italy's leading satirist, Dario Fo, in his stories of fifteenth-century miracles, faith, and exploitation. Their religious pageants humanize the Madonna and the saints the way Fo does in his plays, enabling the villagers to communicate directly with their religious icons as if they were members of the family. Fo also presents characters like Christ and the

Madonna as intimate acquaintances in stories that satirize the hypocrisy of religious institutions that exploit their names.

Like characters in Fo's comedies, my cousins in Venafro believe devoutly in Jesus but are skeptical of the church's representatives. When a golden statue of Saint Nicandro was stolen from a village church, Celeste's husband, Amato, reenacted the theft for me with gestures and winks that made it clear he believed the culprit was a local priest.

I had assumed that the feuds between peasants and landlords played out in Fo's comedies were a thing of the past, but Amato was living through a similar crisis. After a lifetime of faithfully farming the land he lived on, and giving the owner half his harvest, Amato was being evicted. He mocked his landlord with the same tone I had heard Fo use so often, lashing out with laughter at the injustice of his situation. "I'll murder whoever he sends to take my land," joked Amato with grotesque pantomimes to demonstrate the death that awaits his landlord's cronies.

Amato's comic account of his problems epitomizes Italy's complicated relationship among wealth, power, and the church described in Fo's comedies. "Only rich people like my landlord can carry the saints in our procession," sneers Amato as he explains the system by which the honor of carrying the saints' effigies is given to the citizens who make the largest contribution to the church. He acts out a mock auction in which piles of money are exchanged in a frenzied competition to carry the saint.

Outraged at church-sanctioned inequities, Amato and my other relatives have developed an intimate relationship with the saints of Venafro that bypasses the corruption of religious institutions. The satires of Dario Fo are infused with a similar spirit of direct accessibility. Their simple faith is echoed in Fo's comically humanized versions of the Gospels. He reenacts stories like the resurrection of Lazarus and the wedding of Cana in a way that makes the audience feel they could have been there themselves, making bets on Jesus' chances of raising the dead or getting drunk on the water Christ turned into wine.

The key to Fo's technique is his ability to make direct contact with his audience. His asides and improvisations create an intimate

The metal clowns in Archaos try to survive the urban wasteland. *(press photo by Morten Abrahamsen)*

A Balinese mask caricatures the Dutch soldiers who colonized the island and massacred its inhabitants at the turn of the century. *(photo by Rebecca Carman)*

A Balinese clown wears a frog mask that comically portrays the adaptability of the culture. *(photo by Ron Jenkins)*

At an election rally, a Balinese clown holding a camera wears the mask of a tourist. *(photo by Ron Jenkins)*

A Balinese clown wears the mask of Sidhya Karya that traditionally teases children at the end of the temple ceremonies. *(photo by Rebecca Carman)*

I Made Bandem, former temple clown and current member of parliament, holds the mask of a king, given to his father by a monarch for whom he performed. *(photo by Ron Jenkins)*

Puppets mock the meeting of Mikhail Gorbachev and George Bush at Malta in a production of Lithuania's Sepos Theater. *(press photo)*

An abused servant contemplates suicide in a Lithuanian adaptation of Chekhov's *Cherry Orchard. (press photo)*

A barricade of anti-Soviet satirical drawings and slogans surrounds the parliament in Vilnius during Lithuania's struggle to evict Russian troops from the city. *(photo by Stansilavas Kairys)*

Residents of Palm Springs, South Africa, joke with one another as they dance the *toyi-toyi* in a town meeting called to protest policies of the apartheid government. *(photo by Ron Jenkins)*

South African actors Percy Mtwa and Mbongeni Ngema wear clown noses to mock the ignorance of white racists in the Market Theater production of *Woza Albert. (photo courtesy Brandeis University)*

An effigy of the Pope with Dario Fo's face is suspended from the ceiling of a deconsecrated church as part of an exhibition featuring sets and drawings from Fo's satirical plays.

A page from Fo's sketchbook depicting scenes from *Johan Padan*, a comedy that includes Fo's bawdy rewriting of the Gospels.

Dario Fo with a model of Harlequin, the character he has reinvented as a *guillàre*, a comic champion of the oppressed. *(photos on this page by Ron Jenkins)*

Satomi Yojiro strikes a pose that encourages *taishu engeki* fans to make donations.

Yojiro's troupe takes a curtain call during a *taishu engeki* performance.

Yojiro quivers with mock fear after breaking the rules of social decorum.

Yojiro jokes with the audience, creating the mood of intimacy that draws audiences to his iconoclastic *taishu engeki* performances. *(photos on these two pages by Sally Schwager)*

The Bread & Puppet Domestic Resurrection Circus satirizes American culture. *(photos © 1987 Ron Simon)*

The author wearing the clown makeup he developed at the Ringling Brothers College for Clowns.

bond between the spectators and the world of miracles he describes. In the same way that Amato's pointed pantomimes were intended to initiate me into his world, Fo adopts a confessional tone and never lets his viewers forget that they are the most important characters in the play. His public feels as if he is giving them the inside story on the Gospels, a more personal perspective than they would ever hear in church.

I spent a year watching Fo create this intimacy with audiences when I traveled with his theater company in Europe, but it was only after he invited me to serve as the onstage simultaneous translator for his American tour that I directly experienced his rapport with the public. Translating his stories and improvisations phrase by phrase gave me an opportunity to eavesdrop on his inner dialogue with audiences. It also gave me a daunting responsibility. Fo performs all over the world. He knew he was funny. If people didn't laugh, there was no one to blame but me.

For other performers a translator might have set up a barrier between the audience and the stage, but Fo incorporated me into his seduction of the spectators, commenting to them about me and to me about them with jokes that enhanced our collective intimacy. When Fo sensed the rhythms of my voice falter, he would assume I was having difficulty translating a phrase and use the opportunity to stop and tease me. Since Fo doesn't speak English, I had to dutifully interpret his comic insults about me, but that was part of our game. When I shortened his sentences in translation, he pointed at me and quipped, "Americans are experts at synthesis."

Fo often speaks of a clown's relation to an audience as that of a fisherman with a trout on a line. Both have to be careful to maintain the right level of tension, pulling in and letting go with a sense of rhythm that keeps the connection taut. "If you relax too much," says Fo, "the fish gets away, but if you try too hard the hook rips the fish's mouth off."

As the intermediary translating between Fo and his American public, I often felt like Fo's fishing line, being gently pulled and teased to draw in the audience. Recreating his rhythms and the timing of his pauses was just as important as translating the meaning of his words. Fo was constantly adjusting his delivery to the

cadences of the audience's laughter, silence, and applause. "The
public is my co-conspirator," declares Fo. "My texts have been
shaped and changed by their reactions."

Onstage as Fo's translator, I too became his co-conspirator,
helping to eliminate the division between the audience and the stage.
One of the ways we did this at the Kennedy Center in Washington,
D.C., was to stop the show and introduce my grandmother from her
seat in the orchestra. Born in Venafro, she had maintained a rela-
tionship with saints and miracles that was as intimate as the one Fo
portrayed in his comedies. Making her part of the play for a moment
was part of the fun that drew the audience closer to Fo's perfor-
mance and invited them to participate the way my cousin's daughter
did when she asked to eat the saints' spaghetti. The informality
made it easier for the spectators to imagine meeting Fo for a bowl of
pasta after the show. My grandmother, of course, invited him home
for just that.

In the overgrown gardens of a rat-infested mansion, fifteen thousand people watch the dizzying antics of the controversial Italian
clown, Dario Fo. Long-limbed and rubbery-faced, he whirls
through space with ferocious energy, shouting out blasphemous
puns in an intoxicating stream of earthy dialects. Suddenly he
stops for a moment of intimate eye contact with the huge crowd.
"I used to be a peasant, a farmer," he confides, "but I will tell you
about the miracle that made me a *giullàre.*"

According to Fo *giullàre* were traveling storytellers in the
Middle Ages, and he is resurrecting their defiant comic spirit to
battle against the social injustices of modern Italy. It is the summer of 1974 and Fo's performance as a *giullàre* is part of a mass
protest against the city council of Milan. Fo has been evicted from
the dilapidated public building adjoining the gardens that his theater collective has been trying to turn into a community center.
Volunteers from the working-class neighborhood had helped the
actors renovate the crumbling art nouveau palace and now they
had turned out to support Fo's call to occupy the building.

When council members of the conservative Christian Democratic Party (known as the DC) ordered a fence erected to keep the squatters from continuing their renovations, Fo issued leaflets that read, "The rats thank the DC." Now he was continuing his satiric attack on the politicians with a one-man comic parable called *The Birth of the Giullàre*. It tells the story of a medieval peasant who defies the attempts of greedy priests and politicians to throw him off his land. With the miraculous assistance of Jesus Christ, the farmer becomes a *giullàre*, unmasking the hypocrisy of his adversaries with ridicule.

An obscene gesture directed toward the corrupt priest is greeted with particular delight by a crowd that has grown skeptical of the Vatican because of its isolation from the problems of everyday life. Fo's performance, though set in the Middle Ages, is recognizably relevant to the current conflict between the neighborhood and the municipal government in Milan. His twentieth-century audience roars its approval of the peasant's resistance to the unjust authority of church and state. Fo speaks to them as if they are the *giullàre*'s audience in a twelfth-century piazza. "Here comes the *giullàre*," he sings out. "I'm here for a satirical battle with the landlord, ready to puncture his pomposity with the sharpness of my tongue."

Fo's interpretation of the *giullàre*'s place in Italian society is fundamental to understanding his vision of laughter. He sees the *giullàre* as a comic provocateur who performed for the masses in the town piazzas. Using satirical songs and stories to challenge the authority of corrupt church officials and nobility, the *giullàre* was a primitive prototype of commedia dell'arte clowns who were later gentrified by their wealthy patrons in the European courts of the Renaissance. "The *giullàre*," says Fo, "is Harlequin before he was castrated."

Taunting their landlords with the same humor displayed by the *giullàre*, Fo and his followers took only a few months to win the right to use the city's building for their community center. They christened it "Palazzino Liberty" (Little Palace of Liberty), and audiences flocked there for years to see Fo's subversive comedies.

The occupation of Palazzino Liberty, declares Fo, "was one of the most important performances we ever produced."[1] During particularly turbulent periods in recent Italian history, Fo, his wife, and collaborator Franca Rame and their company demonstrated the power of popular comedy to undermine the repressive forces of religious and political authority. In Italy the seventies were a time of terrorism, bombings, and kidnappings, often perpetrated by right-wing extremists and blamed on left-wing advocates of social reform. Police killed members of leftist political parties while they were in custody. Activities like these were indirectly sanctioned by the dominant Christian Democrats, whose long history of corruption finally led to their fall from power in 1993.

Fo and Rame had been satirizing the unethical activities of the Christian Democratic Party decades before its downfall, using laughter to attack the bribery, scandals, and injustices that were eating away at Italian society. Traditions of comedy are built into the cultures of Bali, Lithuania, and South Africa, and people pay attention to the clowns as a natural part of social intercourse. In a fully industrialized country like Italy that has lost contact with its traditions, clowns are far more marginalized, and it is left to extraordinary individual artists like Fo and Rame to revive the once flourishing heritage of laughter.

With medieval clowns as his models, Fo became a modern-day *giullàre* who used ridicule to challenge the hypocrisy of a political party that had a monopolistic hold on Italian political power in the name of Christianity. The impassioned response he elicited from the audiences who helped free "Palazzino Liberty" from the city bureaucracy was a natural extension of the bond he established with audiences in all his performances. "I want to create a moment of solidarity," says Fo. "It comes from my desire to make the public feel that we are struggling together for something in an atmosphere of complicity."

What Fo and his audience are struggling for is freedom from exploitation. His satirical performances play out the fantasies of the disenfranchised, turning powerless figures like peasants, foot soldiers, and housewives into masters of their own fate.

Fo and Rame create stories that focus on the tension between freedom and oppression. They then skillfully orchestrate their comic climaxes so that they coincide with the victim's escape from tyranny, making laughter and liberation part of the same phenomenon.

This basic pattern of Fo's subversive comedy is evident in *The Birth of the Giullàre.* The satire depicts a peasant who endures unfair humiliations at the hands of corrupt politicians, priests, and landowners. Playing all the parts himself, Fo vividly conveys the peasant's growing frustration in each ensuing encounter with authority. The priest tries to cheat him out of his land with an oppressive litany of religious double-talk that Fo builds to an intolerable intensity before depicting the peasant's long-awaited moment of revenge: a good old-fashioned slapstick kick in the pants. The same rhythmic pattern of oppression, frustration, rage, and liberation is repeated in Fo's other plays.

The Birth of the Giullàre was part of a larger epic comedy called *Mistero Buffo* (Comic Sacred Play), a play seen by more than five million Italians in a 1977 television broadcast originating at the Palazzino Liberty. *Mistero Buffo* was a daring populist reinterpretation of the biblical legends and church history that evoked a phenomenal response from Italian mass audiences. It infused religious dogma with a carnival spirit of liberation from the passive acceptance of religious and political dogma. Theaters alone could not satisfy the public demand, so Fo and Rame performed the piece in opera houses and football stadiums as well as on television. The segment in which Fo satirized a twelfth-century pope was denounced by the Vatican as sacrilegious, and Fo was subsequently banned from the national airwaves for seven years.

Two decades after its premiere Fo's satiric portrait of the medieval Pope Boniface VIII is still among the most popular pieces in his repertoire. The piece begins with Boniface berating the choirboys helping him to prepare for a public procession. As they dress him in fine robes and jewelry, the vain pope is more concerned with improving his appearance than conveying spirituality. He polishes his mirror in time to the rhythms of a Gregorian chant and admires his image while barking orders to the choirboys between the beats of the chant. When they fail to lift his train high enough off the ground, the pope complains that they are leaving him to carry the weight of the robes like a beast of burden. "What do I look like," he growls, "a pope or an ox?"

Every time the choirboys are slow to please him, the pontiff explodes in comic fury and threatens to have them hung by their tongues from the church door. Fo took this detail from historical accounts of the punishments Boniface inflicted on clergy who dissented against his papal decrees. The nail through the tongue is a stark emblem of censorship, but Fo turns it into fantastical slapstick through sly gestures that reinforce the threat with a pantomimic rendering of the choirboy's body swaying in the breeze as it hangs from the door. "Better watch out," smiles the pope through gritted teeth, suggesting that they'll end up squirming in the wind if they don't fulfill his desires more efficiently. Fo plays Boniface's barely suppressed rage like Jackie Gleason warning his wife that he's going to send her to the moon.

The satire concludes with an anachronistically absurd meeting between the pope's procession and Jesus on his way to the Crucifixion. Boniface is so self-absorbed that he doesn't recognize the gaunt, bearded martyr even when the choirboys tell him that it's Jesus. Eventually the pope figures out who is in front of him and tries to cover up his blunder by blaming the choirboys. "Oh, *that* Jesus," he laughs. "Jesus Christ! He's got two names. Why don't you use them. I was confusing him with somebody else."

Fearing that Christ's renunciation of all worldly possessions might make him skeptical of a pope dressed in gold and silk, Boniface quickly sheds his robes and jewels and orders the choirboys to cover him with mud. Jesus doesn't fall for the charade and gives the pontiff a kick in the tailbone, which according to Fo is the origin of the coccyx's nickname "sacred bone." Even more humiliating is Christ's assertion that he never authorized Saint Peter to establish a papacy in the first place. The pope reacts to the news of his illegitimacy with hysterical silent laughter.

Fo's retelling of Boniface's story is the centerpiece of *Mistero Buffo*, the epic monologue that defined Fo's aesthetics and established his reputation as one of Europe's great clowns. He has been performing it regularly since 1969. Like the other episodes in the monologue, "Boniface" presents religious history from a peasant's point of view the way Fo imagines it would have been performed by *giullàre* in the Middle Ages.

The *giullàre* mocked the tyrannies that constrained the lives of ordinary people. Sometimes the tyrant being ridiculed was a pope, sometimes a landowner, sometimes a noble. Whatever type of exploitation was being satirized, the *giullàre* unleashed a spirit of carnival revolt that encouraged audiences to stand up for themselves. The portrait that Fo paints of the *giullàre* as revolutionary might be somewhat idealized, but even though his historical assumptions are based partially on conjecture, they have served Fo successfully as guiding principles for his art. He and Rame have reinvented the *giullàre* in modern terms.

In an effort to recreate the spirit and technique of the *giullàre*, Fo has studied medieval paintings and mystery play processions to see how religious stories were conveyed in the folk tradition. "When painters tell a story," explains Fo, "they don't show the perspective of only one person. They show diverse points of view. In the sacred presentations of the Mystery plays from the Middle Ages, people would play a variety of scenes from the life of Christ, showing the actions of Jesus, the Madonna, the devils, etc. And when the painters designed their religious frescoes, they recreated mechanically the things that they had seen in the theater of the religious festivals. The painters show the processions as they are seen from different points of view: the same scene from behind, from the front, from a distance. The techniques of cinema were not born with the invention of the camera. They have been used by painters and storytellers for hundreds of years."

In bringing to life these medieval techniques, Fo uses a performance style that is a one-man theatrical equivalent of cinematic montage. His method was particularly effective when he reenacted John Paul II's trip to Spain, where he was shot in a failed assassination attempt. Alone onstage, Fo manages to recreate the pomp and frenzy of a papal visit. He becomes the crowd of faithful worshippers shouting their greetings to John Paul. He also becomes the pope's airplane, advertising its sacred status with a huge papal skullcap on the top of its cockpit. Religious fanatics in the airport crowd think the pope himself is flying over their heads and have to be informed that "the pope doesn't have little windows."

Fo playfully elaborates on the pope's superhuman image when he depicts him emerging from the plane on top of the runway staircase. Using some of the same gestures that form his characterization of Pope Boniface, Fo describes John Paul's beautiful robes blowing behind him in the wind, his pectoral muscles bulging through his chest, and his jeweled red belt. "It's Superman!" exclaims Fo, tracing the airborne path the pope might make as he soars to the sky in the imagination of his followers, leaving behind a yellow trail of smoke that spells out, "God is with you. And he's Polish!"

Fo plays all the roles himself. Images and characters appear and dissolve with a rapidity that gives the audience the impression of watching a televised documentary of the event, with the camera angles changing every few seconds. Fo portrays the gunman waiting to shoot the pope, the Bulgarian agents with walkie-talkies directing the gunman's movements, the police asking the gunman what he is doing with bullets in his hand, and the gunman replying that they are a new kind of rosary bead. He sings a prayer as he loads each one into the pistol's chamber, and the guards leave him alone.

Shifting back into the role of narrator, Fo wonders why no one was able to stop the gunman, given that so many photographs were taken of him as he prepared for the assassination. Then Fo becomes a one-man slide show, reenacting a series of still photographs that lead up to the gunshots. Another round of theatrical jump cuts enables Fo to act out the fall of the wounded pope, the television commentator's announcement that he has been shot in the sphincter, and an indignant Vatican spokesman who refuses to acknowledge that the pope has a sphincter, insisting that the pontiff's bowels be referred to as a divine conduit.

Fo's loony tune version of religious history shocks his audiences into a spiritual double take. The persuasive absurdity of his vision forces them to stop and reexamine their culture's assump-

tions about the church and its influence in their lives. The montage-like structure of his comedy is designed to encourage this
kind of reassessment. Jumping back and forth in time, shifting
perspectives from one character to another, superimposing elements of one situation into another, Fo constructs a landscape of
zany surprises that emphasizes unexpected connections among
faith, hypocrisy, exploitation, and compassion.

Fo scrambles the relationships among history, religion, and
everyday experience so that the truths to be learned from them
can be set free from the preconceptions in which they have been
enshrined. In the segment of *Mistero Buffo* dedicated to Lazarus,
Fo demystifies the resurrection by presenting it from the viewpoint of peasants who come to the graveyard to watch the miracle. Jesus is reduced to a peripheral character as Fo singlehandedly portrays all the faces in the surging crowd, pushing their way
through the cemetery to get the best possible view of Lazarus's
tomb. In a succession of rapid-fire transformations, Fo plays
scores of characters, including the groundskeeper selling tickets
to the miracle and the worm-infested body of the corpse.

Fo offers the resurrection as it would be seen on the evening
news, complete with advertisements. Mocking the commercialization of religion, he gives us glimpses of a charlatan renting
chairs to the onlookers. "You don't want to fall down in amazement when you see him come back to life," shouts Fo in the role
of the pitchman trying to convince customers they need his
chairs to cushion the shock of the spectacle. In this earthy rendition of the sacred story, everyone tries to cash in on the miracle,
from gamblers taking odds on Jesus' chances of success to sardine
vendors selling snacks to the crowd. Fo's eyewitness coverage
ends with a metaphor for the exploitation of the faithful. A peasant kneels in awe of Christ's power while a pickpocket snatches
his purse.

Fo's comic technique makes the audience feel that they too
are part of the crowd watching the resurrection. With the supple
twisting of his body and the changing timbres of his voice, Fo
gives them the illusion that they are witnessing a mud's eye view
of the miracle. His skill at shifting characters and points of view

brings a sense of immediacy to what most people remember as an austere fable of divine power. The intimacy of Fo's version is enhanced even more by his prologue.

Speaking directly to the audience, Fo explains that the story might remind them of other acts of greed perpetrated in the name of the church. He suggests that the Vatican's collection of gold and jewels reflects a far more materialistic view of the world than was preached by Jesus, and launches into a discourse on the forgery of religious relics and the black market for bone fragments purported to be from the bodies of saints. "One dealer from Genoa sold the skeleton of Saint George to an Irish church," recounts Fo, "but it turned out to be the mummy of a crocodile from the Nile. What blasphemy! Not only was the body fake, it wasn't even Christian!"

With the irreverence of a *giullàre* Fo turns the sacred legend into a parable of earthly contradictions. His intention to offer a populist alternative to the official church version of Christ's story is made even more explicit in his retelling of the wedding at Cana. This episode from *Mistero Buffo* begins with Fo playing the part of two angels who argue over the proper way to recount the story. A demure angel wants it be told with decorum, but a drunken buffoon insists on a bawdier account of the wedding feast, with particular emphasis on Jesus' miracle of turning water into wine. The drunk prevails by plucking out the angel's wings as if they were chicken feathers.

With his nemesis out of the way, the boozing angel is free to describe the nuptial celebration as a bacchanalian orgy of the senses. Having been there himself, the reveler describes the wine in vivid comic detail, inviting the audience to feel, taste, and smell the beverage with him as he relives the pleasures of Jesus' miracle. At one point he depicts himself bathing in the wine, mimes the passage of the delicious red liquid through his veins, and expresses his pleasure in a gigantic burp that sends the wine's aroma across the countryside to a man on horseback who smells it and cries out in ecstasy, "*Jesu, sei divino*" (Jesus, you are divine/maker of wine). The exclamation is a pun that equates Christ's divinity with his expertise as a wine maker. The scene gives Bible stories an immediacy that makes them seem more like anecdotes about friends and neighbors.

Franca Rame also makes a significant contribution to *Mistero Buffo*'s demystification of the Gospels. In her portrayal of Christ's mother Italians saw the sacrosanct image of the Madonna interpreted as an ordinary mother who is exhorted by the angel Gabriel into bearing a child and suffering through his crucifixion. Rame's Mary is no saint. She tries to bribe the soldiers guarding the cross and blasphemes the angel Gabriel for deceiving her. The passion in Rame's grief-stricken performance leaves no doubt that *Mistero Buffo* is a play conceived with reverence for Christ's story. At the core of its buffoonery, satire, and irony is a respect for the misery of a mother and her persecuted son. It reinterprets the Gospels as a challenge to the hardships of an unjust world.

Though most of Rame's characters are comic, she often plays tragic roles like Mary to emphasize that her comedy is rooted in the tragic aspect of women's role in Italian culture. Italian women, particularly in the seventies, when Rame's one-woman plays were first staged, battled against a much more traditional set of sexual stereotypes than those that limited the freedom of women in the United States. Many housewives in rural Italy wrote to Rame after watching her televised scenarios to say they felt she was telling their story. For some, Rame's absurd and tragic tales of sexual abuse were only slight exaggerations of the confined lives the women experienced every day.

Rame and Fo conducted seminars, workshops, and public discussions at the Palazzino Liberty that eventually led them to write a collection of monologues about women's issues. Based on true stories of women who had been abused by men, the pieces were performed by Rame under the name *Tutta Casa, Letto & Chiesa*. The title, which could be translated as "It's All About Home, Bed, and Church," reflected the male stereotype of a woman's place in society that emerged from the women's stories Fo and Rame had collected.

With these sharply satiric monologues Rame took the spark of rebellion that Mary had shouted against the angel Gabriel in

Mistero Buffo and developed it into a devastating comic critique of
a male-dominated culture where abortion was banned by the
state and birth control was banned by the church. As the title of
the play suggests, many of the attitudes that lead to the subjuga-
tion of women in Italy can be traced to the church, particularly
the prejudices against abortion and divorce, which trapped thousands of women in abusive marriages. But Rame goes beyond
religion to wrestle with fundamental issues of sexual inequality.

She begins her piece with a prologue that cuts to the core of
male prejudices by making fun of the phallus. She announces that
the phallus will be a central character in each of her monologues.
"It's like a little tail," she jokes. "The devil has it in the back. Men
have it in front." Conceding that the phallus will not be seen on
stage with her in the flesh, Rame claims that it is an invisible
presence that "is always here among us . . . huge, enormous,
looming over us. It crushes us!"

To free society from the stifling influence of the phallus,
Rame performs a series of comic monologues that show women
breaking out of their traditional subservience to men. Her heroines are working mothers and housewives whose stories were
drawn from the hundreds of conversations Rame had with ordinary women throughout Italy. One of the characters gets so fed
up with nursing her bed-bound, lecherous relative, fielding
obscene phone calls, and being locked in her apartment by a jealous husband that she ends up taking on the men in her life with a
shotgun.

In another monologue a mother tells her daughter an ironic
bedtime story about a little girl who is enslaved in a sterile, abusive marriage with an engineer until she is rescued by a magic
rag doll that comes to life, tells her dirty jokes, and makes the
husband pregnant by inserting herself in his rectum. The husband is unable to bear the pain of childbirth; his belly gets bigger
and bigger until he explodes, leaving only the laughing dolly in
his place. "Now you're free," she tells the girl. "You're in charge of
your body, your choices, your self." As happens so often in the
work of Fo and Rame, the absurd comic climax coincides with a
liberation from social tyranny.

At the end of *Tutta Casa, Letto & Chiesa* Rame takes what she refers to as a *"salto mortale"* (fatal leap). Circus acrobats use the term to describe their most dangerous stunts. Rame uses it to describe the leap from comedy to tragedy. Throughout her show the vignettes become increasingly serious in tone, using fewer and fewer props until she is left alone on a bare stage with nothing more than a chair. She concludes with either a one-woman version of *Medea* or a story about rape. In either case the emotional weight of her performance is devastating.

In *Lo Stupro* Rame sits virtually motionless in a chair as she describes in a detached, first-person narrative the experience of being raped. It is both a metaphor for the exploitation of women and a brutally realistic comment on the crime itself. Hardly ever raising her voice, she evokes the violation with such wrenching intensity that spectators have literally fainted during the performance.

Rame's interpretation of *Medea* is equally challenging. Her goal is to make the audience feel sympathy for a character who murders her children and has been vilified since the time of the Greeks as a vengeful embodiment of female evil. Rejecting the text of Euripides, Rame and Fo wrote a new play based on the Medea legend as it is told in southern Italy. "The writers who created the myth of Medea were men," says Rame one evening after rehearsals for another play. "Even the actor who played her part in Greece was a man. My version tells the story from Medea's point of view as a woman." Rame reasons that Medea had no choice but to murder her children. Her husband, Jason, was preparing to marry a younger woman, which would have resulted in Medea's enslavement in the palace as a cast-off second wife. "Whenever Medea tried to assert herself, everyone told her that she must remain silent for the good of her children," says Rame. "In Medea's culture, children were the yoke that society put around women's necks to make it easier to oppress them." Rame believes this is still a problem in modern Mediterranean cultures like Italy, where the church discourages women from divorcing husbands for having mistresses, forcing them to accept the role of second-class wife for the sake of their children.

These and other painful Italian truths are at the core of Fo and Rame's comedies. Even their funniest plays are inspired by tragic circumstances. Throughout the politically repressive 1970s they played the roles of *giullàre*, confronting government atrocities with satirical comedy intended to make audiences challenge the legitimacy of the Christian Democratic Party. One of their most provocative antigovernment plays was based on the 1970 death of an Italian railway worker named Giuseppe Pinelli. Pinelli died in police custody while being interrogated about a terrorist bombing that was later proved to have been committed by right-wing extremists. Police had tried to link the 1969 bombing, which killed seventeen people and wounded one hundred, to left-wing activists like Pinelli, and claimed he had jumped out a window during questioning. The mysterious circumstances of Pinelli's death and the ensuing political scandal inspired Fo to write *Accidental Death of an Anarchist*, a play that he described as "a grotesque farce about a tragic farce."[2]

Based on trial transcripts, court documents, and newspaper reports, Fo's play struck a nerve in a society that had been plagued for years by terrorism, kidnappings, police brutality, and political corruption. During its four-year run from 1970 to 1974, *Accidental Death of an Anarchist* was seen by over a million people in theaters, town halls, and football stadiums. This period coincided with a government investigation of the bombing, Pinelli's death, and related scandals that lasted almost as long as the run of the play. Fo changed the script regularly to include new information as it was released, and audience discussions were held after the shows.

The absurd situations in Fo's play became a springboard for public discussion of the equally absurd inconsistencies in the results of the government investigation. Franco Quadri, the theater critic for one of Italy's major weekly newsmagazines, wrote that Fo's farce "dismantles and continually reassembles the false and conflicting versions of the outrageous judicial case presented by the police . . . the wild inventiveness of the writing blends harmoniously with the aims of counter-information and succeeds in having a concrete effect on consolidating public opinion."[3]

The central character in *Accidental Death of an Anarchist* is a madman that Fo describes as a "histriomaniac." The madman is yet another incarnation of Fo's *giullàre*, challenging authority with outrageous wit as he changes roles with dizzying rapidity. Played by Fo, the histriomaniac infiltrates a police station by posing in turn as a government magistrate, a forensic investigator, and a bishop. This gives him access to information the police are trying to cover up as well as an opportunity to wreak havoc on their already confused inquiry into a case that mirrors the circumstances of Pinelli's.

Terrifying the authorities into believing that their ruse has been discovered, the histriomaniac convinces two police inspectors to throw themselves out of a window to prove their innocence. He also persuades his right-wing antagonists to join him in a hilarious sing-a-long of Communist solidarity tunes. By the end of the play the madman has handcuffed the police, set off a time bomb, and announced that he is going to the mass media with a transcript that will reveal everything.

The lunacy of the madman's antics are motivated by the same drive that led Fo to write the play. "I was pre-occupied with the issue of justice," explains Fo. "I realized that a criminal act had been conducted by the state, but people were calmly accepting the results of the official investigation. When I injected absurdity into the situation, the lies became apparent. The maniac plays the role of the judge, taking the logic of the authorities to its absurd extremes, and he discovers that there are incongruities. For instance, if the police testimony were true, the victim would have had to have three feet. The clown maniac uses this incongruity to establish the truth of the situation. Absurdity becomes a form of logical reasoning based on paradox."

In Fo's formula for comedy, laughter liberates the public from ignorance and points the way toward truth. In the same way that church-inspired satires like *Mistero Buffo* tried to provoke a reassessment of religious traditions, plays about current events like *Accidental Death of an Anarchist* tickle audiences into rethinking their opinions of the state. Fo describes the process in terms of a scientific experiment: "My plays are provocations, like catalysts in a chemical solution. When you want to know what elements a particular liquid is composed of, you put in another liquid, and perhaps the mixture turns blue, or it boils, or it changes, forming precipitates. I do the same thing as a clown. I just put some drops of absurdity into the calm and tranquil liquid which is society, and the reactions reveal things that were hidden before the absurdity brought them out into the open."

Although many examples of violence and police brutality in Italy were as outrageous as those found in more turbulent cultures like South Africa and Lithuania, the majority of Italians were content with the status quo. This situation resulted in the tranquil society that Fo described, and his comedy was designed to stir things up in a way that revealed the agitation beneath the surface. This comic style differs from that found in cultures on the brink of revolution, where laughter was used to incite opposition to regimes whose repressiveness was clear to everyone from the start. Performing in a culture where not everyone wanted change, Fo and Rame were also more marginalized than the political clowns in Bali, Lithuania, and South Africa, whose subversive comic messages were recognized by the majority of their audiences as urgent, relevant, and necessary.

Although it was based on a specific event in contemporary Italian politics, *Accidental Death of an Anarchist* turned out to be one of Fo's most frequently produced plays in translation abroad. It was staged in over twenty different nations, including productions in London's West End and on Broadway in New York. The success of Fo's plays in translation abroad coincided with a growing international demand for Fo and Rame to tour their work in person. In the mid-1980s Fo and Rame performed *Mistero Buffo* and *Tutta Casa* to standing-room audiences and critical praise throughout Europe. Initially they were denied visas to enter the United States on the basis of their political views, but eventually the State Department relented and the couple played to enthusiastic audiences in Washington, D.C., Cambridge, New Haven, and New York City. Their satire of social and political tyranny proved to have a universal appeal that led them to expand their vision of the *giullàre*. Italy was not the only industrial culture to face the problems of bribery, corruption, and police brutality. Fo and Rame adapted their performances to include local references to the countries they visited and encouraged translators and adapters of their texts to do the same.

One of the plays that expressed the widening international-ized scope of Fo and Rame's comedy was their 1984 production of *Elizabetta: Almost by Chance A Woman*. Like most of Fo's plays, it began as a response to a specific set of cultural circumstances in Italy, in this case a flurry of politically motivated kidnappings. But unlike *Accidental Death of an Anarchist*, which played with the headlines in a mock documentary style, *Elizabetta* achieved its satiric impact by relocating the action to another time and coun-try, the sixteenth-century English court of Queen Elizabeth. Fo used the intrigue of Elizabeth's court, the political implications of Shakespeare's plays, and the crumbling of the British Empire to give his kidnapping story a complex comic resonance that cros-sed the barriers of language, time, and geography.

During rehearsals for its first foreign production in 1985, Ronald Reagan began responding to the Beirut hostage crisis with lines that seemed to have been lifted directly from Fo's script. "We cannot lower ourselves to making deals with crimi-nals," says Elizabeth in a scene where Fo makes it clear that the queen is hypocritically making secret arrangements with the kid-nappers and taking advice from her double-crossing, power-hun-gry advisers. By the time the play had its American premiere in 1987, virtually the same scenario was unfolding at the Iran/ Contra hearings. Fo wrote a new prologue to the play, noting the ironic parallels, but did not have to adapt the main body of his text. His farce, inspired by the devious dealings of Italian politi-cians and embellished by sixteenth-century intrigue, seemed as if it had been written with Oliver North in mind all along.

At its most basic level *Elizabetta* is a multilevel rumination on the subversion of power, and as always in Fo's work, much of the subversion is orchestrated by a *giullàre*-like character who ridicules the figures of authority. In this play the *giullàre* is a maidservant named Donazza, played by Fo in drag. Donazza uses her skills as a beautician to mock Queen Elizabeth, who is played by Rame as a lovesick tyrant trying to recapture her lost youth and beauty as her empire disintegrates around her. Promising to thin the Queen's thighs with leeches and puff up her breasts with bee stings, Fo's character humiliates the monarch mercilessly.

The clown's rebellious relationship to authority is expressed most eloquently in Fo's one-man reenactment of *Hamlet*. Attempting to convince Elizabeth that Shakespeare's play is actually a veiled satire of her regime, Donazza acts out the tragedy in the queen's bedroom, playing all the parts herself. In a wacky two-minute condensation of the play Fo argues that the laconic prince of Denmark is a transsexual portrait of Elizabeth's indecisiveness. The queen is so insulted by this interpretation of the play that she tries to suppress it by putting her hand over Donazza's mouth. Refusing to be silenced, Fo continues to tell the story of the play with his hands. When Elizabeth grabs his right hand, he continues gesturing with his left hand behind his back. When she manages to tie up both arms, Fo tries to pantomime the conclusion of the tragedy by wiggling his feet. The slapstick encounter makes it clear that the queen's clumsy attempts at censorship are no match for the irrepressible satiric impulses of the clown. The issue was a personal one for Fo, who had been censored by Italian television on numerous occasions and denied permission to perform in America in 1980 on the basis of his political views, but cases like the attempted silencing of Salman Rushdie have made censorship a global issue.

The spirit of wry antagonism between Queen Elizabeth and the clown mirrored Fo's relationship with the contemporary targets of the play. The prologue to the American version of *Elizabetta* includes a letter from the playwright to Ronald Reagan that disingenuously denies the performance's satiric intent. Fo hails the president as a fellow actor and thanks him for the free publicity the State Department gave to Fo's past American appearances by refusing to grant him a visa.

"After all the help you have given me," reads the letter, "I don't want you ever to think that I would be ungrateful enough to satirize you in any of my plays. Just because my play is about an aging leader whose advisors don't tell her what they're doing behind her back, a leader who tends to get confused and forgetful about certain details, don't think for a minute that it has anything at all to do with you. Also be assured that the minor urinary problems Elizabeth suffers in the play have nothing to do with your well publicized prostate operations and that her obsessive concern with her image and cosmetic beauty treatments has no relation whatsoever to the dyeing of your hair, your face-lifting, or the polyps that disappeared mysteriously from your nose."

While *Elizabetta* broadens the scope of Fo's subversive humor by transposing it to Elizabethan England, his newest monologue is the most complex realization of his vision of the *giullàre* as an agent of comic liberation. *Johan Padan* is the story of an Italian vagabond who escapes persecution from the fifteenth-century Inquisition by stowing away on one of Columbus's expeditions to America. Padan is a *giullàre*-like hero who not only defies the tyranny of the church in Europe but continues to mock Christianity in America as the source of a New World of oppression and injustice. He teaches the Native Americans to resist the invading European armies by exposing the hypocrisy of the Christian faith they use as justification for an invasion that is in fact motivated purely by greed. Padan's skills as a storyteller and confidence man lead to his acceptance by the Native Americans as a shaman. By performing a series of comic miracles, the lowly vagabond ends up being revered as the savior of his adopted tribe.

Like all his plays, *Johan Padan* begins with a prologue in which Fo connects the story's themes to current events. He takes devilish delight in linking his fifteenth-century fable to the latest scandal's of Italy's Christian Democratic Party. In an ironic reference to the rise of neo-Nazism in Germany, Fo reminds the audience that Spain's Queen Isabella expelled the Jews from her country in 1492 and confiscated their wealth, making her "the first Nazi in history." Fo enjoys recounting the reactions of Spanish audiences who heard him make that disparaging remark about their queen during the campaign to have Isabella declared a saint by the Roman Catholic Church. The prologue sets up Fo as the con-man *giullàre* telling a story about a con-man *giullàre*, so that

by the time he launches into the tale of Johan Padan his audience
is swept up in a swirl of laughter that opens the boundaries
between history, current events, and poetic imagination.

Fo performs *Johan Padan* as an epic monologue, playing all
the parts of the Native Americans, the conquistadors, the horses,
the turkeys, and the vagabond—by himself on the stage. The
most striking element of the epic is its depiction of laughter's
concrete impact on human survival. More directly than in any of
his other works, Fo is painting a portrait of the *giullàre* as a secular miracle worker whose comic impulses come from the heart
and cut to the bone. The minor miracles Padan performs are all
linked with laughter. When a drought threatens the village with
starvation, Padan performs a comic dance that makes the son of
the rain god laugh. His father, the rain god, is so moved to see his
son laughing that he cries with joy and his flood of tears pours
down from heaven as rain. Later Padan entertains sick members
of the tribe, who respond to his comedy as if it were a benediction
and begin dancing in a carnival celebration of the heroic clown
who has saved their lives.

As the story progresses it becomes clear that Johan Padan is
Fo's vision of the *giullàre* as pagan saint. Condemned by the tyrannical church authorities of the Inquisition, Padan has escaped from
the hypocrisies of European civilization to a new realm where a
blasphemer can be elevated to the status of saint by the simple
faith of the people whose lives he has touched. In his earlier stories Fo simply mocked the doctrines of the church. In *Johan Padan*
he accomplishes a total subversion of the religion in which the
clown has become a secular pope who frees his followers from all
constraining aspects of church dogma at the same time that he liberates them from the tyranny of politics based on greed.

Johan Padan elaborates the Gospels with a steamy love
affair between Christ and Mary Magdalene. His tribe of listeners
celebrate the resurrection with lewd dances and lovemaking of
their own that makes a mockery of Christian decorum. Padan's
unorthodox preaching is all part of his wacky plan to convert the
Native Americans to Christianity and save them from being
enslaved by the Europeans.

In an iconoclastic satire that attacks both religious and political corruption, Fo turns Johan Padan into a subversive portrait of Christ himself as a confidence man and clown. Fo believes that this version of Jesus is the one supported by the *giullàre* who challenged the conservative authorities of the church in the Middle Ages. "In my research of medieval texts," says Fo, "I came across this figure of Christ, transformed by the people into a kind of hero against the authorities and church hierarchies . . . a different, more humane Christ, always on the side of the underdogs. He possesses a pagan, almost Dionysiac joy for love, festivity, beauty, and worldly things. At the same time he is full of hatred and violence towards hypocritical priests, the aristocracy who tried to lord it over the poor, and the arrogance of the church and its temporal power. This probably isn't the Christ of history, but it is the Christ produced by the great cultural tradition of the people."[4]

Fo's description of the populist Christ could serve as a model for Johan Padan. Padan declares himself an enemy of the Inquisition and takes sides with the underdog Native Americans in their battle against the conquistadors, who claim to be seizing the New World in the name of the church. When the Spanish soldiers capture Padan and prepare to hang him, he is saved by the Native Americans, who are willing to risk their lives on his behalf. Their chief tells the Spanish general that Padan has brought them a spirit of joy, laughter, and hope as opposed to the onslaught of death, slavery, and despair offered by the Christian soldiers. "You arrived on horses with armor and guns," says the chief to the Spaniards. "He arrived naked on the back of a pig."

The contrast between the tyranny of the Christian soldiers and the liberating laughter of Johan Padan is clearly established. And in the end of Fo's carnival clash between the forces of repression and freedom, it is Padan and the Native Americans who emerge victorious. Padan is set free when they use the trickery he taught them to sabotage the Spanish forces. The Native Americans render the Spanish canons useless by urinating on their gunpowder supply in the night. They put hallucinogenic intoxicants up the noses of the Spaniard's horses. And they frighten the Europeans with displays of fireworks that Padan taught them to set off during their village feasts. In another of Fo's comic miracles of reversal, the seemingly omnipotent Spaniards are forced to sail home in defeat, vanquished by the resilient ingenuity of ordinary people who refuse to accept the stifling of their humanity.

The play closes with an account of the brief but idyllic period during which the Native Americans of the Florida peninsula were able to resist the continuing attacks of European colonialists. Padan lives out his old age feasting, singing, dancing, and raising a family in the loving embrace of his new village home. He infused his adopted tribe with a comic spirit that gave power to the powerless and led to the flourishing of simple human pleasures.

As Padan lies on a hammock at the end of his life, he sings a religious folk song he learned as a child in Italy. It expresses a peasant's joy at the news of Christ's resurrection. As the lights fade into blackness Fo's sonorous voice sends the song sailing into the rafters of the theater as his arms trace a slow, circular path toward heaven. In spite of its blasphemies *Johan Padan* ends with a sacred chant that links the play to its roots in the simple faith of the medieval peasantry that laughed at the first *giullàre*.

Fo's vision of himself as a contemporary *giullàre* is played out to its fullest in *Johan Padan*. During the prologue and performance he pauses occasionally to hold up a large book of paintings and sketches. Fo explains that he has culled Padan's story from a collage of historic documents and diaries of the fifteenth century, and that his book of drawings represents his responses to those sources as the story began to take shape in his mind. Fo is a revisionist storyteller at heart. Flipping through the pages that play havoc with color, composition, and point of view, he is clearly prepared to turn history upside down.

In and out of the theater, Dario Fo uses laughter to subvert the official historical record, empower the powerless, and ridicule the sacred cows of authority. His slapstick victories are minor miracles, far more immediate than the distant miracles discussed by priests in church. They are intended by Fo to inspire his audiences with the will to produce small miracles of their own.

During a student strike at the University of Bologna Fo offered his support by telling students the story of a comic miracle that occurred during a fourteenth-century battle between the soldiers of the pope and the people of Bologna. Based on historical facts filtered through Fo's fertile imagination, the monologue tells how the papal army seized the city's castle and barricaded themselves inside the fortress gates with all the food and wine from the municipal storehouses. Left with nothing to eat and no weapons with which to attack the impenetrable castle, the population of Bologna loaded catapults with animal manure and showered their enemies with shit.

The unconventional assault lasted for weeks, and when the supply of dung ran low, loyal citizens lined up to contribute their own feces for the cause. Farmers from around the countryside came to cheer the humiliation of the pope's men. The battle became such a popular tourist attraction that signs had to be posted, "Entry restricted to those carrying shit." Worn down by the barrage of filth that rained on them daily, the pope's men eventually waved their manure-stained white flags of surrender.

Fo's fable glorifies the power of ridicule as a weapon against authority. As in all of his work, the comedy is fueled by the turbulent musicality of his delivery. "I try to make the rhythms of the language allude to the rhythms of the violence," says Fo. The dialect Fo uses echoes the thrusts of attacking soldiers and the sudden release of springed catapults. The unrelenting cadence throbs with the irreversible momentum of an ambush that can't be stopped. "You don't have to understand any of the words," says Fo, "but you sense that it is about a war."

On one level all of Fo's stories are about war. Liberation is the through line of his comedies. They chronicle the battle against the tyrannies of everyday life in a Catholic consumer democracy. Like the *giullàre* of old, he uses ridicule to inspire the powerless to challenge authority. His comedy is charged with the immediacy of a newspaper headline, the rhythmic drive of a jazz improvisation, and the epic scope of a historical novel. Carrying on a tradition that assaulted the feudal injustices of the Middle Ages, Fo and Rame use laughter to combat the subtler tyrannies that plague the world today: bribery scandals, sanctions against abortion and divorce, homelessness and hunger in the face of arrogance and wealth. Products of a Catholic culture dominated by the power of the Vatican and the well-documented corruption of the recently discredited Christian Democratic Party, the couple has created a defiant theology of clowning in which Christ is a con man and the *giullàre* is a patron saint of laughter.

Female impersonator Satomi Yojiro welcomes his audience into the iconoclastic world of taishu engeki. (photo by Sally Schwager)

6

Mocking Conformity in Japan

My initiation into the mysteries of Japanese laughter came at an ancient Buddhist temple in Nara when I got stuck inside a hole in a sacred wooden pillar. It was supposed to bring luck to anyone who crawled through it, but I got wedged in with my shoulders on one side and my hips on the other. A crowd gathered to watch the foreigner try to wriggle out, but my squirming got me nowhere. Looking around in panic at the stern-faced Japanese, I imagined their dismay at the prospect of an American infidel installed as a permanent feature of the temple architecture. I prayed to the giant Buddha behind us for a graceful exit.

To my surprise I felt tiny hands pushing at the soles of my size thirteen sneakers. Children were trying to help me through. Old women and businessmen joined in the effort by pulling on my arms. After a few well-placed shoves, I plopped unceremoniously onto the floor of the temple courtyard. The crowd greeted my release with laughter and applause. In the course of my absurd dilemma a miniature community had come into being and forgiven me for disrupting the temple's decorum. I had entered the hole as an outsider, but by the time they pulled me through to the other side, I had been accepted into their clan, at least temporarily.

My comic plight and rescue in Nara mirrored a Japanese rite of passage I witnessed regularly in Tokyo's popular theater performances, known as taishu engeki. *Strangers pass through the threshold into an inviting world of laughing camaraderie where breaking the code of etiquette is part of the fun. Japanese live under a highly constraining set of cultural rules that dictate behavior in all social settings.* Taishu engeki *is one of the few places where these rules are openly broken.*

As a foreigner accustomed to the reserved demeanor of the Japanese, it was shocking to see spectators walk up to the stage, interrupt the play, and present their favorite actor with a six-pack of beer. Even more astonishing was the reaction of the actor, who would stop the show, converse with his fan, and step back into the story without missing a beat. The rest of the audience would laugh and applaud, caught up in the contagious pleasure of defying etiquette. Strangers shared meals of fried octopus and seaweed crackers they brought in plastic bags. People called to one another using diminutive rather than honorific names. (I was known as "Mr. Beard.") Onstage and off, emotions were expressed brazenly, as if the release of long-stifled impulses was making everyone giddy with glee.

Even before I understood the details of what went on in the dances, sketches, and plays, I was attracted to the shabby ambiance of taishu engeki. *The theaters are located in rundown Tokyo neighborhoods where people congregate beneath paper lanterns for festivals, shopping, praying, gambling, and other public amusements. A slightly disreputable atmosphere is combined with the spirit of a far-flung family reunion. There is an ongoing dialogue between the performers and their public. Regular customers come to sit in the same seats every day, commenting on the skill of the leading performers, known as "zacho," between mouthfuls of sushi and beer.*

I didn't know any taishu engeki *fans when I first began going to the performances, but once they noticed I was becoming a regular customer, they began saving seats for me, buying me snacks, and sharing rumors about the* zacho's *latest offstage activities. Wrinkled old women and weather-beaten drunks often waved to me from the far side of the theater when I walked in. As an awkward foreigner I appreciated these small gestures of greeting, and after a few months I started to see the plays through these fans' eyes.*

One of the moments of the show I most looked forward to was the goaisatsu *(welcoming), during which the* zacho *took a few minutes to speak directly to the crowd. Formal* goaisatsu *are a part of*

most social and business encounters in Japan, but zacho Satomi
Yojiro's goaisatsu was so casual that people felt comfortable shouting out questions and calling him by his nickname, "Yo-chan!" The
zacho sat on the edge of the stage and responded to everyone with an
amiability that made us all feel like guests at a private party. After
a while he even began talking to me.

Like all Satomi's fans I was flattered to be included in his dialogue, but my limited Japanese language skills were not suitable for
extended conversation. Once when he asked what I thought of the
show, I mustered up the courage to shout "Terrific," but instead of
saying subarashi I said something closer to suribachi, which means
"mortar and pestle." The zacho smiled diplomatically at my absurd
response and went on to the next question. In spite of the regularity
with which I embarrassed myself, Satomi's actors and fans slowly
accepted me as an honorary member of their club.

At the taishu engeki theater in the Jujo neighborhood of Tokyo
the intimate atmosphere of our gatherings was enhanced by the
absence of chairs. We all sat together in stocking feet on the tatami
mat floor. On crowded evenings six of us were squeezed onto a single mat. "Move up. Push together. Make room for more people,"
grunted Yo-chan during the goaisatsu, jokingly imitating the mili-
taristic bark of the usher who managed to pack in a few extra customers no matter how limited the space.

The audience laughed at the zacho's sympathy for their crowded conditions. "We're exhausted from waiting here since ten in the
morning to get a front row seat," complained a woman inches away
from the stage. "Oh, that's why you were sleeping during the play,"
quipped Yo-chan, pretending to be offended. "No," she says. "We're
still tired from being out late last night at the karaoke bar." "I did-
n't sleep much either," says the zacho, continuing the banter as if
they were old friends catching up on each other's weekend activities.
"I was up early playing golf." "We'd love to see you play golf,"
chimes in a voice from across the room. "Why didn't you invite us?"
A look of childlike innocence washes over Yo-chan's face. "You mean
I didn't invite you? How could I have forgotten?"

The audience giggled at the zacho's mock apology, but the
exchange touched on a crucial element of Yo-chan's appeal. In the

impersonal world of urban Japan, taishu engeki *provides a refuge of intimacy. The audience develops a personal relationship with the actors, the stories, and the people around them. The informality makes everyone feel like an insider. Strangers feel welcome and really do hope that Yo-chan might invite them out someday, if not to a golf course, then maybe to a sushi bar or restaurant. Occasionally the* zacho *does just that, sometimes in small groups, sometimes in large, organized banquets.*

The give-and-take between the stage and the audience enables spectators to identify with the actors as part of their family. One elderly woman who recently moved to Tokyo told me that the performers' familiar faces provide her with a reassuring sense of security in a strange city. "When I go to other places in Tokyo I feel afraid, but here I feel safe. If something happened to me, I could go in the dressing room and the actors would help me."

For this woman and the hundreds of fans that pack into the theater each night, taishu engeki is a village, a comforting oasis of human warmth in a city known for its emotional reserve. For a few hours the theater is transformed into a miniature neighborhood where the social taboos of modern Tokyo give way to the intimacy of common tears and laughter.

In a rundown theater near Tokyo's temple to the goddess of mercy, paper snow is falling on the rickety facade of an old Japanese teahouse. It falls on actors in cheap, gaudy costumes as they play out the melodramatic story of an outlaw's anguish over the death of his mother. The snow falls in such abundance that the audience in the front row is covered with white paper flakes. The toothless old women, gawky young girls, and half-drunk men are so absorbed in the action on the stage that they don't bother to brush the snow out of their hair or wipe the tears from their faces.

Impassioned voices from the crowd shout encouragement to the actor playing the enraged son as he raises a samurai sword to avenge his mother. But before the hero can act on his impulse, he is tethered by ropes thrown at him from all directions. Ensnared in a primitive harness that stymies his movements, the son takes the only choice open to him and plunges the sword into his own belly. The paper snow falls even more thickly, its fury tied to the fevered flurry of feelings on the stage. The spectators get whiter and wetter as the dying hero weeps over his mother's corpse. The bond between the actor's storm of emotion and the audience's stream of tears is made visible by the paper snow that blankets both the players and the crowd.

The snow-blurred image of the hero rendered helpless by ropes pulling at him from all sides is a ghostly embodiment of an ageless Japanese dilemma. Like the actor before them, each member of the audience is caught in a metaphoric web of conflicting emotions and obligations. The problem is so deeply embedded in the culture that the Japanese have a label for it: the clash of "*giri*" and "*ninjo*." These terms can be roughly translated as "duty" and "human feeling," but taken together they represent a complex concept rooted in the Confucian belief that the feelings of the individual should be subjugated to the needs of society.

Social expectations are part of every culture, but the amount of self-sacrifice demanded of the Japanese is extraordinary by any standard. An individual is expected to deny personal emotions for the common good in accordance with a complicated hierarchy of loyalties to family, friends, employers, and the government. Japan's economic miracle of the eighties, for example, owed much to its workers' willingness to subordinate their individual feelings to the obligations imposed on them by their companies.

In the play about the anguished outlaw a tyrannical pressure to conform is part of every plot twist, and the protagonist is straitjacketed by cultural restraints that are second nature to the Japanese. He is forced to suppress his natural response to the fate of his mother because her suffering was caused by his father. The Confucian rules of filial obedience place a son's duty to his father above any pity he might feel for his mother, particularly because a wife is obligated to submit to any abuse her husband chooses to inflict on her.

Comic elements of the melodrama begin to emerge with the crowd's reactions to the protagonists. Older women in the audience reveal where their sympathies lie by pointing accusingly at the husband and shouting angrily, "Don't be mean to her." The villain acknowledges the women's sentiments by interrupting the beating of his wife to assure her that she won't be rescued by any of her friends. He accentuates his threat with an evil glare in the direction of the audience. They respond to his challenge with jeers and laughter.

By the time the curtain closes the outlaw hero has chosen death as the only acceptable escape from the irreconcilable demands of the situation, but in Japan not even suicide can free him from the pressure of social expectations. His suicide must be performed according to the rules of *seppuku*, which have been followed by samurai warriors since the seventeenth century. Thrusting the blade sideways into his gut, he falls on his knees to make a cleansing speech of apology to those who have suffered because of his unworthiness (in this case, his dead mother). This codified behavior obligates the police to release him from the ropes and listen respectfully to his dying words. They too must abide by the rules of *giri* and *ninjo*.

The spectators' tears are tears of recognition. Their lives are not lived on the heightened level of the paper snow landscape, but they have all experienced the social pressures that drive him to despair. Like thousands of samurai films, television shows, and Kabuki dramas, the performance confirms the public's concept of traditional values and soothes them into weeping acceptance of the consequences. What is remarkable is that after having their hearts wrenched by this mournful tragedy, they leave the theater laughing. After being confronted by a vision of their society's crushing social pressures, they go home with a sense of liberated delight.

The public's pleasure is derived from the extraordinary context in which the paper snow tragedy is performed. Immediately after the drama, the actor playing the hero emerges from behind the curtain (still in costume, but freed from the ropes) to welcome the audience and engage them in informal comic banter. "Ice cream, a hundred fifty yen," he sings out in a shaky nasal voice that jokingly imitates the sales call of the ancient woman shuffling through the aisles with a sack of ice cream sandwiches on her back. He is soon back again in a new costume, doing a warrior dance that concludes with a crowd-pleasing display of samurai swordsmanship. A few minutes later he reappears as a woman, draped in the exquisitely gaudy kimono of a nineteenth-century geisha.

Each new incarnation is greeted with cheers of "Yo-chan" from the audience, who call him by the diminutive form of his first name. He reciprocates by stepping off the stage to shake their hands as he sings steamy love songs in a black tuxedo. Even during the tragic play, he had occasionally stepped out of character to address them directly in erotic comic asides and jokes that poke fun at his pain. The same irreverence animates his postsuicide resurrection as a samurai, geisha, ice cream vendor, and pop star.

Yo-chan's virtuosic display of self-transformation mirrors his country's ongoing self-renewal. Saddled with the burden of defeat in World War II, Japan has reinvented itself by merging traditional values with contemporary innovations. The cultural tension generated by this hybrid fusion of conflicting values is evident in the schizophrenic style in which Yo-chan reinvents himself throughout the course of the evening. He escapes the tragic consequences of humiliation and crushing obligations by slipping out of the bonds of tradition. In an invigorating clash of the old and the new, rap music and electronic gadgets appear regularly in his plays about seventeenth-century samurai, geisha, highwaymen, and monks. In Japan the love of ancient customs coexists with the hunger for the latest trends. All the outrageous paradoxes of the nation's character come to life in the wildly eclectic blend of underworld intrigue, samurai swordplay, domestic heartbreak, and erotic transvestism known as *taishu engeki*.

Yo-chan is the twenty-eighty-year-old star of a fourteen-person troupe that plays monthlong stands in theaters and hot spa resorts from Tokyo to Hiroshima. A typical program of *taishu engeki* lasts three and a half hours and includes singing, dancing, and two forty-minute plays. The repertoire of tragicomic plays changes daily, so a faithful fan can see sixty different plays in a month. There are more than fifty *taishu engeki* companies touring throughout Japan. Each of them is headed by a *zacho* like Yo-chan who draws working-class audiences by combining the quick wit of a Catskills vaudeville top banana with the romantic appeal of a swashbuckling heartthrob. Unlike the more elite theater form of Kabuki, which is marketed for tourists and subsidized by the state, *taishu engeki* offers glimpses into the recesses of Japanese culture that never make their way into the guide books.

Multiply talented as singers, dancers, actors, and clowns, the *zacho* develop a warm, joking rapport with audiences, enlisting them as accomplices in their teasing assault on social convention. The *zacho*'s rebellious charisma is particularly attractive to young and middle-aged women, who are their most dedicated followers. Most *zacho* are also expert at the art of female impersonation, known as *onnagata*, adding a double edge to their erotic appeal.

Midori Kimura and her daughter Yumi are typical fans of *taishu engeki*. They work in offices during the day but spend as many evenings as possible at the theater. During the two months a year when their favorite *zacho*, Satomi Yojiro, is in Tokyo, they go to see him almost every night. When he performs in other cities, they take weekend trips to watch him out of town. In Midori's wallet is a photo of Satomi in white face makeup and an elaborate woman's wig. It is laminated so that she can handle it daily without wearing it out. "Life is boring when the *zacho* is away," laments Midori. "We always count the days until he comes back."

Fans like Midori and Yumi become attached to their favorite performers and return to see them over and over again. Yo-chan makes a point of greeting them personally during the *goaisatsu* and asking where they've been if he hasn't seen them for a while. He makes them feel like long-lost relatives, and they respond by acting like happy members of a big extended family. Many fans come to the theater with books of photographs they've taken of Yo-chan and his company over the years. Midori and Yumi remember when each of their photos were taken, and recite anecdotes about each shot like proud parents showing off a treasured family album.

The origins of *taishu engeki* can be traced to a seventeenth-century priestess, shrine dancer, and prostitute named Okuni. Okuni is also credited with inspiring Japan's first Kabuki troupes, but while Kabuki has gradually gained respectability over the ages, *taishu engeki* remains a marginal form of popular entertainment that is still fueled by the subversive sensuality of the genre's source. Originally, the term "Kabuki" was used to describe behavior that deviated from traditional norms in unacceptably eccentric ways. True to its raunchy, outrageous roots, *taishu engeki* is downtown Kabuki, performed in colorfully shabby neighborhoods like Tokyo's Asakusa, nearby sacred Buddhist temples, sleazy strip shows, offtrack betting, and the massage parlors of the old prostitution quarter.

Taishu engeki is a celebration of the human eccentricities that are not tolerated in the mainstream of Japan's orderly, efficient, and productive society. In a culture where reverence to authority is ingrained in the population from childhood, *taishu engeki* theaters offer their audiences an orgy of insubordination. The national obsession with etiquette is undermined by comic outbursts of unruly passion and uninhibited breeches of decorum.

Japanese social encounters are filled with formal speech and behavior patterns, known as "*kata,*" which everyone is expected to use. There is a formulaic *kata* for almost every situation: a way of bowing, a way of eating, a way of apologizing, a way of expressing gratitude, and so on. These time-honored rituals of propriety are systematically ridiculed, inverted, and ignored by the comic heroes of *taishu engeki.* A samurai with a baby in his arms brandishes a broomstick instead of a sword. A blind masseuse sticks a pair of chopsticks in his ear. The subversive pleasures of *taishu engeki* are rooted in its teasing challenge to *kata* and the cultural expectations they imply.

Patterns of *kata* are so ubiquitous that Japanese follow them without being aware of it. The significance of *kata* is revealed in idioms that are built into the language, like "*shigata ga nai.*" This phrase is a common Japanese response to disappointment and is the equivalent of resignedly saying, "There's nothing to be done." Literally, though, the phrase means that "no *kata* exist for doing it." In Japan the habit of patterned behavior is so powerful that admitting the absence of a formal *kata* for accomplishing something is the same as conceding its impossibility. This built-in cultural respect for patterns makes Japanese audiences particularly susceptible to the comic effect of breaking *kata* on the stage. Because they do not expect a pattern to be ruptured, the effect is doubly delightful when it happens.

Safely hidden away in marginal neighborhoods, *taishu engeki* theaters are year-round festivals of *kata*-bashing nonconformity, but the mardi gras spirit of *taishu engeki* is particularly visible when Yo-chan's troupe performs near Tokyo's Asakusa Kannon temple every year at the beginning of January. This is the time when New Year's festivities are in full swing and the temple grounds are teeming with colored banners, paper lanterns, and kimono-clad worshippers lining up to say their first prayers of the year. Temporary food stalls spring up overnight offering holiday delicacies like chocolate-covered bananas, fried octopus, and hot corn on a stick.

The mood of merriment inside the old Mokubakan Theater is continuous with the atmosphere outside the temple. The stage is adorned by the same red paper lanterns that hang over the doors of the tiny noodle restaurants that line the nearby streets. The corners of the proscenium are piled high with New Year's gifts for the actors from their fans: good luck dharma dolls like the ones for sale at a wooden stand around the corner from the theater and barrels of rice wine like the ones piled up in front of the temple steps. Kannon, the Buddhist deity of mercy, in whose honor the temple was named, appears in one of Yo-chan's plays so he can rejoin the lover that mourns for him in front of her shrine.

The new year is greeted in Asakusa with the midnight clanging of an eighteenth-century gong, but the traditionally robed priests that perform the ceremony walk down a path illuminated by neon signs advertising the electronic products of Japan's multinational corporations. *Taishu engeki* celebrates the new year with a similar display of time-warped paraphernalia. Samurai swords for the plays are stored in a box with the aluminum microphone stands for the rock music segment. The mist from a dry ice machine that greets the goddess of mercy drifts across the stage to the corner where the electric guitars are stacked up against the *taiko* drums that have been used in Japanese religious rituals for centuries. Yo-chan plays both instruments, making a quick change from samurai robes to a sequined tuxedo.

To an outsider there is something jarring about these clashing juxtapositions, but the regular audience takes no special notice. The merging of the old and the new has become an habitual part of their lives. Hearing Yo-chan ad-lib a modern soft-drink jingle in the costume of a samurai is no different than turning on the television at home and seeing the emperor in a business suit give ceremonial congratulations to a half-naked sumo wrestler. The festival atmosphere of Asakusa's New Year's celebration exaggerates the contrasts, but the convergence of past and present has become so common in Japan that its presence in *taishu engeki* is just another of the reassuringly familiar elements that bind the spectators closer to the world on the stage.

Even when there is no paper snow to mark the bond between actors and spectators, the air is filled with other signs of their connection. Refined audiences in Kabuki theaters customarily express their appreciation of a performer by shouting out the actor's family name during the climactic pauses in his speeches, timing the shout so that it fits precisely into the heightened emotional cadences of the speech. *Taishu engeki* actors employ variations of the same emotionally charged speech patterns used in Kabuki, but their audiences respond with shouts of a much more anarchic nature. They break the *kata* of conventional audience responses found in Kabuki and pierce the air with grunts, shrieks, and cries that obey no rules of order.

These impulsive outbursts feed the actors' creativity, even when they verge on being disruptive. One night a drunk in the audience interrupted a scene by shouting abuse at the stage and stomping toward the exit. Yo-chan, who was playing a sake-drinking scene at the time, impulsively decided to include the drunk in the play. "There's a man who's drunker than I am," improvised the actor. "Maybe I'll invite him to go out with me for a bottle of sake." Energized by the audience's laughter, Yo-chan launched into five minutes of impromptu comic dialogue with the drunk before returning to the plot of the play.

This style of self-conscious improvisation seduces the public into an interactive relationship with the stage. The formal barriers that separate the audience from the play are melted by the myriad ways in which *taishu engeki* integrates the audience into the action. Actors drink sake on stage while spectators take swigs of whiskey from bottles passed back and forth across the aisles. Occasionally a comic character will spray the spectators with water or take a pratfall into their laps. Yo-chan even makes sure that his fingers are scented with perfume when he shakes hands with the audience, so that they can watch him sing a tender ballad with a flower in his hand and smell its fragrance from their seats. In Kabuki there is a ramp that runs from the stage through the audience known as a *hanamitchi*, or flower path. It enables actors to get closer to the public by making entrances and exits directly through their midst. *Taishu engeki* theaters are often too small to include a formal *hanamitchi*, but its actors take Kabuki's concept of audience involvement to even greater extremes. *Taishu engeki*'s participatory elements have widened the flower path so that it reaches every seat in the house. From the taste of sake to the touch of a paper snowflake, *taishu engeki* engages all the senses in a theatrical feast of slapstick and sentiment.

At the heart of the relationship between *taishu engeki* actors and their audience is their mutual delight in ridiculing the orderly patterns of Japan's *kata*-bound society. Every performance is riddled with comic challenges to the myth of Japanese social obedience. The liberating anarchy of a *taishu engeki* performance is embedded in the style of its acting. The actors do not have the refined techniques of Kabuki stars, but they make up for their lack of finesse with an exhilarating sense of recklessness.

Yo-chan's stage charisma owes much to his raw impulsiveness. No matter what character he plays, his feelings are so volatile that they can barely be contained. A sudden surge of anger sends him rushing unarmed toward a sword-bearing enemy. A flood of sympathetic tears washes over him as he witnesses a gangster humiliating his lame wife. A nonsensical song flies from his lips as he sits drinking with a fellow traveler, and Yo-chan cannot resist the urge to get up and dance. Sometimes his urges push the plots toward exciting climaxes, and sometimes they lead to absurd digressions, but his improvisations can always be counted on to season the predictable plays with a delicious sense of freedom, risk, and laughter.

The musical interludes between the plays look like a time-warped Japanese parody of an American variety show from the fifties. Electric guitar players behind makeshift orange band-stands are dressed in patterned kimonos and wigs that seem left over from their roles as samurai warriors and *yakuza* henchmen. The singers who precede Yo-chan read the words to their senti-mental love songs from cue cards cupped in the palm of the same hand they use to hold their microphones. The slick master of cer-emonies introduces each song with the guttural intonations of the gangsters he plays in the dramas.

Yo-chan electrifies this atmosphere of warmed-over ana-chronisms with an entrance calculated to surprise. Sometimes he sings part of his song from the wings, leaving the stage empty to build suspense. Sometimes he makes his entrance from the back of the theater. The audience never knows if he will be wearing a tuxedo or a kimono, but whether tailored in an Eastern or Western style, the clothing Yo-chan chooses is always marked by flashy individual touches. Doing anything he can to break the patterns of the tamer singers that have preceded him, Yo-chan jumps into the crowd to shake hands, improvises comic refrains to the songs, and shakes his hips to the beat of the drums. His rambunctiousness is accentuated by the long sideburns and wavy pompadour of the Westernized hairpiece he wears while singing.

When Yo-chan lets loose in this feverish flood of Japanese schmaltz and Western rock and roll, he is breaking the Japanese rules of reserve but paradoxically replacing them with another set of nonconformist *kata*. Dressed as greasers from the era of Elvis Presley, Yo-chan and his band are conforming to images of Western rebels that have become familiar icons in Japanese soci-ety. This duality is what differentiates Japanese conformity from that of other countries. Even if you peel away one level of inhibitions, another will take its place.

Tokyo's teenagers, for example, live such doubly regimented lives that when they break away from their families for a taste of wild music in the streets, they end up dancing in perfect unison to punk rock bands set up in predetermined sites in Harujuku Park. At a party where people hope to transcend the barriers of politeness, the host formally announces that informal behavior will be allowed, but this does not stop the guests from apologizing every time they do something that would be considered rude in a formal setting, like pouring sake into their own cups instead of waiting until someone else pours it for them, as tradition dictates.

In other words, polite formality is so deeply ingrained in Japanese behavior that people automatically obey rules, even when they have decided to break them. *Taishu engeki* actors are caught up in the same paradox. No matter how uninhibited their comedy appears in comparison with normal Japanese behavior, it is still structured with near geometrical precision. The rupture of social patterns is achieved in a predictably patterned way. Not even Japan's most anarchic comedians can escape the regimentation of their society's convention-bound habits. Actors like Yo-chan get their laughs by puncturing official forms of *kata*, but they also reassure their audience by creating an unconventional form of *kata* in its place. This is what makes their humor quintessentially Japanese. Its wildness is tempered by unspoken aesthetic rules. Like a Japanese garden, the comedy is both sculpted and free.

One of the plays that typifies the double nature of *taishu engeki*'s comic *kata*-busting is called *Kenka Bozu* (Fighting Priest). Because Buddhist priests are not permitted to engage in violence, the title of the play is an oxymoron that sets the mood for a humorous assault on the rules of the priesthood. Yo-chan plays the title role, a *yakuza* gangster who escapes the police by taking refuge in a monastery and becoming an apprentice priest. His first indiscretion occurs while chanting prayers at a Buddhist altar. Yo-chan uses the sacred bells to jazz up the rhythms of the chants and can't stop himself from improvising scatological variations on the words. When he is sent on an errand by the head priest, he ends up getting drunk and stealing money from the donation box to help a beautiful young woman in distress.

Throughout the play Yo-chan engages in these unpriestly activities in white holy robes that are loose-fitting enough to reveal the trademark tattoos of a *yakuza* that cover his body under the clothing. *Yakuza* gangsters are among the most celebrated nonconformists in Japanese society, and their startling body tattoos are one of the ways in which they proudly set themselves apart. Interestingly, as do other Japanese attempts at nonconformity, the tattoos of the *yakuza* conform to an accepted standard. Their beautifully ornate patterns are painstakingly composed of traditional designs that cover the torso, legs, and arms. *Yakuza* characters are a staple of *taishu engeki* and emblematic of the Japanese paradox of conformist nonconformity.

While breaking the rules of the priesthood in *Kenka Bozu*, Yo-chan stays faithful to the code of *yakuza* honor that has been established in films and Kabuki plays. Like Jirocho of Shimizu, the archetypal Robin Hood figure in *yakuza* mythology, the outlaw priest comes to the aid of a woman who is being cheated by unscrupulous loan sharks. Ever the polite gangster, he prostrates himself in front of the head priest to apologize for stealing the money to help the woman, and humbly begs for permission to continue protecting her from the threats of her crooked creditors. When the aged holy man grants his request, Yo-chan leaps to his knees and expresses his thanks in formal Kabuki-like phrases of gratitude that end with a stylized gesture of appreciation and the words "Thank you, *oyabun*." The audience roars with laughter at the multiple levels of *kata* that are broken by Yo-chan's calculated satiric choices.

Oyabun makes them laugh because it is a *yakuza* term of respect that is the equivalent of "godfather," and inappropriate for a priest. Yo-chan's heightened Kabuki vocal style sets up the expectation of a serious climax, an expectation comically shattered when Yo-chan ends his florid thank-you with the *oyabun* joke. With one arm upraised and his face looking directly toward the audience, Yo-chan swivels his neck and jolts his head into a frozen position. This arresting pose of condensed emotion, known in Kabuki as a *mie*, is ordinarily used at serious moments and not as the setup for a gag about gangsters and priests.

Yo-chan's irreverent use of the eloquent Kabuki convention in this farcical situation is part of the ongoing parody of Kabuki *kata* that runs through every *taishu engeki* performance. Dozens of *mie* patterns are performed in every play, sometimes seriously, sometimes mockingly, so that the audience never knows what to expect. In this way *taishu engeki* satisfies the public's need for heightened passions to be safely packaged in familiar patterns, at the same time that it mocks the absurdity of depending on a formula for the expression of human feelings.

Comic traditions in countries like Lithuania and South Africa don't have such highly codified patterns to draw on, so laughter there is more unpredictable and can actually inspire rebellion against the prevailing ideology, whether it be communism or apartheid. In Japan there is no outside authority to rebel against. Japanese comedy subverts the restrictive *kata* of social interactions but does not really challenge the basic need for some kind of *kata*. Far from anarchic in its comic tone, *taishu engeki* offers a comforting set of informally communal behavior patterns in place of the more stultifying patterns that dominate formal Japanese interactions. Yo-chan and his troupe are predictable in the way a village family might be predictable in their interactions around the dinner table. Their comedy ridicules dehumanizing patterns of social interaction and frees the audience to participate in the more casual and eccentric patterns of their informal community.

Yo-chan is not the only *zacho* to self-consciously parody *taishu engeki*'s stylistic connection to Kabuki. Tomio Umezawa, whose fame as a *zacho* has been boosted by regular appearances on national television, occasionally stops in the middle of a *mie* to chide his audience for not shouting his name the way the audience does at Kabuki. "I'm working very hard to act in the Kabuki style," jokes Umezawa, "and I'd appreciate it if you'd show your appreciation in a Kabuki-like manner."

A few minutes after Yo-chan has succeeded in mocking the traditions of samurai, *yakuza*, Kabuki, and Buddhism with his shrewdly chosen words of gratitude to the priest, he shifts his focus to debunking the highly esteemed art of wrestling in Japan known as sumo. When the fighting priest in *Kenka Bozu* finally tracks down the crooks that are victimizing the innocent young woman, he discovers they are hiding out in a sumo training stable. The big fight scene that ends most *taishu engeki* plays is usually an acrobatic display of samurai swordsmanship, but this new plot twist leads to the alternate finale of a slapstick sumo match. The bad guys are sumo heavyweights with lots of stuffing in their kimonos for comic effect. As usual, Yo-chan is outnumbered, but he escapes the blows of his opponents by bouncing off their bellies. Shattering the time-honored rules of sumo, Yo-chan subjects his globular-shaped foes to a barrage of humiliating fighting tactics that seem to be borrowed from the tricks of American professional wrestlers. The audience howls with laughter at the incongruous juxtaposition of fighting techniques, and Yo-chan milks the sumo slapstick from every imaginable angle.

The *zacho* is well aware of his audience's enthusiasm for sumo wrestling. Whenever his performance dates overlap with the bimonthly national sumo tournaments, Yo-chan watches the matches backstage during intermission and reports the results to the audience before he starts the next act. Sumo is a ceremonial and tradition-bound affair in Japan. Wrestlers begin each match with a ritual throwing of salt into the air, and the tournaments are often graced by a visit from the emperor. The familiar *kata* of the national sport provide ideal material for the pattern-breaking style of Yo-chan's comedy. As the fighting priest pounds the stuffing out of his opponents, the background music is a pop song about a macho sumo wrestler sung in the style of American rap.

Kenka Bozu is a farcical play from start to finish, so it is to be expected that its characters would shatter the behavior patterns of everyday Japanese life, but even the most tragic plays use comedy to undermine *kata*. No subject is too serious for exemption from ridicule, not even death. Japanese society has developed rigid *kata* for dealing with death, from the stylized gestures of ritual suicide to the behavior patterns observed by mourners attending funerals.

In a tragic play that ends with the hero's father killing himself, Yo-chan introduces the subject of death by mocking the *kata* that are traditionally connected to ritual suicide. He meets a man who is about to jump into the river because he has lost the money he needed to buy carrots for his sick mother. "Go ahead and die," shouts Yo-chan, ridiculing the man's overinflated view of the significance of a carrot. "But if you're going to kill yourself, you should at least do it the right way." Yo-chan proceeds to give a lesson in the appropriate *kata* for doing away with oneself in proper Japanese style. Every step is filled with melodramatic passion and punctuated by an absurdly grandiloquent Kabuki *mie*. Yo-chan also demonstrates the precise length of the dramatic pause the man should use before looking up to the heavens and apologizing to the spirit of his dying mother. This hilarious crash course in suicide technique confuses the man so thoroughly that he gives up the idea of killing himself and sets off instead to find alternative means of procuring a carrot.

The comic tone of this mock death scene does not diminish the impact of the real suicide that occurs at the end of the play. The same gestures of grief that Yo-chan mocked in his encounter with the carrotless son are performed with genuine feeling at the play's conclusion. Yo-chan's Kabuki-style *mie* of apology to his dead father is so compellingly mournful that the audience is moved to tears. The two contrasting suicides highlight the difference between *kata* that is heartfelt and *kata* performed as a rote imitation of form. Paralleling the ridiculous with the sublime, *taishu engeki* offers the public an opportunity to differentiate between the fraudulent and authentic uses of the patterns that shape their lives. Its comedy subverts rote *kata* while endorsing the genuinely personal *kata* that bind families together.

There seem to be no limits to the *zacho*'s attempts to smash the taboos surrounding death. Comic necrophilia is a common gag on the *taishu engeki* circuit, but Yo-chan gives a creative twist to the theme by announcing in mock horror that the corpse he carries on his back has an erection. He then embarks on a series of comic contortions caused by the difficulty of removing the dead man's organ from the backside of Yo-chan's kimono. The

bizarre scene of slapstick erotica concludes with a passionate
tango danced with impeccable timing by Yo-chan and his love-
starved cadaver.

The way in which laughter creates a sense of family while
subverting the *kata* that keep families apart is revealed in some of
the personal exchanges between the actors and their fans outside
the theater. A few nights after performing the double suicide play
about the death of a father, Yo-chan sat in a restaurant with some
of his fans telling them the story of his own father's death. "He
never let me call him daddy or father," said Yo-chan describing
the strictness with which his father adhered to the Confucian pattern of filial respect, "so even on his death bed I called him `sensee`
[an honorific term that in Japanese can mean either "teacher" or
"doctor"]. When I looked at the oscilloscope measuring out the
beats of my father's life, they were getting weaker, so I said,
`Come on, *sensee*, try a little harder,` and the doctor turned
around and said he was already trying as hard as he could. My
mother and I looked at each other, and even though we had tears
in our hearts, our eyes were laughing at the idea that the doctor
thought I was talking to him."

Yo-chan tells the story as if it were a comedy, with a full
pantomimed reenactment of the oscilloscope's trajectory from
fading blips to stillness, but the intimate group of his fans all
knew what it meant to choke back their feelings out of respect for
their parents. Some of their parents were sitting at the table with
them. Two generations of *taishu engeki* fans laughed with him
sadly, just as they would the next night when he told the whole
story again from the stage of the theater. Both in the restaurant
and in the theater an extended family had been created out of a
mutual need to transcend the Japanese patterns that stifled the
expression of emotion.

Much of the family spirit in a *taishu engeki* audience is created by the way in which the plays wreak havoc on social attitudes
toward gender and sexuality. The fans are mostly women, who
are forced to accept rigid differentiations between male and
female behavior outside the theater and take great delight in
taishu engeki's mardi gras of sexual role reversals. Traditionally

women in Japan are trained to speak in high-pitched, subservient voices. Their sense of obligation to men is so strong that the candy industry exploits it for a half-billion-dollar profit, on a holiday called White Day, by selling *giri choco* (obligation chocolates) to women office workers who feel it is their duty to buy a box for each of their male colleagues. Men, on the other hand, are not expected to give White Day presents in Japan, where it is considered unmanly to publicly reveal one's affections for a woman.[1]

Taishu engeki's splashiest assault on the rules of sexual propriety occurs near the end of every performance when the *zacho* does a dance of female impersonation in which he dons the traditional layered kimono of a Kabuki *onnagata*. There is a long history of sexual cross-dressing in Japanese theater, and since the seventeenth century the most celebrated manifestation of that tradition has been the male Kabuki actor's stylized portrayal of a woman. These *onnagata* specialists have become superstars of the contemporary Japanese cultural scene.

Unlike Kabuki, which is still performed exclusively by men, *taishu engeki* troupes include both male and female performers, but in spite of the availability of women to play the parts, *taishu engeki's zacho* have chosen to satisfy the Japanese fascination for *onnagata* by regularly displaying their own skills at sexual transformation. The phenomenon of the *onnagata* is yet another manifestation of the Japanese obsession with form. The term *"onnagata"* is a compound derived from the word for woman (*onna*) and the word for form (*kata*). The *onnagata* actor is not simply trying to act like a woman; he is striving to imitate the ideal form of female beauty. The smooth white makeup on his face, neck, and hands covers up the blemishes of his skin in an effort to achieve an aura of flawless feminine softness. His movements flow with a liquid grace that sculpts his robes into suggestive feminine curves.

Because the *onnagata* creates an ideal pattern of womanhood without being burdened by the natural imperfections of a real female, who might not conform to the ideal, he is often considered more womanly than a woman could ever be. It is symptomatic of Japan's addiction to *kata* that the idealized form of femininity played by a man is viewed as more desirable than the real thing. Women watch the *onnagata* with mixed feelings of jealousy and admiration. "He is more feminine than I am," sighs a young girl during an *onnagata* dance at *taishu engeki.* "If I could be like him it would be much easier for me to find a husband." Other women find themselves attracted to the tenderness exhibited by the man beneath the *onnagata* makeup and confess that they wouldn't mind marrying an *onnagata* themselves. Men are also aroused by the fantasy of female perfection and sometimes approach *onnagata* actors after the show to ask for a date. The dizzying array of psychosexual responses to an *onnagata* is further complicated when one tries to imagine the feelings of men in the audience who occasionally arrive at the theater wearing geisha-like costumes and makeup that rival the flowery ostentation of the female impersonators on the stage.

Yo-chan's *onnagata* dance confounds the audience's expectations by suggesting there is an assertive modern woman beneath the submissive female stereotype. Initially he seems to be conforming to the conventional patterns of *onnagata* performance. He makes his entrance dressed in elaborate layers of delicately patterned kimono, and his features are softened by white makeup that covers every visible patch of his skin. His willowy gestures seduce the space around him, while his bedroom eyes radiate an erotic charm that seems to excite both the men and the women in the crowd. So far he is fulfilling the demands of the *kata* by following the rules that have governed *onnagata* performances for centuries, but when members of both sexes begin approaching the stage to give him presents, Yo-chan's performance catches fire and transcends the limits of tradition.

Teasingly pursing his moist red lips, Yo-chan shatters the elegant persona of a seventeenth-century courtesan with comic flashes of modern greed. He throws kisses at the customers who offer him presents, and playfully covets the banknotes of ten thousand yen ($80) that they slip into the sash that holds together his kimono. Lunging toward the gift-wrapped packages placed on the edge of the stage, he quivers with pleasure as he reads their designer labels. Yo-chan stuffs the cash and the gifts into the folds of his clothing with an acquisitive glee that transforms the *onnagata*'s refined reverie into a samurai shopping spree. He completes his deconstruction of the revered Edo-era archetype by unexpectedly breaking into a pseudo-Brazilian samba, punctuating its rhythms with seductive pelvic thrusts. Shamelessly displaying the socially unacceptable urges of avarice and lust, Yo-chan's old-fashioned *onnagata* shocks the audience into howls of laughter with the thoroughly modern moves of a gold-digging Marilyn Monroe.

Taishu engeki's tendency to simultaneously reinforce and undermine Japan's sexual stereotypes is characteristic of the tension between tradition and innovation that is a part of the genre's heritage. Yo-chan first sensed this tension when he was learning the *onnagata* dance under the strict tutelage of his father, a *zacho* of a generation that clung more tightly to its traditions. Yo-chan's father forced him to learn the demure step of the *onnagata* by walking across the stage with a postcard clutched between his knees. If his steps became too wide, the postcard fell, and he had to start the dance from the beginning. Essentially Yo-chan's father was teaching him a man's fantasy of idealized female behavior, insisting that the only way he would be permitted to break the rules of male behavior would be to follow the rules of the *onnagata* that had been established for breaking them.

Yo-chan's modernized *onnagata* breaks both sets of rules, creating an unsettling comic confusion that makes his character more human and accessible, strengthening his bond with the audience as he challenges the austere and distanced stereotype. Yo-chan recalls that even his tradition-bound father had employed a similar device, rupturing the formal patterns of the dance by pulling his son's hand inside the kimono, and making the audience laugh at the *onnagata*'s surprisingly licentious behavior. Yo-chan was as unsettled as the audience at the sexual ambiguity of his father's playfulness. "He played the role so convincingly," says Yo-chan, "that it felt to me like he had a woman's breasts."

Yo-chan portrays an *onnagata* that acts on all kinds of uncontrollable impulses. None of these actions, however, transcend the *onnagata*'s ultimate accountability to men. The stereo-

type has been updated to the twentieth century, but it is still safely within the boundaries of a man's perception of female urges to
love, to covet, and to shop. Summing up the paradoxes of his
attempts to both preserve and break away from the traditions of
his father, Yo-chan quotes a Japanese proverb, "The son of a frog
is still a frog."

The boundaries of Japanese female behavior are more thoroughly shattered when the *onnagata* of *taishu engeki* moves out of
the dance numbers into the plots of the plays. The plays in which
women are played by men display a wide range of female characteristics. Frustrated by the demands made on them by the male
characters, the *onnagata* sometimes respond with boldness, wit,
ferocity, and intelligence. Other times they end up accepting the
obligations imposed on them by the Japanese system of *giri* and
ninjo. It is usually the comic *onnagata* who shatter their social
restraints most effectively. They get laughs by impolitely eaves-
dropping on all-male conversations, shouting insults in masculine
language patterns, and ridiculing the sexual infatuations of gangsters and samurai. In one play a comic *onnagata* chastises her
profligate husband by lifting him upside down by his legs and
grinding her foot into his crotch. This kind of slapstick independence delights the women in the audience by obliterating all the
pretenses of traditional wifely obedience.

A particularly intriguing play written by Yo-chan's father
features an entire company of *onnagata* playing the roles of court-
ly geisha in the harem of the shogun. Yo-chan plays the part of a
new geisha in the harem who is despised by the others for her
good looks. When the newcomer becomes the shogun's favorite,
her rivals conspire to have her disgraced. The shogun is completely ignorant of the manoeuvering that goes on behind his
back, and the feud in the harem erupts into a bloody battle that
climaxes with Yo-chan stabbing the madam of the brothel and
killing herself as well.

Ironically the character in the harem who humiliated Yo-
chan's *onnagata* the most deeply was played by his real mother,
Mefuji Kieko. One of the few female characters in the play portrayed by an actual woman, her dominance of the stage suggested

a more radical sexual role reversal than the one being performed by the men around her. While the men acting as *onnagata* were trying to embody the form of ideal femininity, Mefuji was redefining the limits of what a real woman could do. In her vibrant stage portrait of a geisha who fearlessly carves out a position of influence in the court of Japan's most powerful leader, Mefuji establishes the image of a woman who pursues power more aggressively than the shogun himself.

Playing against her culture's gender-based expectations, Mefuji portrays a wide spectrum of Japanese female characters and imbues them all with a moral or physical strength that presents surprising challenges to the men around her. Whether she is seductively threatening, coldly manipulative, or self-sacrificingly generous, she is always a potent force on the stage, and women in the audience applaud her every entrance, no matter what persona she happens to be clothed in. Even in the role of a humble mother abused by her children, Mefuji elicits shouts of approval from female spectators for the strength of her passive resistance to the cruelties she is forced to bear. "You're right," shout the voices of support. "They should be ashamed to treat you like that."

The memories of the mother's pain still linger in the theater the next night when many of the same spectators cheer her victories over rival gangsters as Mefuji plays a comically villainous extortionist. This time she has assumed the role of a man, and her character's violence seems fueled by the memories of injustices suffered as a woman the night before. There is spirited laughter when she trades insults with Yo-chan while her foot is firmly planted on his hand. "It's not the play itself that's funny," says a middle-aged mother who works for the Japanese electric company. "It's knowing that the strong man forcing Yo-chan down onto the ground is actually his mother." Sensing how much the audience enjoys the comic sparring between mother and son, Mefuji uses her scenes with Yo-chan as springboards for extended improvisations, subjecting the head of the troupe to ridicule that only she could inflict with impunity.

Mefuji's male impersonations provide a provocative counterpoint to her son's *onnagata* roles as a woman. She matches the

delicate charms of his tender female characters with steely ferocity. Armed only with a sword, she single-handedly vanquishes a
gang of grunting samurai. Sometimes her outlandish triumphs
are calculated to elicit laughter, as she defies the laws of probabil-
ity with ridiculous ease. But underlying many of her male roles is
a self-conscious viciousness that cuts to the heart of masculine
cruelty. Perhaps her most heartless character is a gangster who
steals a sword and demands a human head for its return, only to
spit on the severed head when it is offered by the dead man's best
friend. While the *onnagata* provides a glimpse into the Japanese
male fantasy of a perfectly submissive woman, the Japanese
women who impersonate men reveal their darker vision of the
opposite sex.

The Japanese tradition of women performing male roles on
stage goes back at least as far as Okuni, who spiced her prototyp-
ical Kabuki skits with dances in men's clothing. A Tokyo performer named Ooe Michiko headlined a postwar cabaret boom of
women dressed as men who put on spectacular displays of sword
fighting. Michiko was particularly noted for the kind of acrobatic
swordplay that Mefuji uses in overcoming her opponents on
stage. Mefuji admits to having a lot of fun beating mean at their
own violent game, and Yo-chan confesses that after ten years
onstage, he is still nervous when he performs with her. "After all,"
he blurts out, "she is my mother."

The audience's knowledge of the comically scrambled stage
relationship between Mefuji and her son helps create a bond
between the public and the stage. Fans feel like part of the family
when they recognize Mefuji playing a modern *yakuza* gangster
one night and a seventeenth-century geisha the next. Her son
might be meeting her on stage as anything from a member of her
harem to a gangster in her mob. One night the rapidity with
which Yo-chan was expected to switch sexes seemed to get the
best of him, and he tried to breast-feed a baby while performing
in the role of a man. Playing up the paradox, he pantomimed an
orgasm as the child sucked on his nipple. Comic improvisations
like this invite the audience to play along with the gender confusion of a man whose mother sometimes dresses as a man trying

to kill him with a sword and other times dresses as a vamp trying to seduce him with an erotic joke. "My face may look old," says Mefuji in one of her lustier roles, pointing suggestively to her hips, "but down here I'm only eighteen."

Mefuji is not the only woman in the troupe challenging the limits of acceptable female behavior in Japan. Tsutsumi Terumi, a twenty-seven-year-old member of the company, has been performing since she was three. Her father acted with Mefuji's husband for over forty years, so, like Yo-chan, she was born into the tradition of *taishu engeki*. Staring into stage lights since childhood has affected Terumi's eyesight, leaving her partially blind in one eye. Many of the characters she portrays are also blind, a condition that increases their tragic dependency on men. In a society whose rules limit women's options even when they have perfect eyesight, the heightened helplessness of Terumi's blind heroines calls added attention to the dilemmas faced by all Japanese women.

Terumi brings audiences to tears with her moving depiction of the tortured feelings and stifling obligations brought on by the classic clash of Japanese *ninjo* and *giri*. But she is equally adept at delighting them with the outlandish ways she breaks out of the traditional woman's role. The same actress who plays a girl sold into prostitution to pay her family's debts appears later in the week with a pistol in her hand, swearing to take revenge on the extortionists who murdered her father. Every time she shoots the gun her brother falls down in fright, and she continues comically overwhelming the men in the play to the last scene, when she proposes marriage to Yo-chan with her pistol aimed at his crotch. Though they appear in different plays, the gunslinger with comic determination and the blind girl in pain are both born out of the thwarted ambitions that Japanese women have been learning to live with for centuries.

In a culture where secretaries are called *"shokuba no hana"* (office flowers), unmarried women are known as *"urenokori"* (unsold goods), and mothers are referred to as *"ofukuro"* (honorable old bags), *taishu engeki* defies sexual stereotypes with a wackiness that knows no bounds. Mefuji's swordsmanship, Terumi's

marksmanship, and Yo-chan's samba-dancing geisha are characters in a realm where gender is deliberately turned upside down
and inside out. The sexual status quo is mourned, mocked, and
mutilated by a parade of merciless gangsters, lascivious mothers,
blind geisha, and hermaphroditic samurai who take the concept of
sexual ambiguity to its furthest extremes. "Don't you know a
man when you see one?" ad-libs Yo-chan's mother, brandishing a
sword in the costume of a male gangster. Her son doesn't even
try to answer. He just turns to the audience with an expression of
bewilderment and laughs.

When Yo-chan looks the audience in the eye, he is doing
more than just asking for a laugh. He is adding to the web of self-
reflectiveness that draws the audience into the world of *taishu
engeki* as if they were part of the family. This ongoing invitation
to intimacy is one of the most radically subversive aspects of the
performance, more profoundly disruptive to the prevailing social
order than anything else in the performances. Japanese etiquette
discourages the public expression of emotion, but *taishu engeki*
subverts the culture's isolationism by providing opportunities for
total strangers to interact and form emotional ties. These bonds
between strangers are at the core of *taishu engeki*'s appeal. The
paradox between the subversion and reinforcement of *kata* is reconciled in the spontaneous human interactions that require both
the breaking of old patterns and the formation of new ones.

Breaking the frame of the play to include the public is one of
taishu engeki's most entertaining forms of *kata*-busting. It defies
the rules of tradition while strengthening the emotional bond
between actors and audience in surprising ways that endure from
one performance to the next.

Yo-chan is a master at improvising scenes that involve
direct contact with the crowd. One night while running away
from an actor playing the role of his brother, the *zacho* leapt off
the stage into the lap of a spectator. The plot called for the two
siblings to have a family quarrel over a woman they both loved,
and Yo-chan's stage brother threatened to throw him out of the
house. "She'll protect me," squealed Yo-chan, clutching the arms
of the startled audience participant. "Yes, I'll take care of him,"

she giggles at Yo-chan's assailant. "Are you sure?" quips the brother. "He'll cost you a lot of money." As are the rest of Yo-chan's fans, the woman is familiar with the *zacho*'s expensive tastes, but this does not dampen her determination to help. "That's all right," she snaps back, "I have a lot of money." The brother is impressed. "In that case, maybe you can take care of me too," he says, stepping off the stage himself as if to join Yo-chan and his newfound benefactor in a comically incestuous ménage à trois.

This kind of impromptu encounter between the actors and the audience happens in so many of the plays that the audience begins to feel as if they are participants in the action. This intimacy undermines the repressive patterns of Japanese social behavior that discourage interaction with strangers, while reinforcing new patterns of camaraderie. Sometimes Yo-chan makes his entrance to the stage from the back of the theater so that he can confide his feelings to the audience before he talks to the characters on the stage. The public becomes his confidant and he occasionally calls on them to pass judgment on the villains, as witnesses of their crimes. Other times the audience does not wait to be invited into the plot. When Yo-chan plays a woman who refuses an arranged marriage and wonders aloud what will become of her after she has been abandoned by her family, someone in the audience calls out consolingly, "Poor thing. Come to my house." In another play an innocent man is imprisoned unjustly and a woman in the front row offers him a tin of cold tea through the bars of his cell.

The boundaries between the world of the spectator and the world of the actor are further blurred by the plots of the plays and the irony with which they are performed. Many of the stories are about actors (the most popular characters in *taishu engeki* after *yakuza* gangsters and samurai). One play opens with two fans coming backstage to visit an actor in his dressing room. The actor (played by Yo-chan) says that life in the theater is difficult, and wonders about the hardships endured by the audience after they go home. He imagines the women coming home to complaints from their husbands and children that they are spending

too much time at the theater and not enough time cooking dinner. This comic monologue mirrors real conversations he has
with the audience during the *goaisatsu*. Women tell him they
come home from the theater shouting "Yo-chan! Yo-chan" all
night long. The *zacho* jokes that he sympathizes with "the honorable suffering of your poor husbands."

The audience at *taishu engeki* is always welcomed as valued
members of the theater company's extended family. Frequent
patrons become familiar with the troupe and begin to view their
onstage spats as family squabbles. When Yo-chan is slapped by
his mother with a sword, their clash can be enjoyed on a double
level as samurai hostility or filial discipline. The aging husband
and wife team that performs a nightly comic dance of marital dis-
cord is seen insulting each other so regularly that the looks of
mutual disgust on their faces can be viewed as sympathetically as
the harmless bickering of one's own grandparents. Almost all the
plays involve some kind of family loyalty, whether it is the devotion of a gangster to his *oyabun* and brother mobsters or the
obligation of a samurai to his parents.

The familial bonds that Yo-chan establishes with his audience are layered with all the complex associations that family ties
imply in Japanese culture. In one sense the extension of family
intimacy frees the audience from the patterns of emotionally
inhibiting *kata* they would be compelled to use among strangers,
but the creation of a new family also establishes a new set of less
formal but equally recognizable obligations. The most visible of
these obligations is the giving of gifts. In the exchange of presents between actors and audience, *taishu engeki* gleefully redefines yet another conventional pattern of Japanese behavior in
delightfully unorthodox terms.

One of the most festive moments of gift giving in Yo-chan's
performance occurs during the emotional climaxes of his love
songs, when he pulls autographed scarves, photos, and cigarette
lighters from the deep pockets of his kimono and throws them into
the crowd. The chaos that ensues as the crowd scrambles to grab
the souvenirs cuts through the veneer of social reserve associated
with the ceremonial giving of gifts in other Japanese settings.

Yo-chan's act of generosity sets up a web of obligations between himself and the audience that mirrors the network of *giri* obligations displayed so poignantly in his plays. The difference between the obligations the public feel toward Yo-chan and the obligations they feel toward their own family and business colleagues is that they are freely choosing to enter the world of *taishu engeki*. It is an escape from the rigid *kata* of the Japanese home and office, and though it is permeated with patterns of its own, *taishu engeki's kata* are warm and spontaneous, as opposed to the rote patterns that dominate Japanese society at large.

The audience feels compelled to reciprocate Yo-chan's kindnesses and is given a variety of opportunities to do so. For some the debt of friendship is repaid simply by returning again the next day to buy a ticket to the show. These returnees help Yo-chan sell out almost every show of the year. Others find more elaborate ways to express their gratitude. They bring gifts to the stage during dance solos of their favorite performers. Sometimes the offerings are as humble as a bag of tangerines or a six-pack of beer. More often they are gifts of cash, bills of large denominations that the spectator slips into the sash of the dancer's kimono.

The gifts received by Yo-chan are often quite extravagant. Sometimes the ten-thousand-yen notes he receives are attached to one another in a giant necklace or fan that he graciously incorporates into his dance. Yo-chan's long-time admirers give him elegant handwoven kimonos or boxes of rare imported foods. Regardless of a gift's monetary value, Yo-chan stops his performance to receive every present and honor the people who come to the edge of the stage to present it. He bows, shakes their hand, and thanks them all with formal words of gratitude, as if each were an honored visitor to his home. When he resumes his dance, he finds a place for the gift on the stage, so that it becomes part of the performance as an adornment of a costume or a piece of scenery. This binds the audience even more closely to the actors. Something they have brought with them to the theater has been assimilated into the show. Occasionally a gift being displayed will be greeted by applause, like a new character making an entrance onto the stage. The most beautiful of the gift kimonos are unfold-

ed by an assistant as Yo-chan dances around them. When fully
opened they hide the person holding them up, and the empty
kimonos float ghostlike across the stage, as if their donor's spirit
were dancing a duet with the *zacho*.

This ongoing exchange of gifts and favors highlights the
quirky combination of family intimacy and corporate enterprise
that characterizes the relationship between actors and fans. In
spite of the coziness of the experience, *taishu engeki* is a multimil-
lion-dollar business. Dozens of troupes tour throughout Japan,
filling theaters ranging in size from three hundred to two thousand seats. They are booked by large corporations that also over-
see the recording contracts and television deals of the most
famous *zacho*. Although Yo-chan and his company stand to make
a profit from their relationship with the public, they go out of
their way to make the audience feel more like guests than customers. The intentional ambiguity of their status is heightened
by Yo-chan's use of the word "*okyaksan*" when he refers to the
spectators. In Japanese *okyaksan* can mean either "guest" or "customer," two categories that are often merged in business relationships, where gift giving is a customary way of developing an
informal sense of mutual obligation.

During his *goaisatsu* greeting Yo-chan thanks the audience
for their support, tells jokes about how much he'll miss everyone
when the company moves on to the next town, and calls attention
to the videos, CDs, and souvenir programs that people can buy to
remember him when he's gone. Yo-chan's entertaining sales pitch
is all the more persuasive because he is still wearing the costume
of the hero who won the audience's heart in the samurai play that
ended a few minutes earlier.

Most of the plays in the *taishu engeki* repertory have something to do with money problems and the generosity of strangers. Someone buys a hungry samurai a bowl of noodles, and the
small act of kindness is repaid years later, when the samurai saves
his benefactor's children from a mob of extortionists. Women are
sold into geisha houses of prostitution by their impoverished parents and rescued by a good-hearted anonymous gangster. "From
the top of my head to the tip of my toes I am controlled by cold

money," says Yo-chan's lover in one of the plays, explaining to her little brother why she has to sell herself to a geisha house. Before the play is over, Yo-chan has killed the gangster to whom his lover is indebted and freed her to find love and happiness. Swept away by stories like this that recount grand gestures of noble sacrifice, the audience is perfectly primed to spend a few yen to support a troupe of hardworking actors.

Taishu engeki is a microcosm of the peculiar relationships that exist in Japan among business practices, social etiquette, and cultural values. The performers' excesses and eccentricities are a creative reaction to Japan's traditional system of social patterns. Depending on one's point of view, the patterns can be elegant, reassuring, stultifying, antiquated, essential, or absurd. *Taishu engeki* simultaneously displays all these contradictory attributes in the course of an evening's entertainment. In the end the patterns that are the most fully subverted are the patterns of isolation.

In other theaters the actors can relax when the curtain closes on the last act, but *taishu engeki* performers spend up to an hour every night making personal farewells to everyone in the audience who wants to shake their hands. This ritual of informal good-byes is called the *"okuri dashi"* (send out). No matter how exhausted they are, or how inclement the weather, the actors walk out the stage door immediately after their last exits, circling around to the front of the theater in time to meet the audience as they leave. This gives the most enthusiastic fans an opportunity to continue the banter, gift giving, and picture taking that had been going on during the performance.

Even in the snow, the still-sweating actors wait patiently in their costumes until every fan has had a chance to make some kind of personal contact. "The roads are slippery," cautions an actor in his samurai robes as the spectators wave farewell. Women giggle as they have their photograph taken with the *zacho* in his white *onnagata* makeup and layered kimono. "Take care. It's cold out tonight," he says as they walk away feeling warmed by the expression of concern.

The *okuri dashi* following Yo-chan's closing performance in

Jujo in 1992 was particularly emotional. It marked the end of the troupe's two consecutive monthlong runs in Tokyo, and the fans who had followed Yo-chan faithfully were saying good-bye until the following year. "Don't go," they had shouted to him during the *goaisatsu* in the theater, and now outside in the cold February night air they try to make the farewell last as long as possible. Many of their faces are still wet with the tears they had cried during the *zacho*'s three encores, but Yo-chan makes them laugh, singing silly songs as he autographs their programs and whispering jokes in their ears as they pose with him for a photo.

The emotionally charged scene outside the theater goes against the stereotypes that foreigners have of Japanese society as a culture where feelings are sacrificed to the cold efficiency of commerce. Deprived of the freedom to express their feelings in so many other aspects of their lives, the audience at *taishu engeki* are hungry for a chance to let themselves go.

On the last night of the run the spectators huddle together in the alley where the brilliantly colored kimonos and exotic sets are being loaded into the trucks. They cling to the actors and one another, making small talk, anything to postpone the inevitable departure. Reluctantly they do eventually walk away, but a small group of them succeed in prolonging the evening a little by meeting at a nearby restaurant.

The small family restaurant they choose has a tatami mat floor and folk masks on the wall, creating a sense of continuity with the theater. A table full of slightly inebriated women had tape-recorded Yo-chan's last show and were warbling away to the electronic accompaniment of their idol's voice. They waved to the other fans as they arrived, and their singing made the room full of strangers seem like home.

For the fans in the tiny restaurant Yo-chan was more than a heartthrob to be remembered with autographs, tape recordings, and other souvenirs. That would make him just like all the other movie stars, television celebrities, and famous singers who permeate the popular culture around them. *Taishu engeki* falls into a different category of pleasures than those to be found in the mass media. For Yo-chan's fans the desires of memory are working in two directions at once. Their need to remember Yo-chan is equaled by their longing to be remembered by him.

"Don't forget me," shouted the fans, one after another, throughout the last few nights of Yo-chan's run in Jujo. It would be futile to address such a request to most performers, but at a *taishu engeki* theater there is real hope of a response. "Forget you," replies Yo-chan to a random fan. "How could I ever forget you? I couldn't even forget you if I tried." He accompanies the last remark with an expression of comic disdain, but the joke cuts to the heart of his relationship with his fans. When they talk to him during his *goaisatsu*, shake his hand as he walks through the crowd, and thank him outside the theater at the *okuri dashi*, what they really want is to make an impression on him that in some small way will be remembered the next time he comes to town.

This simple human yearning to be noticed and accepted was the subtext of the revelry at the restaurant where Yo-chan's fans reminisced after his last show. They mocked the *zacho*, blushed at the mention of his name, and sang along with the tape-recorded sound of his voice. The village of *taishu engeki* does not disappear after the last *okuri dashi*. It just moves to the restaurant down the street from the theater, and from there to the memories of the fans who console one another with letters and phone calls until the *zacho*'s next visit.

For Japanese audiences who spend most of their time in tradition-bound offices and homes, the *taishu engeki* theater is an extraordinary place of unrestricted passions, comically scrambled behavior patterns, and fluid sexual identities. Comedy and tragedy intermingle, but it is the catharsis of laughter that offers a taste of freedom from the culture's tyrannical pressure to conform.

Taishu engeki gives ordinary people a chance to feel important, confident that what they do will affect what goes on around them. In marked contrast to the indifference the audience encounters in other realms of their lives, *taishu engeki* gives them a feeling of empowerment. The dialogue changes in response to their laughter, catcalls, and applause. The head of the troupe listens to what they say and looks them in the eye.

In a society dominated by corporate commerce and mass

media, the intimacy of *taishu engeki* subverts the feelings of isolation and inadequacy that eat away at an individual's sense of humanity. By breaking the rules of decorum and turning etiquette on its head, *taishu engeki* transforms a colorless corner of urban life into a carnival of unfettered fun. Order and reserve are overturned by chaos and passion. There is even all the ice cream you can eat. For the weary, obedient, and polite citizens of Japan's highly regimented society, the *zacho* is a modern-day shaman, conjuring storms of paper snow and laughter that transform his shabby theater into a garden of anarchic delights.

Nineteenth-century circus clown Dan Rice performing in the flag suit that later became associated with the image of Uncle Sam. (photo courtesy Harvard Theater Collection)

America's Comedy
of Detachment

Ever since 1967, when the Ringling Brothers, Barnum & Bailey Circus founded America's first college for clowns, the school has struggled to reconcile the tensions between comedy and commercialism that have plagued American laughter for decades. The lumberjacks, nurses, and linguists who studied clowning there with me in 1973 had left their careers to pursue an art form they believed could touch the hearts of children, but the professional realities of clowning in America made it difficult for them to maintain much idealism.

As students of American comedy we could not help but notice that the most prominent function of clowns in America is selling hamburgers. Ronald McDonald is a national icon. IBM's appropriation of Chaplin's tramp was yet another step in detaching the clown from the subversive functions of laughter and turning him into a salesman. Eventually all comics in America are reduced to the status of consumer commodities through their appearances in sitcoms, talk shows, and Hollywood star vehicles.

Our nation's comedy was not always so banal. There is a tradition of American humor that transcends the limitations of the mainstream marketplace. Long before Ronald McDonald became an international symbol of America, a gray-bearded clown named Dan Rice in a red-white-and-blue Uncle Sam costume used his one-ring circus as a comic forum for cultural and political debate. Surrounded by horses, pigs, and mules with names like Daniel Webster, Stephen Douglas, and Ulysses S. Grant, Rice turned his

circus tent into a microcosm of antebellum democracy. His fans
started a short-lived but colorful campaign to nominate him for
president of the United States.

After leaving clown college I spent years reenacting Rice's
comic routines. Rice's socially engaged style of comedy had fallen
from fashion during the Gilded Age, when the Ringling Brothers
were profiting from the country's appetite for spectacle by expanding
their circus from one ring to three. The brothers from Wisconsin
then merged with the celebrated huckster P. T. Barnum to become
the corporate conglomerate, Ringling Brothers, Barnum & Bailey.
As is still true today, politically committed clowns like Rice could
not compete with the slicker entertainment offered by their corpo-
rate-sponsored competitors.

The ease with which America's entertainment industry continues to transform emotionally engaged comedy into detached commercial spectacle was evident during the Ringling clown college's twentieth anniversary celebration. Our class reunion was broadcast as a
CBS special hosted by Dick Van Dyke, and the relentless packaging of
humor was overwhelming.

When I arrived in Sarasota, Florida, to catch up with my fellow alumni, the cameras were already rolling at the airport. A
graduate in a gorilla suit bounded down the steps to the runway. A
woman from the class of '86 stepped off the plane onto a pair of
stilts and waved a pink flamingo in the air. Two brothers returned
to their alma mater dressed as a human locomotive. During the
flight they told me how much they wanted their costume to be
included in the television special and showed me photographs of its
unusual design. "I'm the cowcatcher," whispered one of the brothers
in a conspiratorial whisper. "He's the smokestack."

The urgent sincerity with which the alumni planned their
homecoming gags was countered by the glib insistency of the sales-
men from clown specialty shops who set up exhibition stands in the
hotel lobby. They could barely keep up with orders for slapsticks,
juggling balls, magic flowers, greasepaint, and rubber chickens. A
guy selling oversized clown shoes almost convinced me to pay $125
for a fifteen-inch balloon-toed pair of red-and-white saddle shoes.
"This is our most popular model, and it's practical too," he said.

"They're big enough to be funny, but small enough to wear between shows. You can walk up stairs, drive a car. No problem. Suitable for all occasions."

The ostensible main event of our gathering was an alumni talent show, taped by a television crew who kept asking the performers to repeat the gags and telling the audience to laugh as if it were happening for the first time. Each repetition distanced us a little more from what had once been funny. Watching all this in my Dan Rice/Uncle Sam costume, I kept imagining that the corruption of American comedy was being reenacted over and over before my eyes.

For me, the highlight of the reunion was the performance that featured the current class of graduating clowns. They were not yet jaded by the commercialization of the profession, and their comedy was charged with a raw vitality that ignited the alumni audience of five hundred aging clowns into an kinetic state of attentiveness.

Having performed most of the routines ourselves as students, we knew the moves by heart and were rooting for the rookies to be funny with the fervor of fans at a championship sporting event. Every pants drop in the show got a standing ovation, and when the clown dentist's three-foot pliers extracted a giant molar from the mouth of his hapless victim, five hundred voices sang out the patient's despairing punch line, "You got the wrong tooth!!"

By the time the performers appeared for the finale in their crimson graduation gowns, we were all on our feet, applauding so enthusiastically that the bleachers shook under us. At the height of the delirium an octogenarian master clown named Lou Jacobs stepped into the spotlight, and the students threw their caps into the air as a tribute to their teacher. Lou had taught us all our first gags, and his gruff generosity embodied for us the purest impulses of clowning. We shouted ourselves silly for him.

The collective catharsis of the event continued into the next morning when we threw ourselves into the impromptu delights of a marathon pie fight. The television crew was gone, so we could indulge in this old-fashioned comic orgy as a direct experience unmediated by the camera. The tactile memory of wet pie filling slapping against our faces conjured up the explosive laughter of all the crowds we had ever played for.

Future clowns, current clowns, and ex-clowns hurled pies at one another in an intergenerational brawl of epic proportions. Oblivious to the rules of etiquette, status, and gravity, we were lost in the emotional immediacy of a comic ritual that could never be replaced by the canned laughter of American television. We slipped on the cream that was dripping from our faces, fell over one another in heaps, and abandoned ourselves to the liberating pleasures of primal comedy that has nothing to do with selling hamburgers.

One of the most extraordinary manifestations of emotionally engaged American laughter occurs every summer in the mountains of rural New England. One weekend a year thousands of people gather to laugh in the green pastures of a former dairy farm in Glover, Vermont. The event is never advertised, but information is spread by word of mouth across the country, and on the chosen date a caravan of cars, campers, motorcycles, and pickup trucks encircles the rolling cow pastures that have been the home of the Bread & Puppet Theater since 1970. Families pack picnics. Backpackers bring sleeping bags. Parents come with babies in their arms. There is no charge for the performances, and Peter Schumann, the founder of Bread & Puppet, is on hand to offer free bread to the revelers. Delighted crowds watch as he bakes it himself in a huge clay oven set up in the middle of a field. Some of the visitors roll up their sleeves and help Schumann stir the huge large wooden vats of sour rye dough. While his assistants butter the hot loaves with fresh garlic spread, Schumann slips away and exchanges his white baker's hat for the red-white-and-blue stovepipe headgear of Uncle Sam. He returns on ten-foot stilts, dancing wildly on the grass to a funky washboard band's spirited rendition of "When the Saints Go Marching In." Schumann's star-spangled blue jacket and red-and-white striped leggings give him the appearance of an elongated American flag doing the jitterbug.

"Puppetry is a form of ecstasy," declares Schumann.[1] His annual ritual of comedy and communion is known as the "Bread

& Puppet Domestic Resurrection Circus." Performances of giant puppets, miniature masks, and satirical clowns are staged in fields, barns, and pine forests for two days and nights. The political gags turn laughter and bread into necessary foods for thought.

Every year the stilt-dancing Uncle Sam presides over a carnival that mocks a different aspect of America's history. The two hundredth anniversary of the Constitution was commemorated with giant effigies of the Founding Fathers dedicated to "life, liberty, and the pursuit of property." Bread & Puppet's constitution was a "living document," a giant cardboard baby constructed with body parts that matched various branches of government and aspects of the Bill of Rights. The judiciary was "the long arm of the law." Freedom of speech was the baby's lips. And the right to privacy was a fig leaf between the infant's legs. Another year, the quincentennial of Columbus's voyage, was marked with a huge replica of the *Santa Maria* that floated into a pristine valley and deposited a golden bull that proceeded to defecate all over the landscape. Its feces took the form of placards reading "yours" and "mine," which were attached to a ludicrous contraption of ropes and pulleys intended to represent the absurd mechanisms of capitalism in action. In scenes that depicted a farcically unequal distribution of wealth, the puppets argued that the chaos of our economic system could be traced back to its origins in bullshit.

The crude political metaphors are balanced with moments of homespun poetic beauty. Every year there is a ritual wedding of a thirty-foot-high washerwoman to an equally huge puppet farmer. As a washboard band plays the wedding march, the giant couple is surrounded by smaller masked washerwomen and farmers who do a circle dance in their honor. The homely features of the puppet bride and groom are animated with a touching grace. Schumann has sculpted them in a folk style that fits the natural beauty of their environment.

The pastoral dream of Schumann's puppets is the flip side of their satirical rage. The Resurrection Circus sets up a dichotomy in which the joys of nature and humanity can be enjoyed only

once the tyrannies of greed and consumerism have been overcome. At sunset there is a bonfire in which puppet incarnations of
evil are sacrificed to the flames. In 1987 the military industrial
complex was set on fire by an earth mother puppet whose
embrace was over fifty feet wide. The year before, the ghoulish
specter of hunger was burnt to ashes. These exorcisms free the
audience watching from the hillside amphitheater to move into
the clearings of the adjacent pine forest where evening puppet
comedies play out similar themes of liberation.

The cathartic impact of the Resurrection Circus is enhanced
by the context in which the puppet plays are acted out. Bread &
Puppet has created an environment in which the audience has
been emancipated from the normal trappings of commercial theater. There is no admission fee, no advertising, no corporate
sponsors. This is an astonishing accomplishment for an impoverished theater company that hosts five thousand spectators a day.
People laugh at puppets breaking loose from the clutches of
greedy businessmen while they munch on bread that the puppeteers have given them for free. The festive spirit of the weekend
is rooted in this carnival release from the usual constraints of
consumerism. Donations are accepted, but this only serves to
reinforce the mood of reciprocal generosity. Spectators feel they
are stepping into a vision of small-town America, where cows
and good neighbors are valued more highly than profit. In fact
Bread & Puppet's dairy farm home does function like a small
town. Every summer hundreds of volunteers come to live there,
build the puppets, and rehearse the shows. The communal atmosphere of the festival is not a theatrical illusion but the result of
the genuine commitment of the volunteers and their faith in the
power of puppets and laughter.

The extended community that gathers around the creation
and presentation of the Bread & Puppet Domestic Resurrection
Circus experiences something similar to a Balinese temple festival. A temporary village is created where historic and religious
themes from the public's common heritage can be replayed in a
fantastical form of comic surrealism. Like Balinese clowns who
confront the threats to their village's survival, Bread & Puppet's

satire is aimed at the forces that diminish the quality of their audience's lives. Pollution, nuclear waste, runaway technology, and political corruption as well as consumerism are among the subjects joked about by the tree-sized puppets and the papier-mâché animals that populate the plays.

The problem of survival in the face of adversity continues to fuel the comedy when the audience at Bread & Puppet's festival moves from the fields into the barn, where smaller puppets made of found objects are animated by Schumann's collaborator, Paul Zaloom. While Schumann deflates American political mythology in a cow pasture, Zaloom punctures the same myths on a table-top. In 1986, when the theme of the festival was hunger, Zaloom played the ringmaster in the outdoor circus narrating a sketch about "the death-defying tightrope act of dairy farming in Vermont." The act pitted farmers and their puppet cows against government agents who drove up in an old Chevy sedan waving signs that read Property Taxes, Low Milk Prices, and Dairy Termination Program.

Later, inside the barn, Zaloom performed a sketch called "Farming in America" that dealt with the same conflict using dis-carded household items as the principal players. The dairy farm-house was a school lunch pail, and the grain silo was a thermos. The farmers were garden tools and the dairy herd was made of pint-sized milk cartons painted with the black-and-white patterns of holstein cows. The government representative was a plastic fist with an extended middle finger who assured the farmers he was giving their problems serious consideration, but his visit was followed immediately by bankers in the form of a toy safe who repossessed the farm, silo, and cows, and left the farmers in an empty field. "And that's farming in America," concludes Zaloom darkly, brushing the farmer, farmhouse, and cows off the table. In Zaloom's comedy of trash, the problems of the hungry are ani-mated by the leftovers of the overfed.

The Bread & Puppet Domestic Resurrection Circus is one of the last vestiges of deeply felt American laughter. As its name suggests, it celebrates the revival of simple human values that are often lost in the fast-paced swirl of contemporary society. The company performs for an audience so convinced of the necessity of their satirical shows that some of them are willing to volunteer months out of their lives to construct and rehearse the puppets. Even the spectators who arrive only to watch demonstrate a rare level of commitment to the comedy. They drive for hours and sometimes days to reach an isolated rural corner of Vermont. They respond to the puppet antics with an unqualified enthusiasm that is personal, intimate, and heartfelt. They eat the bread that is offered to them by the puppeteers in a festive ritual of communion. For the day or two that they enter the village of bread and puppets, their public gladly leaves behind the stress of modern America and embraces the simpler pleasures of a world where animated beings serve as liaisons between humans and their natural environment. Temporarily freed from the tyrannies of modern civilization, the audience laughs heartily at the greedy politicians and entrepreneurs who rob them of their peace of mind throughout the rest of the year.

During the fall, winter, and spring, Bread & Puppet transports their comic vision to urban neighborhoods throughout the country, broadening their audience to include those who would never come to Vermont. In keeping with the village spirit of their summer festival, the company recruits neighborhood volunteers to march in their puppet parades. In Boston in 1986 a typical outdoor show took place in the distressed inner-city neighborhood of Roxbury.

For a few hours, a Roxbury park was transformed into a carnival of satirical inversions. Local children played the parts of New York City skyscrapers "on loan from Harry Helmsley, Donald Trump, and Imelda Marcos." Each child carried a cardboard cutout of a big-city building so that they formed a backdrop for a Ronald Reagan puppet in the mock reenactment of the Statue of Liberty's birthday celebration. The tall ships were represented by a toy boat on a twelve-foot pole, and for the "spectacular fireworks" a garbage-collector puppet handed Reagan a five-and-dime sparkler. The president waved feebly as tiny sparks flickered from his hand and a facsimile of Lady Liberty was wheeled out in a rusty wheelbarrow. The community took great delight in mocking an administration that they perceived as hostile to their concerns. They saw Reagan as a president who represented only the wealthy and never supported aid to inner cities. Residents stopped their cars, honked their horns, and waved from their windows, as puppets and stilt dancers paraded through the neighborhood park.

The ragged aesthetics of the Bread & Puppet performance created a grotesque portrait of Reagan's America that was oddly reinforced by the inner-city landscape. The hand-painted lettering on the company's old touring school bus looked like a continuation of the graffiti on the walls of the playground where it was parked. Drawn into the satirical critique of the performance, the Roxbury audience seemed to be making their own connections between their urban problems and the hard times depicted in the show. People in the crowd murmured words of appreciation in the call and response style of a Gospel church service, and a little boy expressed his enthusiasm in a postshow improvisation that may or may not have expressed his political biases. Borrowing the Ronald Reagan mask and two fake butcher knives from the prop truck behind the bus, he put on the face of the president and with a shiny blade in each hand began chasing the kids in the neighborhood. Seldom has the threat of budget cuts been presented in visual metaphor with such ferocious glee.

Bread & Puppet offers a glimpse into the type of audience-performer rapport that characterized now vanished popular entertainments like vaudeville, medicine shows, and rural one-ring circuses. Working-class immigrants would crowd into vaudeville theaters to see ethnic comedians reenact their shared struggle to adapt to a hostile urban environment. Entire towns would come out to listen to a traveling medicine show barker make his comic pitch. The nineteenth-century circus clown Dan Rice turned his tent into a town meeting where he mocked the pretensions of local and national politicians in a red-white-and-blue flag suit that was the forerunner of Peter Schumann's stilt-dancing Uncle Sam.

Today some theater performers still manage to capture a degree of comic intimacy, but America's most successful mainstream comic artists like Johnny Carson, Jay Leno, and David Letterman deliver their material in a detached, ironic style that dilutes the urgency of their comic themes. To varying degree the smoothness of their delivery calms the audience into accepting the incongruities that fuel their punch lines. It is no coincidence that America's most successful comics have found their mass-market niche on late-night network television. Their reassuring comic styles tranquilize the public in preparation for a good night's sleep. This is in sharp contrast to socially engaged comics who, in the tradition of Bread & Puppet, use laughter to unsettle the audience into an awareness that something is wrong. While subversive laughter can be found throughout America, its power is diluted when performers begin adopting the tone of detachment that is key to mainstream commercial success.

The cultural dynamics that have contributed to the increasing detachment of American comedy can be seen in the evolution of Afro-American humor. Some of America's most fiery comic artists have come from the black community. Their heritage of persecution has helped fuel a comic tradition that is emotionally engaged. Racial discrimination has taken many forms throughout America's history, and Afro-Americans, like oppressed blacks in South Africa, have turned to humor as both a weapon and a shield against the tyranny of racism. The unmitigated rage of black comedians, however, has never been acceptable to mainstream white audiences, so the comic power of Afro-American artists has been rechanneled into a variety of styles that are more palatable to mass-market audience of whites. The historical trajectory of Afro-American comedy is as twisted and fraught with paradox as the race's still unfinished struggle for genuine political justice.

The laughter of Afro-Americans is spiked with the collective memory of slavery. No other genre of American popular comedy is as directly linked to freedom and the struggle to survive. Richard Pryor made that connection explicit in his 1976 comedy album, *Bicentennial Nigger*, in which he announced that the country was "celebrating two hundred years of white folks kicking ass." In the epilogue to the album Pryor plays the role of an African who has just arrived in America on a slave ship. He mouths the words of the stereotypically docile black man trying to please his white masters, but the ingratiating laughter that punctuates each line is charged with an irony that grows increasingly grim.

"I'm so thrilled to be over here in America . . . They brought me over here in a boat. There was four hundred of us come over here. (LAUGH) Three hundred and sixty of us died on the way over here. (LAUGH) That just thrills me so. (LAUGH) I don't know. You white folks is just so good to us. (LAUGH) Got over here. Another twenty of us died from disease. (LAUGH) Then they split us all up. (LAUGH) Took my mama over that way. Took my wife that way. Took my kids over yonder. (LAUGH) I'm just so happy. (LAUGH) I don't know what to do if I don't get two hundred and twenty more years of this. (LAUGH) You all proba-bly done forgot about it. *But I ain't never gonna forget it.*"

Pryor's foreboding punch line is spoken in a deep, angry voice that has cast off the facade of phony servility and demands respect. His vocal metamorphosis is foreshadowed by the pro-gressively ominous irony in the laughter that undercuts each phrase of the monologue. With the shifting tones of this brief performance, Pryor recapitulates the evolution of Afro-American laughter in this country, from the minstrel show figure of Jim Crow to the film comedian Steppin Fetchit and the radio-televi-sion stardom of Amos and Andy. In Pryor's comic vision the docile troupe of domesticated entertainers have grown fangs and threaten to turn on the masters who laughed at their helpless-ness. His transformation turns the racist stereotypes inside out and releases a pent-up rage that had festered behind the mask of black comedy for centuries.

Pryor's artful reversal in the slave monologue mirrors the trajectory of his career. He started out in the sixties with a safe, nonthreatening style of comedy that he felt would appeal to mainstream America. In 1970 he became frustrated by the limita-tions of this approach, dropped his facade of reassuring detach-ment, and pioneered a much more directly confrontational style of Afro-American humor that made it clear he wasn't going to forget "two hundred years of white folks kicking ass." Pryor's breakthrough success paved the way for others to smash the taboos that had been imposed on Afro-American comedy by the commercial constraints of the entertainment industry.

These taboos have their origins in the era of slavery, when the overt expression of resentment could have cost blacks their lives. In spite of the dangers, slaves developed a rich comic tradition that satirized the system under which they were forced to live. Their humor was passed on in an underground oral tradition of songs, dances, and joke telling. Former slave Frederick Douglass recorded one of the tunes slaves sang to mock the stinginess of their masters:

> *We bake de bread*
> *Dey give us de crust*
> *We sif de meal*
> *De gib us de huss*
> *We peel de meat*
> *Dey gib us de skin*
> *And dat's de way*
> *Dey takes us in.*[2]

Singing comic songs like these while no whites were around enabled slaves to vent their aggressive impulses without suffering the consequences of their masters' anger. In this sense the joking might actually have saved some lives. Sometimes the slaveholders did witness the mocking behavior but were too dim-witted to realize the humor was directed at them. This enabled the slaves to enjoy a double joke at their masters' expense. According to the testimony of ex-slaves, black parodies of plantation ballroom dances were among the satirical messages that whites had difficulty decoding: "Us slaves watched white folks' parties where the guests danced a minuet and then paraded in a grand march, with the ladies and gentlemen going different ways and then meeting again, arm in arm, and marching down the center together. Then we'd do it too, but we used to mock 'em every step. Sometimes the white folks noticed it, but they seemed to like it. I guess they thought we couldn't dance any better."[3]

The slave's assumption was right. Whites didn't give their slaves credit for being able to do much of anything properly. In the decades before the Civil War, while slaves mocked their masters both openly and in secret, whites developed an enduring and degrading form of popular entertainment based on their ludicrous belief in the ineptitude of the black race. This was the minstrel show, in which white actors painted their faces black and made audiences laugh by portraying black characters like Jim Crow as ignorant, incompetent fools. These minstrel shows were the most successful theatrical spectacles in nineteenth-century America. They were full of songs and dances that expressed the white artist's twisted view of the black's nature. The performers didn't realize that some of the minstrel show dances, like the cakewalk, looked silly because slaves had invented them to parody the pretensions of their masters. This led to the ironic situation of whites dressed as blacks mocking black dances originally created by blacks to parody the dances of high-society white folk.

In an act of cultural castration white minstrel performers disengaged black humor from the harsh reality that engendered it. The emotional intensity and visceral power of genuine slave humor was too disturbing for the white public to accept, so it was watered down to a far less passionate form of comic expression where black men never talked back to whites, slaves were too stupid to revolt, and huge choruses of Afro-Americans were content to laugh and sing without ever complaining about their lot in life.

The minstrel show was one of the first significant uses of comic detachment to dilute the power of American popular comedy. The performers disengaged themselves from the social and emotional implications of their material. The resulting performance was more restrained and less threatening to the subjects being ridiculed, neutralizing the potentially subversive elements of the satiric impulse and rendering them harmless. The rich and deeply felt tradition of black slave humor was diluted, diminished, and de-fanged by minstrel performers who catered to the prejudices and fears of mainstream white audiences.

While minstrel shows maintained the uninhibited comic energy that nineteenth-century whites associated with slave culture, the performances diffused and redirected that energy so it seemed to have no point and could be laughed off as a childish diversion. Controlling the image of the black race gave whites a sense of safely distant superiority. They could laugh at Afro-Americans fighting with each other for ridiculous reasons and conveniently ignore the possibility that their real anger might be directed at the whites that had enslaved them. In his autobiography Mark Twain describes the absurd argument between the black-faced Tambo and Interlocutor that occurred with some variations in almost every minstrel show. "Sometimes the quarrel would last five minutes, the two contestants shouting deadly threats in each other's faces with the noses not x inches apart, the house shrieking with laughter all the while at this happy and accurate imitation of the familiar negro quarrel."[4] In sketches like this the wrath of the Afro-American was rendered harmless by white performers who parodied the race's fury in a context that robbed it of its true meaning.

Although the theatrical appropriation of the black persona was perpetrated by white artists who were probably unaware of its underlying social ramifications, the rise of the minstrel show did have an insidious long-term effect on the Afro-American comic tradition. Not only had their caricatures robbed black men of their dignity in the minds of white audiences, but the stereotypes they perpetuated were so enduring that black artists had to re-create them if they had any hopes of making a living as comic entertainers. White audiences grew accustomed to the stereotypical black buffoons, and up until the middle of the twentieth century Afro-American comedians had to imitate the white man's parody of their race to achieve commercial success.

When black performers began forming their own minstrel troupes in the late nineteenth century, they had to darken their skin with blackface and perform in the caricatured style that had been fixed in the public's consciousness by white minstrel troupes. The stereotypes continued into the twentieth century. When the great Afro-American comedy duo of Bert Williams and George Walker began headlining variety and vaudeville theaters, they wore blackface and billed themselves as "Two

Real Coons" to distinguish themselves from the white "coons" to which audiences had become accustomed.

Williams eventually became a star of the Ziegfeld Follies, but the demeaning persona he was compelled to assume onstage was an affront to his dignity. He could never speak directly about his feelings during his performance, but the subtext of his comic material spoke eloquently of the black man's confused identity. He got a lot of laughs by wiggling his eyes during the trademark song that closed his act. The goofiness of his mugging was heightened by the contrast between the bulging whites of his eyes and his burnt-cork makeup, but the lyrics of the tune told a sadder story of a man who had lost his self-esteem. Williams had written the song himself and entitled it "Nobody." He made the audience laugh by detaching himself from the suffering he had put into the words and delivering them with a carefree and silly nonchalance.

> *When life seems full of clouds and rain*
> *And I am filled with naught but pain*
> *Who soothes my thumpin' bumpin' brain?*
> *Nobody.*
> *When winter comes with snow and sleet*
> *And me with hunger and cold feet*
> *Who says "Here's two bits. Go and eat."*
> *Nobody.*
>
> . . . .
>
> *When I try hard and scheme and plan*
> *To look as good as ere I can*
> *Who says, "Look at that handsome man."*
> *Nobody."* [5]

Williams's nonchalant style had something in common with the distancing techniques used by white actors in the minstrel shows. Like them, he soothed the sting of Afro-American suffering by presenting it as something that could easily be laughed away. He separated pain from its disturbing consequences. Still, his comedy was not entirely whitewashed. It was riddled with troubling hints of doubt and ambiguity that white minstrels eliminated completely from their routines. Williams's accomplishment becomes clearer when one compares the plaintive comic intelligence of "Nobody" to the mindlessness of a typical minstrel ditty:

> *Me sing all day*
> *Me sleep all night*
> *Me have no care*
> *Me sleep is light*
> *Me tink no what tomorrow bring*
> *Me happy so me sing.*[6]

The growing popularity of genuine Afro-American performers like Williams did not limit the success of white racial caricaturists. The stereotypes of happy, hapless Negroes soothed the racial anxieties of the American majority and took on a life of their own that transcended the skin color of the actors who performed them. The black actor Lincoln Perry became a film star in the 1920s and 1930s with his slow-walking molasses-mouthed portrayal of the chicken-brained Steppin Fetchit. During the same decades a white duo, Freeman Gosden and Charles Correll, achieved stardom on national radio with their glib characterizations of two Afro-American bumpkins named Amos and Andy.

In 1929 Gosden and Correll embarked on a live stage tour of the Amos and Andy show that was extraordinarily self-conscious in its use of detachment as a comic technique. The performance began with an empty proscenium and offstage recordings of Amos and Andy radio routines. Eventually the two white actors entered and performed a skit in the same exaggerated black dialect they used on the radio. To highlight their virtuosity as racial ventriloquists, Gosden and Correll surprised the audience with a magical transformation during which they tossed off their kinky black wigs, stripped away the shabby outer garments that had concealed their tuxedos, and stepped into a pool of light that changed their skin tone from black to white. They accompanied the metamorphosis with upper-class white dialogue but then switched again to black vernacular without changing costumes. This heightened the comedy by presenting the spectacle of white aristocrats in morning suits speaking and acting like dim-witted, lower-class darkies. The audiences roared with laughter.

No theatrical exhibition could have more bluntly demonstrated the white man's manipulation of the black man's image. Gosden and Correll were displaying the masterful control they had perfected over the Afro-American caricature. They could turn it on and off at will. Not only had the black man's voice been trivialized and demeaned, it had been disembodied as well. Audiences could hear a pale facsimile of black speech from the mouths of white men who had written the script, appropriated the accent, and rendered the black man himself entirely superfluous. Even the imitation black makeup was gone. Audiences could sit back and laugh innocently at the ease with which Afro-Americans were being systematically erased from the American theatrical landscape.[7]

The popularity of Amos and Andy continued into the fifties, when two black actors were hired to play the roles on television. The actors were given direction by two white stars on how to perform the "black" mannerisms and dialects they had created for the comic pair. It wasn't until the sixties and seventies that Afro-American comedians were able to redefine the image of their race in the popular media. Before that comedians like Redd Foxx, Godfrey Cambridge, and Moms Mabley had offered genuine portraits of Afro-American life, but they played primarily for black audiences. These segregated performances displayed a comic verve and involvement that was absent when Afro-Americans imitated the caricatures of their race that proved to be so successful throughout the first half of the twentieth century.

Moms Mabley personified the emotionally engaged style of Afro-American humor that flourished from the twenties through the sixties. She performed in Harlem and on the black vaudeville and nightclub circuit for audiences that responded warmly to her references to their common predicament in the world of whites. Mabley assumed the kind of cozy, confidential tone that made the public feel as if they were part of her large, extended family. She would sit down on a stool and say, "I got something to tell you," as if she were giving them some intimate advice. Her fans often

called out to her during the show, voicing their approval and support as if they were engaged in a two-way confessional dialogue
rather than a comedy routine. In her hands a monologue becomes
a communal ritual of inclusion. "Thank you, thank you, children,
and home folks and kin folks," she begins. "I'm telling you I'm
glad to be at home and I had my first real meal in months (laughter). My niece cooked me some hog mawwws (laughter), and
some cracklin' corn b-r-e-a-d (laughter) and a few greens on the
side (laughter). Thank the lord I'm talking to people that know
what I'm talking about" (laughter and applause).[8]

Mabley's rock solid sense of black identity contrasted
sharply with the confused portrait of the race communicated in
mainstream comedy by comedians who would not go beyond
stereotypes divorced from any real-life experience. In the sixties
Dick Gregory became one of the first Afro-Americans to challenge these stock characterizations by speaking directly to white
audiences in a voice that made no effort to mask the authenticity
of its black identity. Moms Mabley performed a few times on
national television and in Playboy clubs, but Gregory was able to
make the crossover more successfully because of his cooler, more
intellectual approach to comedy. His wry, rational style appealed
to a nation that was gingerly beginning to come to terms with
the civil rights movement, but it was not until Richard Pryor's
meteoric rise to fame in the seventies that mainstream mass-
media audiences were truly exposed to the fiery core of Afro-
American humor.

Richard Pryor had entered show business trying to placate
white audiences with a subdued comic persona that gently poked
fun at shallow racial stereotypes, but by the peak of his career he
was mocking racism with an impassioned delivery that burned
through the hypocrisies of prejudice like an acetylene torch.
Pryor's success in films and concerts led to a network television
series in 1977, but his comic persona was too hot for NBC executives, who tried to censor his material and eventually canceled the
show after only four weekly installments. Pryor's comedy was
disturbing because it touched nerves of Afro-American pain and
anger that had never before been exposed to mass audiences. He

was often forced to compromise his work by the commercial demands of film and television producers, but his three major concert films capture Pryor's comic rage in all its unleashed fury.

Pryor creates laughter out of raw emotional experiences. Raised in his grandmother's brothel in New Orleans, Pryor had firsthand exposure to the black subculture of prostitutes, drug addicts, and pimps. In an astonishing sketch about a junkie named Motif, Pryor takes his audience into the inner workings of an addict's mind. He incisively exposes the man's humiliation, disappointment, and bewilderment in what amounts to a comic autopsy of despair.

His portrayals of America's underclass connect his characters' personal misery to the failures of American democracy. With only a few disjointed phrases, Pryor poignantly suggests his character Motif's frustrated past of unemployment and rejection. "Work ethic . . . you can't have a job, but you can fill out the application . . . Talk about I ain't responsible. I got a $200-a-day habit and I ain't missed a payment."[9] The fragmented speech patterns of the junkie are followed by a pantomime of his physical reaction to a drug injection that is simultaneously terrifying and hilarious. For almost a minute Pryor lapses into total silence, drooping forward and sinking almost to the floor in a stupor of ecstatic desperation. Catching himself just before he hits the ground, Pryor reverses the fall and lifts himself up, only to tilt backward like a rubber mannequin with no center of gravity. Motif is teetering on the edge of death, and Pryor uses comedy to illuminate his struggle to survive the drug habit that plagues the black underclass in America.

At the visceral center of Pryor's comic genius is a life-asserting scream that signals a refusal to submit to the tyrannies of drug addiction and racism. Like the Afro-Americans he portrays, Pryor has personally confronted these demons and draws material from his experience that gives authenticity to his observations. In his *Live in Concert* film, the audience can literally hear him screaming for his life. Pryor jokes about his terror when he awoke one morning and his oscilloscope reading was approaching the fatal horizontal line. He responds to the machine's indifference

with a long, piercing scream of anger, fear, and pain that sets the
oscilloscope bouncing back to life. The scream is a funny and
defiant declaration of his will to stay alive and beat the drug habit
that put him in the hospital

The echoes of that scream are heard frequently in all of
Pryor's performances. Even on his aborted television program, he
found a moment to let out an uncensored yell. Playing a militant
activist, Pryor condensed the man's speech to a single word:
"Black!" He stretched the word into a long, passionate scream
that released all its suppressed implications. Everything that
blacks were forbidden to say for centuries came roaring out of
that one-syllable assault on the censors.

Another variation of Pryor's primal scream appeared in his
concert film *Live on Sunset Strip*. Made shortly after his recovery
from a drug-related accident, the film shows how the comedian
turns a life-threatening experience into a comic masterpiece
about the nature and causes of drug addiction. On June 9, 1980,
Pryor suffered third-degree burns over most of his body when a
mixture of ether and cocaine blew up in his bedroom. He ran
down the street in flames and by the time he was hospitalized
doctors described his chances for survival as slim. Pryor's reenactment of the incident is the climax of his film. Remembering
the moment when he first realized he was on fire, he moves from
contentment to panic in mid-sentence. "You know what, that
looks like FIRE!!!!!" His scream erupts from the gut and expresses the awakening of a drug addict to the consequences of his self-
destructive impulses.

Again Pryor compresses a multitude of meanings into a single, heartfelt yell. When he screams, "FIRE!" Pryor is sounding
an alarm that goes beyond his personal pain to call attention to
the fires of racial violence, economic injustice, and drug addiction.
These were the themes of the comic sketches that built to the
film's climactic scream, and Pryor structures his material to suggest that they are all linked together. He jokes about a visit to the
Arizona State Penitentiary and wonders why 80 percent of the
inmates are black in a state that doesn't seem to have any black
people anywhere else. Later Pryor draws an implicit parallel to

the incarceration of blacks and the caging of animals in a zoo. He compares the power and beauty of the free wildlife he encountered in Africa with the pitiful conditions of lions and monkeys in the zoos.

Shifting his focus back to America, Pryor delves into a routine about drug addiction, another form of enslavement that, like time in the penitentiary, is experienced disproportionately by Afro-Americans. Pryor comically dissects the mechanisms of addiction by giving a voice to his cocaine pipe. When his friend Jim Brown tries to intimidate the comic into breaking his habit, the pipe comes to his rescue. "Don't listen. He's trying to fuck with you," implores the instrument of his addiction. "I understand, Rich . . . It's your life. They don't have the right to fuck with you. Where were they when you needed them? Come on in here with me, cause I love you." Lulled into a somnambulant stupor by the seductive voice of his pipe, Pryor can be awakened only by the physical pain of fire. "Fire is inspirational," he announces. "When that fire hits your ass, that will sober your ass up quick."

Pryor's scream of fire epitomized his uncompromising commitment to comedy as a survival tactic. Like his televised shout of "black" and his inarticulate yell at the fading oscilloscope, all of Pryor's comic screams condense pain, terror, and hope into a bolt of vocal energy that keeps him alive. When the audience laughs at these cries from the heart they are affirming his will to persevere. These screams defined Pryor's comic persona, but like so much of American comedy, their sound was eventually muted by the demands of commercial success in the American marketplace. His silly feature films, written and directed by whites, showed him battling against the Ku Klux Klan, unemployment, racial injustice, and white police officers, but the roles trivialized his real comic fire. They captured some elements of Pryor's comic rage, but his heartfelt screams became more and more distant until the advent of muscular dystrophy led to his semiretirement.

The same evolution toward detachment can be seen in the career of Eddie Murphy. Murphy started out doing live performances that imitated Pryor's ferocity in a style that often exploded

the stereotypes of racism. He was particularly effective in performing the reverse racial stereotypes that Pryor had pioneered, making whites laugh at themselves as nasal-voiced weaklings intimi-
dated by the power and sexuality of a truly liberated Afro-
American. These caricatures reincarnated the Steppin Fetchit figure as an ineffectual, cowardly white man. The symbolic reversal
of power is reminiscent of the white comic caricatures performed
by black actors in South Africa who use parody to diminish the
stature of their oppressors. On *Saturday Night Live*, Murphy went
even further than Pryor in exposing the absurdity of past black
stereotypes by performing parodies of characters like Buckwheat.
Murphy's feature film comedies like *Beverly Hills Cop* and *Trading
Places* also played with racial role reversals, but they were performed in a clean-cut, safely predictable style that made mass
audiences feel comfortable. The formula of reversals became so
familiar that some of his films (*Beverly Hills Cop* and *Forty Eight
Hours*) were followed by sequels that were little more than
warmed-over rehashes of his past adventures. On the surface Murphy's comic style is always emotionally outrageous, but its core of
genuine feeling has gradually become as hollow as his trademark
grinning laugh.

The empty detachment of Murphy's comic persona can be
seen most clearly in his concert film *Raw*, where he creates shallow comic stereotypes of women and homosexuals that steer his
material away from the hard-hitting confrontational themes that
made Pryor's live concerts so dangerous, frightening, and true.
Murphy rarely mentions racism and seems to inhabit an exalted
realm of power and sarcasm. There is no sense of authentic suffering beneath his slick delivery, no real threat to his survival, so
the laughter he elicits is shallow and easy, relying on acceptance
of the stereotypes he sets up as straw opponents. Because nothing
crucial is at stake, there is no need for Murphy to scream from
the gut as Pryor did before him. Supremely self-confident,
Murphy has exchanged the anguished comic scream for the cool
ironic guffaw.

Murphy projects the image of an Afro-American who is so
sure of himself that he never has to worry about anything. He can

talk about prejudice and racism, but there is never any real threat that it can wound him, so black and white audiences can relax, as if Murphy's stage presence reassures them of what they wanted to believe all along, that racism doesn't really exist anymore, at least not in a form that can hurt anybody. Murphy's super-cool detachment soothes his audience into complacency, where Pryor's jittery vulnerability once disturbed them into confronting their worst fears.

As cool as Murphy is, another Afro-American humorist takes the style of detachment to even further extremes. Bill Cosby is probably the only Afro-American comic who earns more money and reaches a wider audience than Murphy, and he owes his commercial success in no small part to his low-keyed and reassuring comic persona. In *Raw* Murphy does a telling imitation of Cosby, chastising him for using foul language in his routines. Cosby's slow, deliberate phrasing gives the impression of a reasonable man who thinks out every word before he says it. This delivery separates Cosby even further from the emotional volatility of a comic like Pryor, who screams before he thinks. Like Murphy, Cosby has his moments of emotional outburst, but they are always circumscribed by rational boundaries that make him acceptable to even the most conservative mainstream audiences. Cosby's television family was a natural extension of his non-threatening character. In his top-rated sitcom, they lived in a safe, middle-class world that had barely been touched by prejudice or the pain and suffering of racism. Although discrimination was sometimes raised as a topic of conversation, its impact was diminished by the gentrified context in which it was discussed.

Afro-Americans are not the only emotionally committed comic artists who become more distanced from their material when they achieve mainstream success. Women comedians also follow the typically American career trajectory from engagement to detachment. The television program that eventually replaced Cosby as America's number one prime-time program is *Roseanne*. In the eighties Roseanne Barr created a comic persona that expressed the pent-up rage of housewives and particularly blue-collar women. The situation comedy written around this character climbed to the top of the national television ratings, but in the process of achieving mainstream popularity Roseanne mellowed her character's confrontational comic delivery. She still succeeds in smashing old television stereotypes of submissive housewives and has devoted episodes to exploring the harsh economic realities of today's America, but her abrasive fury has been tempered by comforting doses of sentimentality. To see the effect of popularization on Roseanne's comedy, one need only compare her sitcom to her nightclub routine and television appearances outside of prime time.

Roseanne's live comedy act began as a brazen attempt to transform the stereotype of a meek housewife into an all-powerful "domestic goddess." She struck a chord of recognition among middle- and lower-class women who did not identify with the media's representation of feminism but could connect to the raw frustration expressed in Roseanne's raunchy routines. Roseanne Barr came from the brazen tradition of American women comics from Fanny Brice to Mae West to Lily Tomlin who have tested the limits of public tolerance for their ironic commentary on the inequalities of the sexes. Roseanne brought this tradition to new levels of provocation in her comedy club denunciation of the idea that women were fighting for the right to engage in military combat missions. "Yeah, like I want to go over there and die for your racist, sexist country where I don't even have equal rights."

Roseanne was at her most subversive when she sang a comic version of the national anthem at a baseball game, but her humor backfired. The American public did not react kindly to her suggestion that there was a hint of absurdity in the time-honored male ritual of saluting the flag before getting drunk and shouting obscenities at pampered millionaire athletes. The furor stirred up by the incident reflects the visceral levels her comedy is capable of reaching. "I was really scared," recalled Roseanne. "I thought they were going to fuck me over, you know, brand me a communist and do the whole blacklist thing to me, kill me or what. I had so many death threats, you wouldn't believe it."[10]

Because of the constraints of commercial television, where a reassuringly detached comic style is a prerequisite for success, nothing as controversial as the national anthem satire has ever been included in Roseanne's network sitcom. On television Roseanne's comic rage is always tempered by the certainty that eventually she will stand by her family. In one episode she actually gets down on her hands and knees in front of her husband and begs his forgiveness for being irrational.

The more emotionally volatile comedy that Roseanne performs beyond the confines of her weekly series is far less tame. In clubs she puts down male hecklers with a ferocity that leaves the audience wondering if real violence might break out. On late-night and cable television appearances Roseanne is equally unrestrained in playing out the comedy of sexual role reversals. Some of her most trenchant sketches ridicule famous American patriarchs from their wives' point of view. Playing Mary Todd Lincoln, Roseanne lashes out wildly at the president who freed the slaves but drove his wife mad. "You're not a man, you're a joke," shouts Roseanne as Mrs. Lincoln, hitting old Abe with a chair, grabbing him by the throat, and finishing him off with an insult. "You're a lousy lay."

In her 1987 HBO special, then President Ronald Reagan is subjected to similar ridicule. Scoffing at Nancy Reagan's remark that she and Ronnie still play games in bed together, Roseanne imagines what kind of games the First Lady is referring to: "He farts and holds her head under the covers. Can you see that? 'Here's one for the Gipper, Nancy.'" Taken out of context Roseanne's attacks on Reagan and Lincoln might seem tasteless, but within the framework of her wider comic vision they reinforce the sense of empowerment she gives to her female fans. Sexual humor is a particularly potent weapon in the arena of gender politics, and Roseanne uses it shrewdly. She is an overweight woman whose career accomplishments and comic rhetoric coalesce to prove that women don't have to be young, beautiful, and submissive to succeed in a male-dominated society. She is constantly challenging male authority figures, in the fantasy of her comic routines and in the real world of the entertainment business, where her clout at forcing network executives to accede to her demands is legendary. Like Afro-American artists who use humor to subvert the tyrannical force of racism, Roseanne uses laughter to undermine the power of patriarchal mythology.

While Roseanne's weekly television series tends to dilute the emotional immediacy of women's humor, female artists who work in more intimate settings continue to demonstrate the power of laughter as a subversive influence in a society dominated by men. Innovative performers like Lily Tomlin, Ann Magnuson, Laurie Anderson, Karen Finley, and Reno use different degrees of emotional intensity to satirize American sexual stereotypes, but one of the most intriguing uses of contemporary women's humor can be seen in the work of an anonymous band of artists who call themselves the Guerrilla Girls.

Founded in 1985, the Guerrilla Girls are a collective of female visual and performance artists who use guerrilla comedy tactics to call attention to discrimination against women and minority groups in the art world. When the Guerrilla Girls make public appearances, the rationale behind the pun in their name becomes apparent. They always wear gorilla masks to preserve their anonymity and protect themselves from retribution by gallery owners and curators without a sense of humor. The wearing of the masks intensifies the interest of the public, which laughs appreciatively at the satirical slogans and slides that are part of a typical Guerrilla Girl presentation. One of their most popular comic creations is a poster of a naked woman wearing a gorilla mask that reads, "Does a girl have to get naked to get into the Met?" The message refers to the fact that 85 percent of the nudes in the Metropolitan Museum of Art in New York City depict female bodies, while only 5 percent of the artists represented in the Metropolitan's collection are women.

Different masked women represent the group at different performance lectures, and they refuse to reveal how many members are in the organization, but the number is probably in the hundreds. The unusual tactics of the collective invariably involve the audience in question-and-answer sessions that lead to improvised comedy amid the serious statistics. In addition to slides of their posters and flyers, the Guerrilla Girls arrive at their lectures with a bunch of bananas. The fruit is used to reward members of the audience for particularly insightful questions. Throwing bananas to individuals in the crowd highlights the interactive sense of inclusion that the comic agitators elicit from their public.

The tactics of the Guerrilla Girls can be traced back to the sixties, when agitprop guerrilla theater was used by counterculture protestors to demonstrate their opposition to the war in Vietnam, racial injustice, and discrimination against women. Laughter was one of the elements that united these performers and their audiences in a common cause. The most impassioned and enduring of the sixties guerrilla theater groups was the San Francisco Mime Troupe, which is still performing today. Like Afro-American humorists battling against the tyranny of racism and women comics assailing oppressive sexual politics, the Mime Troupe aimed their comedy at a repressive force that threatened their freedom—censorship. In 1965 the Mime Troupe, allied with the Berkeley Free Speech Movement, had been threatened with arrest if they followed through on their plans to perform an updated sixteenth-century Italian comedy called *Il Candelaio* in a city park. The department of parks and recreation had deemed the text obscene, but the Mime Troupe was convinced that the real reason for banning the play was its left-wing politics and criticism of the police. The stage was set for a confrontation that blurred the boundaries between comedy and political action.

Knowing they would be arrested, the Mime Troupe went ahead with their plans to perform and self-consciously staged their encounter with the police as a comic spectacle. Actors in the clown masks of the commedia dell'arte were led away by the police. Undeterred by the police officers' interruption of their original comedy, the actors reveled in the improvised creation of a new one, with the police as their straight men. "Ladies and gentleman," shouted the company director, Ronnie Davis, at the height of the confusion, "Il Troupo Di Mimo di San Francisco presents for your enjoyment this afternoon . . . AN ARREST!"

The audience jeered the police as if they were villains in a melodrama and shouted encouragement to the clowns, some of whom stayed in character during their forced walk from the outdoor stage to the paddy wagons. Many came prepared for the encounter and carried placards reading Mime Troupe Si! Park Commission No! Fights broke out. Journalists knocked off policemen's caps in the melee. The conflict between the clowns and the police was a physicalization of the tension between censorship and free speech. The audience participated joyfully in the slapstick battle against repression, and the performers responded with heightened comic bravado.

Public participation in the comedy did not end when Davis and his performers were taken to jail. Thousands of people contributed to the Mime Troupe's legal defense fund by showing up for a benefit concert that celebrated the actors' stand against censorship. Rock promoter Bill Graham produced the event, and entertainment was provided by the Grateful Dead (known then as the Warlocks), the Jefferson Airplane, and Lawrence Ferlinghetti. The Mime Troupe's defiant comedy had inspired San Francisco's seminal counterculture movements of psychedelic rock musicians, beat poets, and community activists to work together for a cause that reflected their shared belief in freedom of expression. Eventually the right to perform uncensored in the parks was granted to all theater groups, and the Mime Troupe still performs there every summer.

Nearly thirty years after their heated confrontation with city police, the San Francisco Mime Troupe continues to maintain an extraordinary rapport with its public. One of their recent satires, called *Steeltown*, was about unemployment in small-town America. When the show toured the Midwest, the actors handed out leaflets to workers outside factories and talked to them about the economic hard times they were all experiencing. The informal advertising continued in local bars, where troupe members found unemployed workers who were willing to talk about losing their jobs. The actors commiserated and got people laughing by singing some of the doo-wop harmonies from the musical numbers in their play. This kind of personal contact helped fill the theater with curious townspeople, some of whom had never seen a live play before. The comedy in the play elicited a laughter of recognition, and afterward audience members expressed surprise and delight at seeing people onstage whose stories were so much like their own.

Like the Bread & Puppet Theater, the San Francisco Mime Troupe has mocked America's injustices for over thirty years. Working on opposite coasts, the two groups specialize in an emotionally committed form of comedy that places a high priority on the involvement of spectators. Over the years the themes of their shows have ranged from war, unemployment, and hunger to racism, sexual prejudice, and drug addiction. Their comedy grew out of America's most painful problems, and they can be seen as low-tech, living newspapers that document the ongoing issues of their times. Collectively, along with socially engaged Afro-American and women humorists, their work represents a form of American documentary comedy that chronicles the dissenting voices of the country's least powerful citizens.

These forms of documentary comedy reflect America's democratic impulses at their most basic level. They represent attempts of marginalized citizens to assert their rights to equality, justice, and the pursuit of happiness. The subversive laughter generated by countless American humorists is a tribute to our collective resilience, even as that laughter is muffled by the mass media through which performances in this country are disseminated. Americans do not dismiss the truth expressed in these comic chronicles of injustice; we simply learn how to detach ourselves from their troubling implications by diluting their emotional impact.

More than any other culture in the world, Americans have skillfully perfected the techniques of distancing themselves from their own laughter. Comic performers like Lenny Bruce who challenge audiences to face the disturbing implications of their humor are limited to marginal venues. Americans have developed a complex structure of popular entertainment in which the pinnacle of a comic's success is his or her appearance on television talk shows or a starring role in a situation comedy. Both these formats are defined by an implicit aesthetic of comic detachment designed to minimize the emotional depth of a comic premise and promote the smooth delivery of reassuring punch lines.

As seen in the trajectory of Afro-American laughter from slave humor to minstrel shows to modern comics, and in the careers of individual artists like Roseanne Barr, American comedy tends to evolve toward ever-increasing modes of detachment. The lack of emotional engagement leaves America with mainstream comedy whose subversive and liberating power has been diminished. The culmination of this development toward increasingly anemic American humor is found in television talk shows where comedy is completely detached from any unpleasant implications and makes no attempt to engage the audience's emotions or social conscience.

The most important and influential representative of television talk show humor is Johnny Carson, whose slick delivery epitomizes American comic detachment at its most popular. Carson's phenomenal success was predicated on a technique that dulled the audience's emotional responses, encouraging them to stay at a safe, polite distance from their society's problems. An analysis of his performance style can reveal more about the nation's tastes and values than any poll or census. For thirty years Carson entertained nearly twenty million Americans a night. No comedian in our history could boast such consistent loyalty and mass audience appeal.

From 1962 to 1992 Carson was the quintessential American humorist, devoid of all subversive intentions or effects. He performed a nightly monologue of jokes about political corruption, homelessness, hunger, poverty, and war without ever suggesting that any of these issues should be a cause for concern. The secret to Carson's success was his unflappable congeniality. Nothing seemed to bother him. He never allowed the slightest hint of deeply felt emotion to cloud his sunny delivery. His mild brand of comic social criticism was spoken in the same easygoing tone he used to joke about Hollywood gossip, sex scandals, and fast-food restaurants.

This lumping together of the trivial and the profound was central to Carson's technique of emotional detachment. It reassured his audience that no problem was more troubling than the declining quality of McDonald's Big Macs. His glib one-liners shifted quickly from commentary on the Gulf War to the television ratings war at NBC, from factory closings and unemployment to game shows and movie stars. Occasionally he would say things that might be interpreted as scathingly satirical, but the blandness of his delivery negated the potential sting of his words. In a reference to Reagan's cuts of social welfare programs, Carson advised viewers to give their elderly relatives useful gifts, like "life-size replicas of their grandchildren made out of cat food."[11] When his studio audience booed his implication that the elderly were eating pet food, the comedian threw up his hands and said, "Don't blame me for the economy." Pulling back both physically and verbally from the response he had evoked, Carson maintained the emotional distance from his material that had been characteristic of his approach to comedy since the beginning of his career.

Carson's most effective technique for distancing his audience from the emotionally disturbing implications of his political humor was to distract them with an ongoing barrage of references to consumer products and famous entertainers. Name brands punctuated many of Carson's jokes, giving a comforting sense of familiarity to whatever subject he was discussing. The mention of political turmoil and social unrest was accompanied by corresponding comments about movie stars, pop musicians, and television celebrities. By the end of his monologue all the names had melted together into a banal stream of consumerism. Consciously blurring the distinction between the marketplace and the political arena for comic effect, Carson proposes a new soft drink called "Ayatollah cola" and envisions the participants in the Iran/Contra affair as characters in a TV miniseries. Entertainers, politicians, and commercial trademarks became interchangeable commodities in his rapid-fire summary of the day's events.

Carson's carefree comic litany was reinforced by the commercials that followed his monologue, promoting some of the same products he had talked about in his jokes. The upbeat parade of consumerism continued when his guests joined him at his desk to promote their movies, record albums, and books. The boundary between marketing and entertainment was nonexistent. When politicians like Nixon and Reagan appeared on Carson's show, the cultural confusion was intensified even further. They would exchange banal jokes with Carson as if budget deficits and nuclear weapons did not exist. Like all the rest of Carson's guests with something to sell, former and future presidents used his show as a platform for public relations. The atmosphere of comic detachment on the *Tonight Show* made it safe for a politician to appear without fear of being challenged to discuss emotionally charged political issues.

Ronald Reagan's 1972 appearance on the *Tonight Show* revealed an intriguing connection between the style of comic detachment that won ratings points for Carson and the rhetoric that eventually enabled the former movie star to win two landslide elections to the White House. Then-governor Reagan joked with Carson using a low-keyed, genial comic delivery that was remarkably similar to that of his host. Eight years later the same good-humored amiability helped Reagan win the presidency. Reagan's sense of humor was always cited as one of his great political assets, and he self-consciously used it to win the public's support, directing his writers to open all his speeches with a joke. His political colleagues acknowledged the importance of Reagan's jokes to his political image by quoting them endlessly in their tributes to him at the 1988 Republican national convention.

It has become a cliché to attribute Reagan's popular appeal to his skills as an actor, but few look beyond this superficial parallel to examine the particular type of acting technique in which Reagan excelled. He was not a tragedian, or leading man. His talents were best suited to light comedy, which is predicated on the actor's sense of lighthearted emotional detachment. An understanding of the remarkable similarities between Reagan's rhetoric and Carson's talk show delivery underscores the significance of comic detachment as a significant mode of American public discourse in the late twentieth century. Television audiences and voters found its appeal irresistible.

Like Carson, Reagan developed a comic tone that was perfectly suited to the electronically distanced medium of television. Using the techniques of light comedy he first learned in Hollywood films of the fifties, Reagan spoke to Americans in a style that seemed to make their troubles evaporate. His delivery imbued even the bleakest circumstances with a spirit of contagious optimism that eliminated the need to worry. Budget deficits disappeared with a smile. Economic inequities were rendered inconsequential by an upbeat spirit. Reagan accomplished all this with a speaking style that made shrewd use of comic detachment. He instinctively understood what Carson and other American comics had known for decades. The mainstream American public doesn't want to be disturbed by performers who display excessive amounts of emotional involvement. Jimmy Carter couldn't detach himself from the emotional burdens of his office, but Reagan achieved enormous popularity with a "teflon" personality that enabled him to maintain a healthy distance from his policy mistakes as well as his one-liners. Pundits who marveled at Reagan's ability to emerge untainted from the political scandals and blunders that surrounded his administration never made the connection between the president's persona and his shrewd use of comic detachment, but Reagan himself used humor quite deliberately.

Reagan's self-consciousness about the public's perception of his comic style was demonstrated by his quick retraction of a joke he made criticizing Michael Dukakis in the early weeks of the 1988 presidential campaign. Reagan had laughingly referred to Dukakis as an invalid in response to the controversy over the Democrat's medical history, but the president sensed immediately that the joke was inappropriate for his comic persona. "I don't think I should have said what I said. I was just trying to be funny and it didn't work." Like a stand-up comic trying out new material, Reagan swiftly summed up his audience's unfavorable response to the line and excised it from his act. Calling Dukakis an invalid was too personal and emotionally charged for the president's style, and he blithely disclaimed the joke as if it had been composed by a gag writer who had temporarily stepped out of line.

This strategy of detachment was also one of Carson's trademarks. No one was better than Carson at turning bad jokes to his advantage by wryly distancing himself from their consequences. As soon as he sensed that a line had not gone over well with the

studio audience, he would get them to laugh at his embarrass-
ment at being stuck with such poor material. "I knew that one
wouldn't work," he would say, winning the audience's sympathy
for his plight as he maintained a safe distance from the content of
his routine. Because it was created by a team of anonymous writers, Carson, like Reagan, did not have to accept responsibility for
its inadequacies.

The similarities between the performance style of the
Tonight Show host and that our fortieth president were made
most explicit whenever Carson impersonated Reagan in extended
comic sketches. Carson captured the president's personality with
an uncanny accuracy that owed much to the stylistic attributes
they naturally share. In a routine where Reagan invited Leonid
Brezhnev to a summit meeting in a hot tub, the Soviet leader dis-
cusses his wartime experience as a soldier in Leningrad. Carson's
incarnation of Reagan counters with his own military experience.
"I fought in *Hellcats of the Navy* for two hours and fifteen minutes." The sketch was not as farfetched as it seemed. Reagan often
boasted about how he developed a personal rapport with Soviet
leaders by telling them jokes. Carson did not have to stretch his
acting skills to deliver the line with the same carefree nonchalance that the real Reagan used when telling jokes to Brezhnev
and Gorbachev to lighten up their meetings. The comedian and
the president were operating on the same rhetorical wavelength.

Reagan also shared Carson's fondness for one-liners that
linked American politics with free enterprise and show business.
This was another form of comic detachment that distracted the
public from the emotional intensity of what was really being said.
Faced with troubling political issues, the president frequently
quoted motion pictures to give the situation the predictability of
a film that was sure to have a happy ending. "Go ahead, make my
day," borrowed from movie star and mayor Clint Eastwood,
became Reagan's ironic challenge to members of Congress who
proposed raising taxes to help the poor. At the 1988 GOP convention he urged George Bush to "go out there and win one for
the Gipper," likening the election to a Hollywood football game
by referring to his role in the Knute Rockne film biography.

At the same convention, a film biography of Reagan featured clips of the president praising free enterprise in a Ronald McDonald sweatshirt. Delegates in the crowd waved Reagan Country placards of the president in a cowboy hat. Borrowing the Hollywood cowboy imagery of a Marlboro cigarettes advertisement, the placard sums up Reagan's success at mixing the worlds of salesmanship, showmanship, and electioneering. The president's appearance at the convention blurred the boundaries between government, business, and entertainment with the same light-hearted tone of comic detachment employed by Carson when he joked about politics between commercial endorsements on the *Tonight Show.*

Given the similarities between the comic styles of Reagan and Carson, it is not surprising to learn that Carson's television director, Fred de Cordova, was also the director of the film comedy Reagan made in the fifties entitled *Bedtime for Bonzo.* This was the film in which Reagan stopped a chimpanzee on a window ledge from committing suicide by convincing him that the future would be brighter. At the 1988 Republican convention his soothing voice carried the same upbeat message. "Twilight? Not in America. Here it's a fresh sunrise everyday." Reagan made Americans feel good about themselves in the eighties with the same optimistic tones of detached humor that fueled his Hollywood career in light comedy.

Johnny Carson and Ronald Reagan served as role models for a generation of young comedians and political communicators. They shared a detached style of humor representative of America's tastes. Their decades of success in selling products and winning votes demonstrate how susceptible we all are to the power of laughter. Carson and Reagan employed a persuasive form of comic rhetoric that is the antithesis of subversive comedy. Instead of using laughter to defiantly mock injustice, they joked about the comic incongruities of our culture with a detachment that relieved both themselves and their audiences of any sense of responsibility for the social, political, and economic inequities of their times. Truly subversive laughter leaves the audience with an unsettling awareness that something is wrong and needs to be changed. The comforting brand of humor performed so skillfully and successfully by Reagan and Carson had the opposite effect of reassuring everyone that there was no real cause for alarm.

Driven by the demands of the mass media, most contemporary American comedy dilutes, commercializes, and diminishes laughter to the point where it loses its force as a weapon of dissent or challenge. America's instinctive need to laugh was demonstrated by the public's deep sense of devotion to a comedian like Carson. His retirement unleashed an astonishing outpouring of public affection. Carson was on the cover of major news weeklies and appeared on television constantly during his last weeks as host of the *Tonight Show*. It was as if the country's late-night viewers were losing a member of their family. They longed for him to give them some sign of affection or emotional involvement, but he kept his reserved stance and remained aloof up through the final show of his thirty-year career.

Like the villagers of Bali who gathered by firelight to watch their temple clowns, Americans were attracted to the collective sense of community established by Carson's nightly monologues. But while the Balinese were united by the warmth of torches in the temple courtyards, Americans were sitting in isolated bedrooms, huddled around the blue lights of their television tubes. They were drawn to Carson's comedy by the vestige of some primal need, but it had become less recognizable in America's disengaged electronic environment.

America is blessed with many subversive comic artists who link their art to survival, but they usually perform along the margins of society. Clowns visit hospitals to offer some remnant of ritual healing laughter to the sick. Rodeos employ clowns to save the lives of cowboys who fall off the backs of deadly Brahman bulls. For the most part, though, American comedy is an art of one-liners, the comic equivalent of the sound bite. With canned laughter as a primary expression of amusement, American mass audiences seem content with a detached style of laughter that voices little dissatisfaction with the status quo. David Letterman, who appears to be the successor to the late-night comedy throne, has a delivery that is even more ironic, cool, and detached than Carson's.

Only rarely do Americans have the opportunity to laugh with performers who use comedy to challenge the injustices that have accumulated around us. This style of defiant comedy is found at home among friends or at odd intervals on Vermont hillsides, in San Francisco parks, and even occasionally on television or movie screens. These occasional bursts of subversive humor are triggered by resistance to the forces of consumerism, racism, and technology. The laughter they evoke is the sound of democracy coming to terms with its flaws.

The method of America's most subversive comic heroes is similar to what great clowns employ around the world. They all use variations of the classic slapstick double take. In traditional comedy the double take occurs when the clown stops to look again at something he or she had passed by without noticing the first time around. The clown responds to the new observation with a sudden shift in behavior, like jumping to the rescue or running away. In *The Gold Rush* a double take sends Chaplin charging out of his cabin when he realizes his famished partner imagines that he is a chicken and is about to eat him alive.

Subversive forms of modern comedy elicit a subtler double take in the minds of the spectators. These mental double takes present the public with the irrationality of social conventions they had assumed to be reasonable, and shock them into taking a fresh look at their cultural assumptions. The nature of the double take matches the specific needs of each society, but in every case it undermines the stereotypes of a culture's mythology by rendering them absurd.

Laughter alone cannot free a society from the prison of its preconceptions, but cultures like Bali, Lithuania, and South Africa, which have integrated comic traditions into the fabric of daily life, have enjoyed some success in finding adaptive solutions to the problems of modern life. More fully industrialized cultures like Italy, Japan, and the United States, which have distanced themselves from the subversive power of humor, are less prone to transform the insights of comedy into widespread social benefits.

The degree to which laughter's power is acknowledged as an essential part of social and political intercourse varies widely across the globe. The Balinese incorporate comic performances into all their important civic and religious ceremonies and pay close attention to the implications of their clowning. Consequently, Bali's comic artists can be given some credit for the extraordinary resilience with which the island has maintained its traditions in the face of modern Western development. The United States is at the other end of the spectrum, as its truly subversive comedians play to small audiences, while its mainstream comedy is diluted to a level of banality that inspires no genuine change.

The through line that connects all these comic traditions goes beyond Chaplin's "attitude of defiance" to a deeper function of humor that can turn an audience of individuals into a community. The laughing resilience of the world's comic heroes defies the forces that threaten their freedom, humanity, and survival. But in waging a war of humor against the modern tyrannies of tourism, totalitarianism, racism, hypocrisy, conformity, and injustice, these clowns are agents of cohesion as well as subversion. They bring audiences together in intimate villages of common laughter. Traditional cultures like Bali, Lithuania, and South Africa use comedy to create a common spirit of resistance against outside invasions. In industrialized cultures like Italy, Japan, and the United States, humor can serve as an antidote to alienation. Even Johnny Carson's most tepid monologues created a bond among the twenty million people who heard them every night. By providing common targets for ridicule, contemporary clowns give audiences common ground for laughter and free them from the isolation that pervades so much of modern life.

The global persistence of laughter as an adaptive response to human hardship makes one suspect that at its most visceral level comedy is linked to our species' instinct to survive. As great clowns like Chaplin have proven, a universal thread links our common sense of humor to our common sense of humanity. A double take can set off a subversive chain reaction that unites an audience in collective protest against the stifling social and political forces of our times. Whether the jokes are told in Balinese, Lithuanian, Zulu, Italian, Japanese, or English, the things that strike us as funny have the power to set us free.

Notes

Chapter 1   Prologue

1. Charles Chaplin, *My Autobiography* (New York, 1984), p. 303.

2. Ibid., pp. 303–4.

3. All quotes from Bidon and other members of Archaos are taken from personal interviews conducted in London in October 1991.

Chapter 2   Sacred Laughter in Bali

1. Ni Made Wiratini, in her unpublished thesis on the Condong female servant character in *ardja*, suggests convincingly, "The condong may act as a model figure for Balinese women, advocating equality with men in the Balinese communal structure, especially in present times. Her intelligence and authority indicate the changing social status of women in contemporary Balinese society." "Gambuh and Calonarang" (thesis, UCLA, Los Angeles, 1991).

2. Clifford Geertz, *Negara: The Theatre State in Nineteenth Century Bali* (Princeton, 1980).

Chapter 3   Revolutionary Laughter in Lithuania

1. All quotes in this chapter are taken from personal interviews conducted by the author.

Chapter 4   Ridiculing Racism in South Africa

1. From *Sophiatown*, a documentary film produced in 1987 by Channel 4 in London.

Chapter 5   Clowns and Popes in Italy

1. Claudio Meldolesi, *Su un Comico in Rivolta: Dario Fo Il Bufaloe Il Bambino* (Rome, 1978), p. 164.

2. Dario Fo, from introduction to *Knock, Knock, Who's There?* (Milan, 1973), p. 11. Cited in *File on Dario Fo*, edited by Tony Mitchell (London, 1989), p. 45.

3. *File on Dario Fo*, p. 45.

4. Ibid., p. 100.

Chapter 6   Mocking Conformity in Japan

1. *Japan Times*, February 14, 1992, p. 3.

Chapter 7   America's Comedy of Detachment

1. Peter Schumann, *Bread & Puppet* (Burlington, Vt., 1985), p. 10.

2. *The Life & Times of Frederick Douglass*, reprinted (New York, 1962), pp. 146–47.

3. Lawrence Levine, *Black Culture and Black Consciousness* (New York, 1977), p. 17.

4. Joseph Boskin, *Sambo: The Rise and Demise of an American Jester* (Oxford, 1986), p. 83.

5. Ann Charters, *Nobody: The Story of Bert Williams* (New York, 1970), pp. 135–36.

6. Boskin, *Sambo*, p. 74.

7. Melvin P. Ely, *The Adventures of Amos 'n' Andy: A Social History of an American Phenomenon* (New York, 1992), pp. 60–63.

8. Levine, *Black Culture and Black Consciousness*, p. 363.

9. From the 1983 concert film, *Richard Pryor Here and Now*.

10. Frank Swertlow, "Big," *L.A. Style*, September 1992.

11. Carson's monologue, *The Tonight Show*, September 16, 1982.

Index

Abortion, 120

Accidental Death of an Anarchist, 122–25

Adapt or Dye, 94–97

Africa. *See* South Africa

African National Congress (ANC), 79, 80, 82–84, 89, 102

African National Congress Youth League, 99

Afrikaans settlers, 89–90, 98

Afro-American humor, 180–93

Aleksynas, Kostas, 52–53

Amos and Andy show, 186–87

ANC. *See* African National Congress (ANC)

Anderson, Laurie, 196

Anom, Ibu, 13, 15

Anom, Ida Bagus, 44

Apartheid, 86–88, 90, 92, 94, 103

Archaos, xviii, 4–10

Ardja (all-female temple love stories), 32–35, 209n

Aristophanes, 2

Artimo, 102

Asakusa, 143, 144–45

Attitude of defiance, 3–4, 207–208

Audience with Evita, An, 97–99, 103

Awakening, The, 56–57

Bali
    ardja (all-female temple love stories) in, 32–35
    author's experiences in, ix, 13–17
    bondres clowns in, 26
    clown interloper in temple festivals in, 17–19, 176–77
    cosmology of good and evil in, 20–23, 29, 45
    Djimat's troupe in, 13–16
    frog dance in, 13, 15–16
    Hindu-Buddhist religion in, 17, 19, 22, 38
    history of, 21–22, 29–30
    penasar clowns in, 20–21, 26, 33, 36, 39, 44
    politics in humor of, 19–20, 34–44
    polyglot fluency of clowns in, 22, 31
    prembon in, 32
    sex in humor of, 30–32, 33, 35
    shadow puppet plays (*Wayang Kulit*), 24–25, 39
    Sidhya Karya in, 26–27, 28, 42–43
    significance of clowns in, 43–45
    street pageant of Rangda and Barong, 23
    topeng (masked performance) in, 25–32, 40, 41–43
    topeng pajegan in, 27–28, 41–43
    topeng panca in, 29–30
    tourism in, 17–22, 26, 37–38, 43
    view of birth in, 25
    and Westernization, 17–25, 37–39, 41, 43–45, 208

Balinese National Academy of the Arts, 39

Bandem, I Made, 38–41, 44

Banyan tree, 38

Barnum, P. T., 172

Barong, 23

Barr, Roseanne, 193–96

Beckett, Samuel, 64

Bedtime for Bonzo, 205

Beirut hostage crisis, 125

Berkeley Free Speech Movement,
     197

Beverly Hills Cop, 192

Bezuidenhout, Evita, 94–99, 102,
     103

Bicentennial Nigger, 180–81

Bidon, Pierrot, 4–5, 8

Biko, Steve, 91

Birth control, 31–32, 120

Birth of the Giullàre, 111, 113

Blacks. *See* Afro-American
     humor; South Africa

Boipatong massacre, 83, 102

Bologna, Italy, 131

Bondres clowns, 26

Boniface VIII, Pope, 113–15, 116

Boston, Massachusetts, 178

Botha, Louis, 84

Botha, P. W., 86–87, 94, 95, 97, 99

Brazauskas, Algirdas, 58

Bread & Puppet Theater, 174–80

Brezhnev, Leonid, 51, 52–53, 73,
     204

Brice, Fanny, 194

Brooks, Peter, 87

Bruce, Lenny, 199

Buddhist priests, 148–51

Bush, George, 204

Buthelezi, Sipho, 102

Cambio, Amata, 108–109

Cambio, Carmelina, 107

Cambio, Celeste, 107

Cambridge, Godfrey, 187

Campaigns. *See* Election campaigns

Cana, wedding at, 118–19

Capetown, South Africa, 102–103

Carang Sari, Bali, 26–28, 31

Carson, Johnny, 180, 200–206

Carter, Jimmy, 203

Castration, 67–72

Catholic Church, Fo's satires on,
     107–19, 127–30

Catra, I Nyoman, 12, 18–20, 44

Cause, The, 102

Censorship
     in Italy, 113, 126
     in Lithuania, 58
     in South Africa, 92

Chaplin, Charlie, 1–8, 10, 66, 67,
     69, 70, 171, 207, 208

Chekhov, Anton, 46, 53, 62–67

Cherry Orchard, The, 46, 62–64

Christ
     in Fo's comedy, 107–108, 114,
          117–19
     in Fo's *Johan Padan*, 128–29
     in Mystery plays, 115
     in *Woza Albert*, 88–91

Christian Democratic Party (DC),
     111, 112, 122, 127

Circus
     author's experience in, x–xi,
          172–74
     Bread & Puppet Domestic Res-
          urrection Circus, 174–80
     Ringling Brothers Circus, x,
          171, 172

City Lights, 10

Clown
     and audience, 109
     author's experiences as, x–xi,
          172–74
     and Bali shadow puppet plays,
          24–25
     Chaplin as, 1–8, 10
     commercial uses of image in
          U.S., 171
     Djimat's troupe in Bali, 13–17
     Fo as, in Italy, 107–19
     for hospital visits, 206

in Italy, 107–19, 112, 124–26, 128

metal clowns, xviii, 4–10

19th-century U.S. circus clown, 170–72, 179

Dan Rice as, 170–72, 179

in rodeos, 206

school for, x, 171–74

slapstick double take of, 207

in South Africa, 82–84, 85, 88, 90–91, 93

and survival, 1–10

temple clowns in Bali, 17–24, 176–77

in *topeng* (masked performance), 25–32

Comedies. *See* Theater

"Communist Nostalgia," 58–59

Communist Party

Gorbachev as head of, 58

in Lithuania, 58

Lithuanian resistance to, through humor, 48–75

propaganda of, 48, 55–57, 68

in *There Shall Be No Death*, 60–62

Correll, Charles, 186–87

Cosby, Bill, 193

Dalang Lukluk, 24–25

Dalang (puppeteer), 24–25, 39

Dapsiene, Daiva, 61

Dapsys, Arvidas, 74

Davis, Ronnie, 197–98

DC. *See* Christian Democratic Party (DC)

De Klerk, F. W., 80, 82, 84, 85, 94

Death, in *taishu engeki*, 138–40, 152–53

de Cordova, Fred, 205

Defiance, attitude of, 3–4, 207–208. *See also* specific countries

Dhibia, Wayan, 34

Dingane, King, 89–90, 98

Djimat, I Made, 13–16, 41–43

Douglass, Frederick, 182

Dubu, Prince, 79, 92, 93

Dukakis, Michael, 203

Dukun (healer), 40

Eastwood, Clint, 204

Ekhaya, 101–102

Election campaigns

in Bali, 36–39

in Lithuania, 54

Elizabeth, Queen, 125–27

Elizabetta: Almost by Chance A Woman, 125–27

Engels, Friedrich, 58

Euripides, 121

Family planning, 31–32, 120

"Farming in America," 177

Female impersonation

in Bali, 31–32

Evita in South Africa, 94–99, 102, 103

in Japan, 134, 141, 142, 154–58, 166

Ferlinghetti, Lawrence, 198

Finley, Karen, 196

First, Ruth, 91, 102

"Flea Killers, The," 54–55

Fo, Dario

Accidental Death of an Anarchist by, 122–25

author's work with, x, 109–10

Birth of the Giullàre by, 111, 113

Elizabetta: Almost by Chance A Woman by, 125–27

as *giullàre* (storyteller), x, 107–19, 122, 123, 125–32

Johan Padan by, 127–30

Medea by, 121

[Fo, Dario]
    Mistero Buffo of, 113–15,
        117–20, 123, 124
    and occupation of Palazzino
        Liberty, 111–12
    photo of, 106
    and student strike at
        University of Bologna,
        131
    technique of, 108–10
Forty Eight Hours, 192
Foxx, Redd, 187
Frog dance, 13, 15–16
Fugard, Athol, 91

Gamelan gong orchestras, 37
Geertz, Clifford, 35
Gender roles
    in Italy, 119–21
    in Japanese *taishu engeki*, 153–61
    in United States, 193–97
Ghetto, 47–49
Gift giving, 163–65
Giri, 139, 140, 160
Giri choco, 154
Giullàre (storyteller), 110–19,
        122, 123, 125–32
Glasnost, 53, 58, 67
Goaisatsu (welcoming), 136–37,
        142, 163, 165, 167
Gogol, N. V., 67, 69, 71–72
Gold Rush, The, 1, 3, 7, 8, 207
Golkar Party, 35, 38
Gorbachev, Mikhail, 53, 57–58,
        59, 73
Gosden, Freeman, 186–87
Graham, Bill, 198
Grahamstown, South Africa, 100
Grateful Dead, 198
Great Dictator, The, 3, 6
Gregory, Dick, 188
Guerrilla Girls, 196–97
Guerrilla theater, 196–99

Gulem, Dewa Made, 15
Gunung agung (home of the gods),
        29

Hamlet, 126
Hanamitchi (flower path), 146
Hanuman, 39
Harlequin, 2
Hellcats of the Navy, 204
Hindu-Buddhism, 17, 19, 22, 38
Hippolytus, 34–36
Hirohito, 30
Hitler, Adolf, 3, 6, 52, 57, 58
Hlongwane, Mlungisi, 82
Holland, 22, 29–30, 44
Homelessness, 8, 102
Humor. *See* specific countries

Il Candelaio, 197
Inquisition, 127, 128
Isabella, Queen, 127
Italy
    Accidental Death of an Anarchist
        in, 122–25
    author's experiences in, x,
        107–10
    censorship in, 113, 126
    Christian Democratic Party in,
        111, 112, 122, 127
    clowns in, 107–19, 112,
        124–26, 128
    comedy of saints' spaghetti in,
        107, 110
    *Elizabetta: Almost by Chance A
        Woman* in, 125–27
    Fo's *Birth of the Giullàre* in,
        111, 113
    Fo's *Johan Padan* in, 127–30
    Fo's *Mistero Buffo* in, 113–15,
        117–20, 123, 124
    Palazzino Liberty in, 111–12, 113
    peasant culture of, 107–108
    Pinelli's death in, 122

Rame's *Tutta Casa, Letto &*
    Chiesa, 119–21, 124
television in, 113, 119, 126
theater in, 109–10, 113–30
women's issues in, 119–21

Jacobs, Lou, 173
Japan
    author's experiences in, ix,
        135–38
    female impersonation in, 134
    gender roles and sexuality in,
        152–61
    music in, 147–48
    New Year's festivities in,
        144–45
    social expectations in, 139–40,
        143–44, 146–48, 150–52,
        154–55, 160–63, 166, 167,
        169
    taishu engeki in, 135–69
    television in, 150
    in World War II, 22, 30, 141
Jefferson Airplane, 198
Jesus Christ. *See* Christ
Jews, 47–49, 127
Jim Crow figure, 181
Johan Padan, 127–30
Johannesburg Police Union, 99
Johannesburg, South Africa,
    79–80, 87, 95, 99, 100
John Paul II, Pope, 115–16
John Vorster Prison, 79–82
Jujo, Japan, 168

Kabuki, 143, 145, 146, 149–50, 154
Kalpokaite, Larissa, 60
Kannon, 144
Karangasem, Bali, 41
Kata (formal speech and behavior
    patterns), 143–45, 147,
    149–54, 161, 163, 164
Kebyar dancer, 41

Kecak (monkey dance), 44
Kenka Bozu (Fighting Priest),
    148–51
Kennedy Center, 110
KGB, 53, 55, 56, 57, 68, 75
Kodi, Ketut, 36, 38, 44
Kredek, I Made, 39–41, 43

Landsbergis, Vytautas, 49–50, 51,
    58, 75
Laughter. *See* specific countries
Lazarus, 117
Lenin, V. I., 58, 61, 68, 72
Leno, Jay, 180
Letterman, David, 180, 206
Liku (crazy queen), 32–34
Lincoln, Abraham, 195
Lincoln, Mary Todd, 195
Lithuania
    annexation by Soviet Union,
        52, 57, 58–59
    author's experiences in, ix–x,
        47–50
    Cherry Orchard production in,
        62–64
    history of, 51–52
    humor as resistance to
        Communist domination
        of, 48–75
    independence of, 51, 53, 58, 75,
        86
    jokes in, 47–50, 52–53
    1990–1991 massacres in,
        61–62, 74
    Nose production in, 67–72
    parliament barricades in,
        72–75
    parliamentary debates in, 54
    puppet shows in, 49, 53, 57–59
    Saja's comic dialogues in,
        54–55
    Skema's play *The Awakening*,
        56–57

[Lithuania]
  Stonys' satiric revue in, 55–56
  television in, 57–58, 74
  theater in, 47–48, 53–57,
    59–72
  There Shall Be No Death pro-
    duction in, 59–62
  Uncle Vanya production in,
    64–67
Live in Concert (Pryor), 189–90
Live on Sunset Strip (Pryor),
  190–91
Lo Stupro, 121
Lontar, 21, 39
Luthuli, Albert, 91

Mabley, Moms, 187–88
McCarthyism, 3
Magnuson, Ann, 196
Mahabharata, 24
Male impersonation, 158–60
Manaka, Matsemela, 101–102
Mandela, Nelson, 82, 84–86, 89,
  94, 95, 97, 103–104
Market Theater, 87, 99
Marx, Karl, 53, 57, 58, 73
Mary Magdalene, 128
Mary the Madonna, 119
Masekela, Hugh, 88
Medea, 121
Mefuji Kieko, 157–60, 163
Metal clowns, xviii, 4–10
Midget, paraplegic, in Archaos,
  8–9
Midori Kimura, 142
Mie, 150, 152
Milan, Italy, 110–11
Minstrel shows, 181, 183–86
Mistero Buffo, 113–15, 117–20,
  123, 124
Modern Times, 3, 5, 10
Mokubakan Theater, 144
Monroe, Marilyn, 156

Moscow Art Theater, 62, 65,
  118–19
Mtwa, Percy, 87–88, 90, 91–92
Murphy, Eddie, 191–93
Music
  of minstrel shows, 186
  of slaves, 182
  in *taishu engeki*, 147–48, 163
  of Bert Williams, 185
Mystery plays, 115

Nabucco, 64
Nara, Japan, 135
Native Americans, 127–30
Nazis, 47–49, 93
Necrophilia, 152–53
Nekrosius, Eimuntas, 64–72
Neo-Nazism, 127
"New South Africa," 82, 86,
  95–99
New Year's festivities (Japan),
  144–45
New York City, 178–79
Ngema, Mbongeni, 87–88, 90,
  91–92
Ninjo, 139, 140, 160
Nixon, Richard, 202
"Nkosi Sikeleli Afrika," 103–104
North, Oliver, 125
Nose, The, 67–72

Odalan in Bali, 18
Okuni, 143
Okuri dashi (send out), 166–68
Onnagata (female impersonation),
  142, 154–58, 166.
  See also Female impersonation

Palazzino Liberty, 111–12, 113,
  119
Palm Springs, South Africa,
  80–82
Palm Springs Civic Association, 82

Pan African Congress, 100
Paraplegic midget in Archaos, 8–9
Penasar clowns, 20–21, 26, 33, 36, 39, 44
Perestroika, 58, 59
Perry, Lincoln, 186
Petersen, Hector, 93
Phaedra, 34–36
Phallus, 67–72, 120, 152–53
Pinelli, Giuseppe, 122, 123
Plays. *See* Theater
Politics. *See* specific countries
Popes, satire on, 113–16
Prembon, 32
Presley, Elvis, 147
Pretoria, South Africa, 82–86, 90, 91
Prisons, in South Africa, 79–82, 89, 92
Pryor, Richard, 2, 180–82, 188–91, 192
Puppetry
  Bread & Puppet Theater, 174–80
  in Lithuania, 49, 53, 57–59
  shadow puppet plays (*Wayang Kulit*), 24–25, 39
Puputan Badung (end of Badung), 29–30

Quadri, Franco, 122

Racism. *See* Afro–American humor; South Africa
Ramayana, 39
Rame, Franca, 112, 113, 115, 119–22, 124, 125, 131–32
Rangda, 20–21, 23
Rape, 121
Ratu Gegek (beautiful lady), 31–32
Raw, 192
Reagan, Nancy, 195
Reagan, Ronald, 125, 126–27, 178–79, 195, 201, 202–206

Religion
  Buddhist priests, 148–51
  Fo's satires on, 107–19, 127–30
  Hindu-Buddhism in Bali, 17, 19, 22, 38
Reno (performer), 196
Retief, Piet, 89–90
Rice, Dan, 170, 171–72, 179
Ringling Brothers, Barnum & Bailey Circus, x, 171, 172
Robben Island, 89, 92
Rockne, Knute, 204
Roseanne, 193–194, 195
Rupik, Ketut, 24–25
Rushdie, Salman, 126
Rusni, Ni Made, 32–34, 43

Saints' spaghetti, 107, 110
Saja, Khasys, 54
San Francisco Mime Troupe, 197–99
Sanur, Bali, 34
Sarafina, 87
Satomi Yojiro
  audience's relationships with, 137–40, 145–46, 153, 161–69
  author's response to, 137–38
  charisma of, 146–47
  comic necrophilia portrayed by, 152–53
  exchanges with fans outside the theater, 153, 167–68
  farewells of, following performance, 166–68
  as female impersonator, 141, 155–57
  and gift giving, 163–65
  improvisations by, 146, 159–62
  Kabuki conventions used by, 149–50
  in *Kenka Bozu* (Fighting Priest), 148–51

[Satomi Yojiro]
  melodrama of anguished out-
      law portrayed by, 138–40
  mother of, as performer,
      157–60, 163
  at New Year's festivities, 145
  photo of, 134
  popularity of, 142, 165
  ritual suicide portrayed by,
      140, 152
  self-transformations of, follow-
      ing play, 140–41
  songs of, 147–48, 163
Saturday Night Live, 192
Schumann, Peter, 174–75, 177
Sebonkeng, South Africa, 102
Sepos Theater, 57–59
Seppuku, 140, 152
Sexuality and sexual stereotypes
  in Balinese humor, 30–32, 33, 35
  of Guerrilla Girls, 196–97
  in Italian humor, 120
  in Japanese *taishu engeki*, 152–61
  of Roseanne Barr, 193–96
Shadow puppet plays (*Wayang
      Kulit*), 24–25, 39
Shakespeare, William, 125, 126
Siberia, 57
Sidhya Karya, 26–27, 28, 42–43
Simon, Barney, 87, 90, 91, 92
Sirvius, Paulius, 60–62
Skema, Antonas, 56–57
Slapstick. *See* Urban slapstick
Slave humor, 182–83
Smelyansky, Anatoly, 65
Smoriginas, Kostas, 66–67, 69–70
Sobol, Joshua, 47, 49
South Africa
  Adapt or Dye production in,
      94–97
  apartheid in, 86–88, 90, 92, 94,
      103
  Artimo production in, 102

An Audience with Evita produc-
      tion in, 97–99, 103
  author's experiences in, ix,
      79–82
  Boipatong massacre in, 83, 102
  Born Again production in, 100
  The Cause production in, 102
  censorship in, 92
  clowns in, 82–84, 85, 88,
      90–91, 93
  Ekhaya production in, 101–102
  irony of slogan "one settler,
      one bullet," 100
  longing for home in, 102–104
  "New South Africa," 82, 86,
      95–97
  political meetings in, 102–104
  political protests in, 79–80,
      82–86
  prisons in, 79–82, 89, 92
  Soweto massacre in, 93
  theater in, 87–104
  Which Way, Ma–Afrika? pro-
      duction in, 92–94
  Woza Albert production in,
      87–92, 94, 99, 100, 102,
      103
Soviet Union
  annexation of Lithuania, 52,
      57, 58–59
  glasnost in, 53, 58, 67
  Lithuanian resistance to,
      through humor, 48–75
  propaganda of, 48, 55–57, 68
Soweto, South Africa, 79, 85, 91,
      92, 93–94
Square, The, 67
Stalin, Joseph, 48, 52–58, 61, 62,
      72, 76
Stanislavsky, Konstantin, 62
Steeltown, 198
Steppin Fetchit, 181, 186
"Stimela," 88

Stonys, Ceslovas, 55–56, 59
Suicide, 140, 152
Sukawati, Bali, 39
Sumo wrestling, 151

Taiko drums, 145
Taishu engeki
    actor's self-transformations
      after, 140–41
    audience's relationships with,
      137–40, 145–46, 161–69
    author's response to, 135–38
    farewells following, 140–41,
      166–68
    female impersonation in, 142,
      154–57, 166
    female performers in, 154,
      157–61
    gender roles and sexuality in,
      152–61
    gift giving in, 163–65
    goaisatsu (welcoming) in,
      136–37, 142, 163, 165,
      167
    improvisations in, 146
    Kabuki conventions used in, 150
    Kenka Bozu (Fighting Priest),
      148–51
    male impersonation in, 158–60
    melodrama of outlaw's anguish
      at mother's death, 138–40
    money problems as theme of
      plays, 165–66
    musical interludes during,
      147–48
    and New Year's festivities,
      144–45
    origins of, 143
    plays about actors, 162–63
    popularity of, 142, 165
    ritual suicide portrayed in, 140,
      152
    significance of, 168–69

typical program of, 141–42
    zacho in, 136–38, 142, 150, 151,
      154, 156, 161–63, 165, 169
Television
    Carson's *Tonight Show*, 200–206
    Bill Cosby's show, 193
    in Italy, 113, 119, 126
    in Japan, 150
    Jay Leno's show, 180
    David Letterman's show, 180,
      206
    in Lithuania, 57–58, 74
    Roseanne, 193–194, 195
Terre-Blanche, Eugene, 94
Terumi, Tsutsumi, 160–61
Theater
    in Italy, 109–10, 113–30
    Kabuki, 143, 145, 146, 149–50,
      154
    in Lithuania, 47–48, 53–57,
      59–72
    in South Africa, 87–104
    taishu engeki in Japan, 135–69
Themba, Can, 103–104
There Shall Be No Death, 59–62
Tokyo, Japan, 135–38, 143, 144,
    167
Tomio Umezawa, 150
Tomlin, Lily, 194, 196
Toner, Jackie, 8
Tonight Show and Johnny Carson,
    200–206
Topeng (masked performance),
    25–32, 40
Topeng pajegan (solo masked per-
    formance), 27–28, 41–43
Topeng panca, 29–30
Tourism, in Bali, 17–22, 26, 37, 43
Toyi-toyi (revolutionary dance),
    84, 97
Trading Places, 192
Traup, Lyuba, 47–48
Tugek, 31–32